Drama and Traditional
Story for the Early Years

Drama and Traditional Story for the Early Years

Nigel Toye
and
Francis Prendiville

Foreword by Jonothan Neelands

London and New York

First published 2000
by RoutledgeFalmer
11 New Fetter Lane, London EC4P 4EE

Simultaneously published in the USA and Canada
by Routledge
29 West 35th Street, New York, NY 10001

RoutledgeFalmer is an imprint of the Taylor & Francis Group

Typeset in Goudy by
Keystroke, Jacaranda Lodge, Wolverhampton
Printed and bound in Great Britain by
St Edmundsbury Press, Bury St Edmunds, Suffolk

British Library Cataloguing in Publication Data
A catalogue record for this book is available
from the British Library

Library of Congress Cataloguing in Publication Data
Toye, Nigel, 1949–
        Drama and traditional story for the early years / Nigel Toye and
Francis Prendiville.
            p.   cm.
        Includes bibliographical references (p.   ) and index.
        ISBN 0–415–19536–5 (pbk. : alk. paper)
        1. Drama in education—Great Britain. 2. Drama—Study and
teaching (Early childhood)—Great Britain. I. Prendiville,
Francis, 1949–   . II. Title.
PN3171.T695   2000
372.13′32—dc21   99–43290
                                                                                CIP

ISBN 0–415–19536–5

Contents

Foreword

This is a much-needed book! There has been a surprising lack of high-quality advice and materials for drama in the early years. The increasing demands made on the curriculum make it even more important that teachers should be supported in using drama as a vital medium for children's learning. The two authors have generously shared many years of experience in compiling this detailed, accessible and stimulating account of drama in action in the early years. Inside these covers you will find tried and tested classroom materials accompanied by step-by-step advice on how to implement drama in the classroom. The book also provides a sound theoretical base for drama which is clearly linked to the Desired Outcomes and the child's first steps into the National Curriculum.

The drama structures all aim to provide meaningful and active contexts for children to explore the relationships between language, identity and human behaviour in social circumstances. At this most important stage in the emerging growth of the child's personal and social identity, the authors demonstrate how drama can be used as a safe play-zone for children to explore, extend and use what they know about the world. Through imaginative role-taking and challenging, but appropriate, problem-solving situations, children are encouraged to think about the needs of others and to develop a caring and socially responsible attitude. The dramas are designed to help children discover the important connections between language and social context and they provide *real* purposes for children to use a wide variety of registers and dialects.

The dramatic contexts suggested here are highly effective in integrating the Desired Outcomes and in demonstrating to children the human importance of the curriculum. The abstract concepts and knowledge of the curriculum are translated into concrete and active situations in which children will discover what they need to know and how to use it in order to resolve the dilemmas and challenges posed within the dramas themselves.

The book makes a connection between drama and the use of familiar traditional tales. Like drama, story is sometimes underestimated as a vital learning medium. Stories are not mere entertainment for children in the early years; they are vital sources of knowledge about the world and its ways. The authors skilfully transform the original stories into a rich variety of fresh situations and encounters with the characters. Often, the character the children meet will be played by the teacher, and one great strength of this book is the use of teacher-in-role. Through the device of teacher-in-role, the authors clearly demonstrate that the teacher can enter into the story world with the children and use her skills and knowledge to lead them into new areas of experience and understanding.

Perhaps the most important strength of this book is that it builds a bridge between the curriculum as planned and the curriculum as it is lived differently by different children and their teachers in the day-to-day world of the classroom. The activities suggested are all linked to the planned curriculum (and they are well planned!) but they also encourage children to work together effectively, to discuss feelings and ideas with each other, to use their bodies freely, to see their teacher and peers in a new light. Through using these ideas, teachers can be sure that they are delivering the Desired Outcomes while also engaging with their children at a very human and direct level. It is possible to play *and* learn together!

Jonothan Neelands

Acknowledgements

Thanks: to all the students we have worked with at Charlotte Mason College and St Martins College; to the experienced teachers of Cumbria, Lancashire and Oldham LEAs who worked with us in Drama on INSET courses, particularly the course for English Co-ordinators; to Liz Smith and Guy Underwood for permission to quote from their work; to Anne Skelding and Sue Matthews and the staff at St Mary's for all their help on the nursery research; to those who read drafts, including Sue Toye, Helen Platt, Denise Evans; to Neil Kitson for reading, supporting and giving unfailing good advice; to all our colleagues and particularly Mike Croft and Sheila Marchant for allowing adapted use of drama ideas; to Kathy Joyce, for having 'trained' both of us; to Jonothan Neelands for all of his inspiration over a period of time, and for permission to use and adapt in Ideas 7, Figure 5 'A Model of Language Learning through Drama' from *Learning through Imaginative Experience* (Hodder & Stoughton, 1992); to QCA, HMSO, OFSTED and the DfEE for permissions to quote from their publications.

Thanks to all children and staffs who worked on these dramas with us, particularly at St Mary's Infants School, Windermere; Ambleside Primary School; Deepdale Infants School and Frenchwood Primary School, Preston; Hitherfield Primary School, London; Sacred Heart Primary School and Prince's End Primary School, Tipton; Hately Heath Infants and Hargate Infants School West Bromwich; Shireland Hall Primary School, Smethwick.

Thanks to all staff in St Martins College, departmental and support staff, who have given us practical help and support.

Thanks to Helen Fairlie and then Jude Bowen, Nina Stibbe, Angie Doran and John Banks for their editorial help in shaping up the book properly.

Introduction

This book is about three things. First, it is about a distinctive method of teaching and learning through drama. Second, it is about using traditional stories as a way to get young children to look at the world. Third, it has a strong focus on moral education, something that is becoming a major concern in schools as we write this. The stories we use and the characters in them all present the children with moral dilemmas. Furthermore, the teaching method we use enables the children to meet these people and therefore open up a dialogue with them. They are able to confront them with the implications for the way they have behaved and give them advice before they make more decisions. The single most engaging element of drama for young children is the opening up of this dialogue. It is as if it is happening now and 'our teacher can be anyone we wish to talk to. We can influence events and witness the success of our efforts!' From a teaching point of view, what feels like a good game to the children allows us to diagnose their knowledge and understanding as well as their skills, in particular in the area of listening and speaking. But, just as importantly, by putting children in the position where they have to examine the moral implications of actions and how all actions have consequences (including taking no action!), we have an opportunity to develop their emotional intelligence. All this is done within the safety of a fiction, where the consequence for making 'the wrong' decision can be looked at without the consequences of real life.

We are centrally concerned with this method for early years work, as children bring skills in pretend play to school with them. If we do not use drama, we are ignoring a key way in which they teach themselves and make sense of the world from a very early age. One of the delights of using drama as a way to teach is the ease with which children will shift into this mode of working; the challenge for the teacher is essentially how to manage this process with thirty or more children. The first part of this challenge arises because you cannot stand outside and 'direct' these dramas; they are the creation of fictional worlds in which you will work in the fiction alongside the children. Therefore there are simple, but important, expectations about the teachers who use this book: you must be able to make that small but crucial step in working within the fiction created.

However, don't worry, you are not trapped in there, as many teachers fear! You can shift in and out of these worlds as the learning demands. You shift roles from demonstrating to questioning to reiterating in any lesson you teach. The difference in drama is the need to establish specific conventions for moving in and out of fiction, from reality to 'as if'. Shifting from being teacher to being teacher-in-role is done quite easily, partly because young children accept this in their own fantasy role-play and therefore will accept it with you. In addition, the kind of the drama we use is minimalist. There are no ornate costumes. There are very few props. Moving from teacher to Pied Piper and back to Pied Piper again can be done by picking up and putting down the child's recorder that represents the Piper's pipe. As long as this convention has been made clear, children will accept it as they accept the shifts in their own play. This is 'Poor Theatre' for the classroom. It is a key plank of our approach and makes the method eminently usable. All you need is yourself, the children, space (and most classrooms are big enough), the idea or structure (many are given here) and the will to talk and listen well.

We have chosen to use traditional story because most, if not all, children bring with them these stories from their homes; they are also part of the pre-school and early years' curriculum. The children have a knowledge of the characters and the events in the stories and this immediately presents us with interesting opportunities to challenge their thinking. Our dramas are not concerned with retelling the stories. That has its place in drama work but is more limited in its scope for learning. By using the characters from the stories, examining and developing the situations already alive with possibilities in the stories, we can create our own stories and dilemmas. The idea for the drama on Goldilocks came from sitting and thinking about the story. Why does the story end after a little girl has gone into some strangers' house, has done damage and then has run off? As educators we cannot leave it there. What example is that for children? The question arose, 'how would her Dad feel when he heard about it?' From that question a rich vein opened up, one that has fascinated many children, *and* teacher groups.

But which traditional stories are we using? The criticism can be justifiably mounted that these stories are essentially Euro-centric and lack the diversity we should demonstrate in a multi-ethnic society. While we accept this, it is a fact that these stories are well known throughout the world. The power of the Disney Corporation and television's all-pervading influence have ensured this. No doubt a book similar to this one is waiting to be written using a broader range of cultural traditions. We are not experts in the stories of other cultures, nor, more importantly, in the meanings of those stories for those cultures. To pretend to be would, at best, mean that we look at the stories in a Euro-centric way and, at worst, that we produce travesties of what those stories are about. The stories we have chosen have versions in many cultures and we have certainly used them successfully in multi-ethnic contexts.

In addition, the stories and the way we recommend working with them are not set in stone, and children will bring to the drama their own traditions, values and perceptions. The nature of this work demands a negotiation of meanings and solutions. Therefore the conclusions a class comes to will represent their view and the diversity of their cultural and life experience. The stories are a vehicle.

We see drama as a vital way of teaching literacy. In an early chapter we look at how drama can work to motivate work in literacy teaching (Ideas 3), but the work throughout the book can be adapted to support work on meaning, word recognition and comprehension.

The style of the book is intended to mix the theory and rationale with many practical examples that have been used with children. We have tried to design the dramas with a particular 'house style' so that you and the children become familiar with the way of working and thus security and confidence grows.

We have started with ways to introduce the strategies for comfort of the user, building up to using more complex structures with more techniques. In all cases we stress the use of role by the teacher as it is essential to the way we work and we do not know of a more powerful way of teaching.

Allied to the role for the teacher, many of the dramas are linked by a common use of roles for the children. Young children, in fact all children, like to feel they are important, and use and re-use of the 'Superhelpers' role we recommend (see Ideas 5) gives the children the confidence and belief for tackling problems, for wanting to talk through problems and for helping others. In drama as in all spheres of life, when we have status and our views are respected, we learn more because we listen better and our self-esteem is increased. This is something that many professionals link with success in education. This 'Superhelpers' role derives from the 'Mantle of the Expert' work of Dorothy Heathcote and is a strong way to empower children within a framework that helps us, the teachers.

The book is divided into two main sections. Part I, the 'Ideas' section, deals with drama methods and relates them to the curriculum and teaching. It also contains example dramas and starting points to use, particularly in Ideas 2, Ideas 3 and Ideas 11. The overall framework is to show how drama can deliver learning to young children in these four key areas:

- the Spiritual, Moral, Social and Cultural curriculum
- development in language and literacy
- the art form of drama itself
- other curriculum content like maths and history.

Parts II and III contain twelve example dramas to be used as models of work, covering a range of areas and of varying demands on the teacher and children, to make development and progression possible.

It is apparent to us that the early years are the powerhouse of education and as such the most vital time for teachers to influence children.

We maintain that drama is one of the most powerful subjects to apply at this time, and is a subject that allows the children to influence the processes of their own development, to learn and yet also to teach us what they see of the world.

CONVENTIONS USED IN THE BOOK

Examples of what the teacher might say in and out of role, and some dialogues with children, are set *in italics*. Examples of classroom experience cited are based on direct experience involving one or other of the authors only and thus are narrated as 'I' in contrast to the general use of 'we'. We use abbreviations for certain key phrases. TiR = Teacher in Role, sometimes numbered (TiR1/TiR3) to show which role is being used. OoR = Out of Role, where the drama is stopped to reflect on what is happening, to discuss what to do, to check that everyone understands, etc.

Where real examples have been used, children's names have been changed.

SUMMARIES OF DRAMAS

At the end of each drama a summary is given. As well as showing the main points of each drama at a glance, with roles, role signifiers and props, the summary makes connections with the objectives and National Curriculum topics discussed in Part I, and has space for notes and evaluation. In the classroom you may find it easier to use this summary than the more detailed scenario.

Part I

Thinking about drama

Why use drama?

DRAMA FACILITATES THE DELIVERY OF THE CURRICULUM

Since the introduction of the National Curriculum (NC) we have witnessed fundamental changes in the structure and content of the curriculum. Alongside these curriculum changes we also have new demands in terms of assessment, recording and reporting of pupils' progress. This means that the need for schools to be accountable has never been greater. The implications for teachers and their ways of working have been enormous. The changes we have seen in schools demonstrate the shift away from the idiosyncratic and largely incohesive curriculum that dominated primary schools before the NC to a far more structured and homogeneous one. We now have an education system where a child moving from school to school, LEA to LEA, has entitlement to a common curriculum with assessments that are based upon common procedures. Not only is there now a common curriculum in terms of content but we also have definitions of learning, attainment and progression that are used when judgements are made about a school's performance. The NC describes learning in particular terms, that is, the acquisition of knowledge, skills and understanding. Furthermore, the knowledge, skills and understanding of pupils are benchmarked by 'level descriptions' so our assessment of pupils is 'criterion-referenced', and 'progression' is seen as gains in knowledge, skills and understanding.

The prescriptive nature of the curriculum is not without its critics. Initially the NC was over-complex and unmanageable, and more recently it has been largely assessment-driven. There is also the added pressure of published league tables for schools as well as published OFSTED (Office for Standards in Education) reports following school inspections. The allocation of time to the literacy and numeracy hours necessitates an 'efficient' delivery of the curriculum so that it can maintain the prerequisite of 'breadth and balance'.

It is one of the purposes of this book to suggest ways of working that make for efficiency in the allocation of time to subjects. Drama in education is, by its nature, a way of working. While many of its functions can be identified within the listening and speaking programmes of study in the NC in English, the fact that it is not limited in its subject content enables teachers to use it for the delivery of many aspects of the curriculum. For example, in our drama about the Billy Goats Gruff (see Ideas 3 and Part III, pp. 233–8) the children will have the role of 'Troll Experts'; they will be required to make a book entitled *Everything You Need to Know about Trolls* (literacy – writing for a purpose and audience, the use of non-fiction books etc.); they will need to design machines to move the Troll's eggs from under the bridge where he used to live to his new home (design and technology); they will have to measure the field where the Billy Goats live and divide it up so that it can be shared (mathematics); and, throughout the drama negotiations with the Troll (teacher in role), they will have demands made on their speaking and listening skills. At a time when external agencies, from central government to school governors, set agendas for teachers to work to, it is imperative that we should find ways to deliver curriculum requirements efficiently. One of the strongest arguments for introducing drama into the curriculum is that it combines into one lesson many of the requirements made by the NC.

DRAMA PROVIDES THE DIALOGUES FOR LEARNING

Throughout the changes that have occurred in the curriculum, teachers have demonstrated the capacity for innovation in their teaching. This book is part of the tradition that claims teaching is as much an art as a science, and, when a teacher is an artist, she is able to go beyond the pre-packaged systems approach that is often born of a prescriptive education. The teacher as artist will spend some of her time planning lessons that encompass a 'negotiation of meaning' with her class. In other words, more than merely transferring a body of knowledge she will be helping children make sense of the world in which they live. It is our intention to enhance the prescriptive elements of the educational culture so that the systems approach is balanced with ways of working that engage children in a dialogue about what they experience in school.

Drama offers a unique experience in that it uses fictional situations and people, in particular the use of teacher role-play, that create a distinctive pupil/teacher dialogue, not only one that engages children and motivates them to learn but one which children, particularly in the early years, *already know how to use*.

Our aim in this chapter is first of all to consider why drama should be used by all early years teachers. One of the strongest reasons is that children find this way of working so accessible. We will examine why that is, and to do this we will look at drama's roots, in children's social role-play.

An understanding of early social role-play gives us a strong clue as to why and how drama works in the classroom. This analysis will lead us to the use of drama as a teaching method in nursery and Key Stage One classes because, while children arrive with the skills to do drama, we as teachers have to make management and organisational decisions so that we can use the methods with groups of thirty or more pupils. We shall do this by describing dramas we have used with classes as exemplars of the method in action.

DRAMA BUILDS ON THE ROLE-PLAY SKILLS CHILDREN BRING TO SCHOOL

Educational drama has its roots in child play, in particular, 'social role' or 'make believe' play. We use the term social role-play (also called sociodramatic role-play) to refer to that kind of play where children behave 'as if' they were someone else, or 'as if' they were themselves in a fictional situation. This feature of children's development, so familiar to anybody who has watched children playing together, crosses cultural, linguistic and socio-economic boundaries. It is a feature of child development that has been with us throughout history. We played this way, as did our parents and their parents.

The combination of imagination and pretending in play is what makes it important in both child development and child learning. The imaginative pretend play directly leads into drama. As Vygotsky noted, 'a child does not symbolise in play, but he wishes and realises his wishes by letting the basic categories of reality pass through his experience, which is precisely why in play a day can take half-an-hour and a hundred miles are covered in five steps' (Bolton 1979 p. 20)

If the child has the capacity to embrace new experiences and meaning imaginatively, then we can utilise it to magical effect in providing content and contexts to take the child even further. Drama operates very effectively in that part of the play space. When children play, what is happening? What sorts of elements are being used that relate very closely to drama conventions? To illustrate how this works we will examine two young children engaged in social role-play.

See Figures 1–6. The stills are taken from a video and the key dialogue is transcribed. Sean, 23 months, and Clare, 2 years 10 months, play together at a family gathering. They play in the living room of their Grandma's house and they are surrounded by visitors, some known to them, some not. The front door is

opened and new visitors arrive with all the associated pleasantries of welcome. Cups of tea are passed around and in the midst of this convivial babble the two children play, and what do they play? They play *house* (Figure 1). Clare: *Come to my house! Can I come to your house? Thank you. Please! Sit down, sit down.*

Figure 1 Clare: *Come to my house!*

The first thing we notice is that they are using symbols, in other words they are transforming objects to help create new meanings. While the adults around her are playing house for real, Clare tells Sean to *Come to my house*, and her 'house' is represented by an upturned coffee table (Figure 2). Sean: *In the house. Close the door*. The table has enough features to be able to represent a house, the table top acts as a roof and entering the enclosed space gives the feeling of being inside (Figure 3). Clare: *Doesn't fit you. Shall I get a little one for you?* While they are both trying to squeeze into the house Clare echoes the language that surrounds her. Clare: *Thank you. Please! Sit down, sit down.*

Figure 2 Sean: *In the house. Close the door.*   *Figure 3* Clare: *Doesn't fit you.*

The room, crammed with guests and visitors, is full of 'Thank yous' and 'Pleases' and in trying to make sense of this situation and the new people around her Clare models the behaviour she witnesses in a 'pretend' game. By 'acting out' situations children can not only practise their responses to them within the safety of it not being real but also explore possible alternative responses to these situations by repeating them. We know there is a strong relationship between practice and learning. Social role-play enables children to practise their responses within the 'no-penalty area' of a fiction.

In our house full of visitors the pretend game takes a new direction, Sean turns a coffee table upside down, gets astride it and tells everyone that he is *Going to the*

shops (Figure 4). This marks a shift in the narrative. From the context of visitors to a house the role-play is now 'a journey to the shops'. All this is done by changing the function of the symbol, i.e. coffee table as house = right way up, coffee table as bicycle = turned upside down, with the announcement, *I'm going to the shops*.

Figure 4 Sean: *Going to the shops.*

Clare follows this by turning her table upside down to represent a bicycle: in this way she contracts into the new direction of the play (Figure 5). Clare's Auntie responds with a question, *Going to the shops?* This is significant for teachers who use drama in their teaching. The intervention of an adult in the children's imaginary play offers the opportunity to raise the level of thinking in the play to a level above the developmental level of the children, what Vygotsky called the 'zone of proximal development' (Vygotsky 1978 p. 84).

Figure 5 Auntie B: *Going to the shops?*

What is fascinating about social role-play is that it is an activity all young children from all cultures engage in. It would seem to be an activity that serves a particular purpose in the development of children's social skills and intellect. The creation of fictional contexts, the use of symbols, the taking on of roles and the generation of narrative that blends these ingredients would appear to be laid down, rather like language acquisition, in the learning blueprint. Children use play to re-create this world and model the social behaviour they see in it. In this way they can experience the world without risking the consequences of reality.

What has this got to do with drama in the nursery or infant classroom? First of all, it may for many teachers and assistants have resonance when observing children playing in the role-play area in the classroom, but can it be useful to the teacher in whole-class teaching? It can have greater use if we can structure these behaviours so that it can happen in larger groups and we can use the skills the children demonstrate towards specific learning objectives.

The implications for us as teachers are profound, because if we can harness the natural ability children have to learn through 'acting out' we can, in our planning, move pupils into fictional worlds in order to explore the real world. Let us consider the points shown in this sequence:

Children arrive at school already equipped with the skills to 'do' drama. As we can see from observing Sean and Clare playing together, they already have an understanding of how to use social role-play to make sense of reality. They can use symbols, create fictional contexts and are willing to play alongside adults who signal they want to be part of the fiction.

Among the skills they bring are the skills to negotiate the rules or conventions of the play. When Clare 'goes shopping' she collects some plastic beakers to represent the milk, bread and eggs the adult has asked her to get. She then picks up a glove puppet to represent a shopping bag. She gives Sean the beakers and tells him: *Put it in there.* Sean looks at the glove puppet and does not realise it is supposed to symbolise a shopping bag. He attempts to put his hand into it to use it as a glove puppet. At this Clare pulls the puppet away and tells Sean: *Put it . . . put them in there*. The change from 'it' to 'them' indicates her attempt to clarify the function of the glove puppet as a shopping bag. Obviously you can put only one hand in a glove puppet ('it'), therefore to refer to 'them' indicates that she is intending the beakers to be put inside the glove puppet. This subtle adjustment in language points to how at a very early age children are able to negotiate and signal the conventions of their role-play.

By using symbols children can find a role for themselves. We have seen that by using symbols Clare and Sean can find a role for themselves. Clare uses the coffee table to make a house and becomes a 'house owner' inviting guests around. Sean turns the coffee table upside down and gets astride it to go to the shops and become a 'shopper' or person making a journey to the shops.

Clare collects some beakers and a glove puppet and also becomes a person on a shopping errand. The use of symbols creates a situation or event, and while most of the play at this early age is parallel play there are times when it is necessary to interact and therefore create a relationship with other players.

Adult intervention can enhance or repress the play. When adults are part of the play they can promote ideas, value children's contributions and enhance their creativity and enjoyment. However, they can also stultify and limit the quality of the experience. Going back to our two children playing, one of the adults in the room asks Clare what she is going to buy in the shops. As long as the adult demonstrates commitment to the play by taking it seriously, as seriously as the children, then their ideas will be valued and acted upon.

The possibilities for learning are therefore opened up by the adult and her more mature thinking, in the case of 'going to the shops' the language development in shopping lists, the mathematical development in counting the items to remember, the use of money to exchange for goods, the social ritual of shopping etc. In the next picture Auntie B says, *I want some bread, milk and cheese. Can you get that from the shops? Do you want some money first? Here's £2. OK?* Clare agrees and goes to get things to fill a glove puppet to represent the shopping.

Figure 6 Auntie B: *I want some bread, milk and cheese.*

When the adult joins in the pretend play she takes it seriously and through her suggestions moves it on to the context of the shop, an errand and a list of things to remember to buy. One of the other adults suggests she gets some fish and chips, but as she does so she laughs and indicates that she does not take the game seriously. Clare ignores this particular adult's contribution and stays with the adult who takes it as seriously as she does. By accepting the use of the coffee table as a house and later a bicycle the adults allow the play to continue and grow. When they play with the children on the *inside* of the make believe they further validate the nature of the activity.

For the child it is a game, but for the teacher the activity of shopping has the potential for a number activity, a sorting activity and a language activity. The teacher working in the drama with the child can focus the learning by introducing planned ideas and challenges. If introduced by the teacher in a manner that demonstrates that the teacher takes the play as seriously as the child, the child will in turn value the adult's contribution and want to engage with the activities the teacher or adult suggests.

They accommodate their playing in and out of a fictional context. Another important feature of social role-play is the fact it does not have a non-stop scenario. It is stopped and started often for negotiation and re-negotiation of the play to happen.

This is unlike the narrative in a children's story which begins at the beginning, goes on to the end and then stops. Interestingly enough, when a teacher reads a story to children they rarely approach it in this way. They stop to discuss events, to look at pictures and ask questions about what might happen next.

When children social role-play they will stop and start their play

- to allow new people in
- to re-establish conventions
- to introduce a new phase of the play
- to change the play context or roles.

We can see this in our household of guests with Clare and Sean playing. There is a moment when Clare 'bumps' her leg and the adults have to help her. This takes her out of the fiction in order to deal with the painful reality. When she has recovered she picks up the play where she left off. This ability to slip in and out of role-play is used by the teacher to negotiate and reflect upon the drama created. What we are going to describe in this book is not a huge step from the way good nursery and Key Stage One teachers work.

The teacher is starting with skills the pupils already have; in doing drama she uses the skills demonstrated by children in their social role-play. She can use these innate capabilities and the intrinsic enjoyment allied to pretend play by structuring and intervening subtly for specific, pre-defined educational purposes. For the child it feels like fun, like a game, but for the teacher it is a potent educational strategy in which children are highly motivated and receptive to learning. The mention here of 'fun' or 'a game' is not to belittle the level of seriousness which young children apply to their playing.

The skill the teacher uses in building a drama, as in most early years teaching, is in balancing the demands of Learning Objectives with the effectiveness of taking part in a 'fun' activity. In drama this means linking the 'play' for the pupils with the learning intentions planned by the teacher. When what Geoff Gilham identified as the two different experiences of 'the play for the teacher' and 'the play for the children' (quoted in Bolton 1984 p. 157) are well balanced, the children are operating *within* the teacher's structure. In other words they have access to *her* objectives *and* they have a sense that they are contributing, to *their own* drama.

In Figure 7 the elements of the balancing act are explored as the two plays that are in operation at the same time, the play for the children and the play for the teacher incorporating the educational objectives.

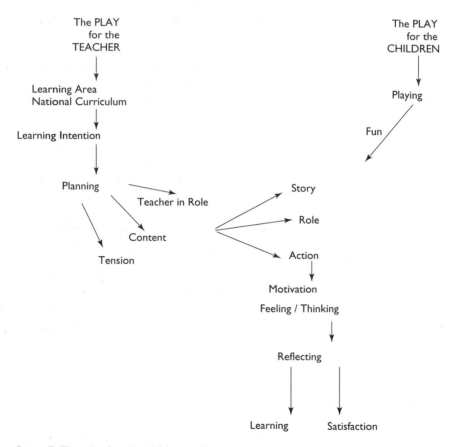

Figure 7 The play for the children and the play for the teacher

HOW TO USE CHILDREN'S DRAMA SKILLS

When children arrive at the nursery or reception class with the skills to do drama, the teacher must choose the most appropriate way in which to approach the work. She will first of all consider the age and interest level of the children.

Children in a nursery will benefit from working in small groups. When they are capable of the basic social skills, the teacher will work with the whole class together. Towards the end of Key Stage One and in Key Stage Two the work will still be whole-class-based but will include some small-group work when the children can work on their own and report back to the whole class.

In a nursery, drama will be one of the tasks or activities that the children can do. It will have one staff member running it, helping to create the drama by using Teacher in Role (TiR).

In classroom management terms for the nursery and reception classes, the approach that we are suggesting is more like a baking or cooking session than a visit to the role-play area. The children are working with the teacher to carefully structured learning objectives. For more on this see Ideas 8.

The kind of drama we are advocating at other stages of Key Stage One will be dominated by whole-class work with the teacher instrumental in the learning. The teacher has to be at the centre of the activity, to manage and enable, to challenge and reflect upon all that has taken place.

The central and distinctive feature of this methodology is the use of TiR. It is this absorbing and potent strategy that distinguishes the approach from any other way of working. Acting skills are not required! All the teacher must be able to do is to adopt a particular attitude within the drama that will stimulate and engage the children's attention.

The use of role makes possible going out of role, which is central to providing reflection on what is being done, reflection that is essential to learning at all ages. Bennett and his associates identified its centrality for the youngest learners in their research into the role of play: 'Learning is a deliberate process, and children need to be consciously aware of what they are doing, learning and understanding in order to make cognitive advances. Again, evidence suggests that the meta-cognitive strategies which can make learning more effective and efficient need to be taught alongside meaningful content' (Bennett et al. 1996 p. 123). Going out of role to discuss 'what is happening' is itself a reflective strategy that children learn in the process of drama.

DRAMA USES THE POWERFUL ALLY OF STORY

If we accept that teachers of early years' pupils see story as having a central role to play in the curriculum and that children they teach arrive with the necessary skills 'to do' drama, the fusing of the two offers an expansive resource for teaching and learning. However, when teachers attempt the fusion of story and drama they can meet problems if they fall into the trap of acting out the narrative as the only way to use story. This can arise because of a fundamental misunderstanding in the relationship between drama for learning and the nature of the narrative form. We would like to spend some time unravelling this understandable confusion.

Our starting point for all the dramas in this book is story. We know the sharing of stories to be a cornerstone of the nursery school and the Key Stage One classroom. In Ideas 2 we look at three dramas, two of them based upon stories: *Where the Wild Things Are* by Maurice Sendak and the traditional story *Goldilocks and the Three Bears*. The other drama takes two elements of a story, a character in a particular situation, rather like a picture in a book, and concentrates on exploring this particular situation. Each of these starting points uses a different way into drama, and they are designed to make increasing demands on the teacher new to using drama in her teaching. The first method we might describe as putting down the book, the second looking at a picture in a book and finally making our own version of the story.

Some of the anxiety that we meet when working on in-service courses with teachers is the fear that drama is such a different way of working from the way teachers usually work, and that attempting it may be inviting chaos. But we would suggest that if we start with the putting down the book method, the *Where the Wild Things Are* example, we are not doing things very much differently from the way we normally work with children on the carpet at story time.

As we have said, teachers rarely read a story from beginning to end without stopping; what usually happens is that the teacher reads the story and stops intermittently to

- talk about and ask questions about what has happened, what may happen next
- talk about and ask questions about characters in the book
- show illustrations
- listen to children's responses.

Stopping and talking about the book is part of the usual way of working. What we are suggesting with the *Where the Wild Things Are* story is that the teacher should stop and talk to the children 'as if' she were a character from the book. In other words, she talks about the book through the point of view of one of the characters. This does not mean she has to put on a different voice or wear make-up or act in a different way. (For more about what she has to do to make it work see Ideas 4.) The point is that this kind of use of drama is a small step for the teacher from merely reading the story. It is usually more accessible for teachers in the nursery and Key Stage One because they already play with the children in the role-play corner.

In the second drama we illustrate how, again using the story time slot, but this time without a book, the teacher tells the children they are going to meet someone who needs their help. In this strategy the pupils, through looking, listening and asking questions, discover a story.

In the final strategy the children meet more than one role and again by listening discover a story before offering possible ways forward to resolve the dilemma they have discovered. What we have planned is a gradual shift from story to drama.

WHAT IS THE DIFFERENCE BETWEEN NARRATIVE AND DRAMA?

Perhaps surprisingly, the most successful fusion of story and drama exists not when stories are acted out but when the narrative is *not* acted out. To explain this we will use the analogy of a train journey. Let us imagine that a railway line represents narrative; the author has laid the track and the narrator of the story is the train that carries us along the route. All stations that we pass through are as the events along the journey until we reach our destination and the journey ends. Just as some stories can be read again, some journeys can be taken again and again. For young children, knowing what is going to happen next in a story can be fun and reassuring and give them a feeling of power and control, the power of the listener who is ahead of the narrator, a feeling of being in control, ahead of the game.

In some stories there are rituals, repetition of phrases or words. These engage children with the narrative. It feels like the narrator doesn't know what is going to happen next and we do. Much of the active participation is going on intern-ally, in the children's imagination. The progress of the story is predetermined: while we may have power over the images we conjure up, we have no power over what is going to happen next. If the story is not familiar to us this can be exciting. If the story is familiar to us we can run the images we have created again and even anticipate them.

This is dissipated when a teacher attempts to get the children to act out the story. As a listener the physically passive involvement is balanced by the intellectual imaginative involvement. The listening child's physically passive involvement is able to create the pictures visually to accompany the story. It is a predominantly individual experience. As with listening to a story on the radio, we might listen with others but it is a parallel play activity. 'Acting out' the story undermines that process, the visualisation becomes redundant and the individual experience is placed in a social context. To hold the shift from individual to social experience together the teacher becomes director, telling the pupils what must happen next; the author remains in control of the narrative and the pupils become mere puppets in the process. Being locked into the narrative makes the predictability of what happens limiting and disempowering. Moving from reading a story to acting it out puts the class in the position of being pushed by the train, with no power to play with the ideas of the story; or, if they do, the lesson becomes chaotic because children are doing so many different things.

DRAMA HELPS US TO EXPLORE AND FURTHER UNDERSTAND STORIES

If we want to fuse drama and story it is far more productive to ignore the narrative and to turn our attention to key moments, key characters and their dilemmas. To return to our analogy, we stop off at the stations on the narrative journey and explore the surroundings. We can meet people who are in the story and even people who are not in the original story but are implicated in the story. We make decisions about what we need to do in the story because from being on the outside we are now on the inside. As stories are retold to us, they usually exist in the past tense, they are second-hand, passed on to us by the narrator. In drama we are dealing with the now, the present tense.

The children feel, *We are on the inside* with *our teacher! Our teacher can be lots of people, she is a living, breathing resource for us to use.* The pupils can be liberated to explore what they understand of the original author's ideas, they can embellish, expand, create new ones. They can actively respond to the characters. They can manipulate the story to resolve any conflict with their own ideas. They become a powerful community with the ability to solve problems and resolve dilemmas.

This book is designed to take teachers gradually from being merely narrators of stories to being expedition leaders on journeys of narrative exploration. The class have an opportunity to deepen their experience of story through their active participation in drama and traditional story.

We have structured these expeditions with a minimal shift of teacher style, beginning with the reading of a story, gradually moving to drama activities to fulfil learning objectives for the story. Finally we offer complete dramas using characters from traditional stories without initially referring to any text.

Where do we begin? We must begin slowly, edging into using role.

SUMMARY

- Drama is a way of teaching and therefore can be applied across the curriculum.
- Using drama in your teaching takes you beyond merely transferring knowledge and building skills as it also involves negotiating meaning in order to gain understanding. This is done through the active participation in a fiction.
- Drama in education has its roots in social role-play or sociodramatic play.
- Like social role-play, drama uses symbols, the creation of fictional contexts and role-play.
- Children arrive at nursery or reception classes with the ability to take part in drama.
- Teachers can use these skills for specific learning objectives by stepping into the fictional work of the children through using drama strategies, in particular teacher in role.
- Drama and narrative form work well together if the drama explores the story rather than merely acting it out.

How does drama work?

Teacher intervention strategies when
using drama with story

STEP ONE: FROM STORY TO DIALOGUE – *WHERE THE WILD THINGS ARE* BY MAURICE SENDAK

There are ways that a teacher using drama can involve children more strongly with story. The use of teacher intervention strategies has great potential for supporting literacy work. It can enhance the children's exploration of the ideas and characters in story. The understanding of the story grows by creating a new fictional context based on the story. The technique builds on the power of the children's own sociodramatic playing, that is their ability to pretend. They use the pretence as a way of making meaning from what they hear or read and in so doing learn from the pretence. The key is for the teacher to enter the 'as if' mode with the children rather than only discussing it. In this way a dialogue can be promoted which will produce active use of the story, including exploration of the words met in the story. What we want to demonstrate is how the teacher can intervene to promote understanding by using the pretend approach.

Although we are using the children's knowledge of dramatic playing, we are not using the approach of acting out the story just as it is given in the book; we set out to present a dynamic situation for the children to engage with, which is new but firmly based on the story.

Dialogue not discussion

We are aiming to get more interaction with the ideas from the story rather than simply discussing the story in the well-tried format of questions from the teacher and answers from the children. The idea is for the children to initiate questions *to a role* from the story, not the teacher outside the story. In its simplest form this can take place on the carpet area as part of story time.

There follows an example based on the popular story *Where the Wild Things Are* by Maurice Sendak. This example demonstrates a method whereby a teacher unused to using role and a class unused to their teacher using role can ease into using the strategy.

Meeting Max's Mother

The Learning Objectives are to get the children

- to think about Max and his behaviour
- to define unacceptable behaviour;
- to think about how his mother feels;
- to think how they might help his mother and Max.

Having read just the first part of the story up to the point where Max has sailed off in his boat, and having talked about the pictures as she might ordinarily do, the teacher asks: *If you had the chance to meet Max's mother, what sort of questions would you want to ask her?*

Some of these are offered and the teacher does not answer them, but listens carefully to the children's preoccupations, as hearing them beforehand gives her a chance to think of possible answers and ways of using the questions. She then says: *You are going to have the chance to meet Max's mother from the story now. I am going to be her. Make sure you ask those very good questions when Max's mother comes in. Will you start, Wesley? I am going to walk away from my chair. When I turn back, having put on this scarf, I will be Max's mother and you will begin asking your questions, one at a time, of course.*

The teacher then walks away from the chair, puts on the scarf and comes back to sit on the chair. There are two key points to remember about taking on role:

- The use of a *role signifier* is very important; it is something held or worn. It can help give information about the role and it shows whether the teacher is in or out of role, because it can be put down or taken off.
- The key to effective taking on of such roles is *not acting* but simply *taking a particular attitude* that will promote thinking and responses from the children aimed towards a specific learning intention.

An actor when taking on a role often has to be expansive in movement, gesture and voice (for example, putting on an accent). An actor may exaggerate all of these signals in order to communicate over distance in the theatre. Actors, in order to characterise, move the invented characters away from being themselves.

The teacher taking a role will need to use physical and vocal signals, but can base the signals on what she normally does, can firmly remain herself. She does not need to perform by creating someone new or by exaggerating (see Ideas 4, Teacher in Role). She need only fictionalise the situation and say she is being Max's mother, not feel that the mother must be other than herself. The teacher has already told the pupils whom they are going to meet, and they know the context from the story, so all that is required is for the teacher to communicate what the person's attitude is at this point.

To promote the learning intentions, Max's Mother can appear to be exhausted and fed up with Max; she can give clear signals in her answers that she is worried that her son never listens to her and behaves too much like a wild thing and she does not know why. She has tried to reason with him but he does not listen. She can ask the children whether they know what she should do.

At its simplest form this technique, known as 'hot-seating' (putting a role on the spot to answer questions – see Ideas 10), is handled by simply answering the children's questions as you think the character from the story might. That would be a way of doing comprehension about the story. In our example we develop the role further by adopting a particular attitude based on the story in order to make them think about the specific Learning Objectives (DLOs). In this way the drama is opened up more for learning.

It is possible to lead the children through a number of such meetings, one per day. This could be part of their literacy hour. They look forward to each occasion and cannot wait to see who it will be this time. Each can be introduced by revealing a large picture from the book or a symbol made up to show who it is. This and the following sections use examples of teacher role sessions for a week based on *Where the Wild Things Are*. Each shows a picture idea, the learning objective and the attitude adopted by the role, how it might be handled.

Monday

Mother: as above or this alternative version.
Learning Objective: to look at the way boys and girls are treated.
Attitude: Mother could be unhappy about Max not doing what he is told but, unlike the above example, she sees him as just being like all boys and never disciplines him: *His sister is different. She always tidies up after her. She'll just have to do his room as well.*

Tuesday

Max (version 1)
Learning Objective: what is selfishness?
Attitude: He is full of himself: boasting about how he chased the dog, refused to tidy his room, ignored his mother and looks good in his wolf costume.
Max (version 2)
Learning Objective: what is the proper boundary between dangerous play and proper behaviour?
Attitude: He is sulky and confused, complaining that his mother never lets him play like he wants to: *What's wrong with chasing the dog? I was only playing.*

Role-playing animals

So far the roles have been human beings, but what if you want to explore the issues raised through the animals in the story? Here is a point worth remembering if you choose to role-play an animal.

If the role taken by the teacher is an animal or toy, like some of the above, she will present it more as a human and signify the sort of role only by the attitude and a role signifier – e.g. a sprig of leaves for the creature (see Thursday below), carrying a lead for the dog. It is misleading and counterproductive to bark as the dog.

Wednesday

Max's dog
Learning Objective: What is the correct way to treat others? To consider the treatment of the dog as bullying and how to deal with it.
Attitude: The dog is very angry (or very scared) about being chased by Max with a fork and wants revenge (or protection). The two different attitudes shown here (one in parentheses) reflect how a different approach can change the focus. In the 'angry' scenario the children are required to calm the role and show how revenge is not the answer. In the 'fear' scenario they will have to help the dog realise how to tackle Max and teach him how he should look after his dog.

Or **Max's Bear** (appears in the first picture in the book)
Learning Objective: the need to think what other people might want; loyalty.
Attitude: He has been left behind by Max and wanted to go on the adventure with him.

Going outside the role described in the narrative

We can also use invented roles who do not appear in the published story but who could have been in the story and provide other viewpoints.

Thursday

The Spirit of the Forest
Learning Objective: to consider how wrong behaviour might damage an environment.
Attitude: He has heard that Max is coming to his forest and has come to check out whether Max is as bad and destructive as he has heard. When the children confirm this, *I'm afraid I will have to stop him coming in case he damages the forest.*

Or **The Forester**
Learning Objective: learning to appreciate what you have.
Attitude: He has found a sad and lonely little boy wandering lost in the forest and wants to find out who he is so that he can go home. *Does he deserve to go home? What should he have to do to show he has changed and deserves to go home?*

Or **A creature from the forest**
Learning Objective: different cultures.
Attitude: S/he has been left after the magic forest disappears and now cannot find her food and where she lives, and wants to behave in ways that do not fit a bedroom.

Friday

One of Max's creatures (version 1)
Learning Objective: responsibility when someone relies on you.
Attitude: Enters very sadly: *He became our king and we are so unhappy and fighting between ourselves since he left. I have come to find him because he should not have left. He must come back with me.*

One of Max's creatures (version 2)
Learning Objective: similar to the above.
Attitude: He enters very angry and says, *I have come to eat him, as we threatened to do, because he has let us down.*

You will notice that we have the same learning objective for both roles. The reason for this is that we can approach the same learning outcome from two different viewpoints or roles. Each will generate a different kind of response. In the first, sympathy is generated towards the creature and therefore the children must tackle Max to remind him of his responsibility. In the second, sympathy is generated towards Max so that the children have to tackle the creature in order to make clear that eating Max is not an answer to someone who has let you down. If you have elements of your class who might support the eating of Max in version 2, it might be a good idea not to use it *or* for the children to see the consequences of that action, by moving the drama forward when the creature leaves and having the class have to face Max's mother and explain why he has disappeared.

Points to note

- Not all of these would begin as with mother in our first example by being asked questions. Some would enter as though looking for the children, needing to talk to them to find something out, e.g. the Spirit or the forester.
- You could change the focus of the work by choosing to read more of the book before the role is brought in or by reading an extract from a different part of the book.

This teaching and learning strategy is known as Teacher in Role (TiR), and it is a very easy way of interacting with the children in a powerful way. It gives the teacher the capability to relate to the class other than as teacher. (For a fuller account of TiR see Ideas 4.)

The use of TiR in the way we have described *Where the Wild Things Are* not only gets the children used to their teaching adopting a role but furthermore does this in the familiar surroundings of the carpet and story area. It is also more secure for a teacher trying role for the first time. This feedback from an experienced teacher trying role for the first time shows how effective it can be:

I have been staggered at how the children allow me to assume another identity. The majority of children let me take on the role when I don the chosen item that identifies me in role and lose it when I take it off. My experience has been that at first there were a few children who took to it straight away while most observed, by the end of the first session half were involved, by the end of the second session three quarters. In the Matthew role play the whole class had allowed me to become Matthew and had responded to his problem.

(E. Smith 1996)

Contrary to some perceptions of TiR, it is close to the usual way of working of early years teachers. They often use simple role-play with children in the theme corner – being a customer in the café or the post office – or slip into role when doing story time with the children. They often work or play with children in activities. It is a very short step towards fuller use of role, as the following example shows. We will describe in detail how a teacher can develop a drama using role.

STEP TWO: INTERVENTION TO CREATE A STORY WITH THE CHILDREN 'LOOKING AFTER BABY'

Background and resources

Here the teacher uses a more extended set of interventions to involve the children more fully, creating more of a context and giving them greater status. To help build the teacher's confidence and give children more chance as individuals, the exercise can be done with a smaller group rather than the whole class, but it works with both.

This is a teacher intervention originally used by Dorothy Heathcote (one of the most influential developers of drama for education: see Wagner (1979) and Bolton (1984) for more information). We have adapted it for use in the role play area when it is set up as a 'home corner' or 'house'.

It uses the teacher pretending and a range of 'props' rather than a story to help stimulate the ideas. We will describe the handling of this session in detail.

The following resources are needed:

- home corner
- bag of materials appropriate and inappropriate to looking after a baby – nappy, *Oxford English Dictionary*, cuddly toy, cotton buds, matches etc.
- doll
- pram or cot.

Stages of the role-play

Stage 1. The teacher is working with a group of five or six children in the home corner and gathers them round her. *I am going to pretend to be somebody who has got a problem and needs help. I am not going to tell you what the problem is yet, I want to see if you can guess.*

The teacher is making clear the rules of the game. She is signalling very clearly when she is in and out of role. She is making clear to the children what is going to happen next, so that they feel secure and have clear expectations about what she wants them to do.

They will know when she is pretending because she will be holding a baby doll. She wants them not to say anything to begin with, just to look and to listen. When she puts the baby down she will be their teacher again and they can talk about what has happened and how they can help the person who has a problem.

Stage 2. The teacher moves to a chair in the home corner and picks up the doll in a shawl. She begins to talk to herself, mulling things over. The teacher is not acting, she is very much herself only with a particular attitude – someone who is worried about looking after a baby. *I don't know what to do. I've never had to look after a baby before. I hope she's not too long. I hope I've got all the things I need to look after this baby.*

Stage 3. The teacher puts the baby down and goes out of role to talk to the children again: *What did you notice about the woman with the baby?*

The teacher listens to the answers and particularly values the answers demonstrating commitment by the children. There is no right or wrong answer at this stage, only the children's understanding. Part of the game they are playing is to find out more as the drama proceeds. The teacher is deliberately valuing those contributions that are offered with commitment and she signals that, while this is a 'game', it is a game that she takes seriously. It is a serious issue, she behaves 'as if' it were someone who genuinely needed help. *I am going to become the woman with the baby again. Have you got any questions you would like to ask her?*

Stage 4. She returns to the chair and picks up the baby and begins to answer their questions. She tells them more about her situation. This could include the following:

- She has to look after this baby for the day.
- She has never looked after a baby before.
- She has brought a bag of things she thinks will help her.
- Perhaps they know something about babies?
- Perhaps they might be able to help?

Stage 5. As the children are drawn into the situation, the teacher begins to take things out of her big bag. The first couple of things are totally inappropriate for looking after a baby, for example, the *Oxford English Dictionary* or a telephone book for something to read to the baby. The obvious inappropriateness of the large *Dictionary* draws some incredulity from the children. Some laugh, some just look very surprised at each other. For very young children she produces a toy that makes a loud noise or is a bit frightening. The teacher maintains her position of the one who does not know and understand. This puts the children in a high-status position of people who can help her.

The teacher does not stay in role the whole time. Sometimes she comes out of role to discuss any disputes or disagreements about the objects presented. She then goes back to the role so that children can explain their agreed position to the woman who has to look after the baby.

The objects are placed into two boxes marked 'yes' and 'no' to indicate what the woman should use and what she should not. In this way it becomes a sorting activity. As the lesson progresses, the objects can become subtler in whether they are appropriate or not, and a box marked 'need to find out' can be used. This can be the source of further research to iron out any disputes or disagreements.

Stage 6. Finally, the teacher thanks them for their help and promises to write to them to tell them what happened.

Other tactics

The static nature of the session so far can be broken by demonstrations of skills required to look after a baby and activities for the whole class to mime. In this way the children practically demonstrate their knowledge, skills and understandings.

As a focus for a follow-up session a letter can be received from the woman thanking them for their help or a short story about the day she looked after the baby.

Looking after Baby – PLANNING SUMMARY

LEARNING OBJECTIVES	NATIONAL CURRICULUM **programmes of study/attainment targets**
• to involve the children in a caring situation to help someone who is inexperienced • to build on ideas they have about looking after children	Relates to a number of areas of the Desirable Outcomes for Children's Learning on entering compulsory education from the SCAA, particularly: • Children are confident, show appropriate self-respect and are able to establish effective relationships with adults. • They work as part of a group. • They are eager to explore new learning, and show the ability to initiate ideas and to solve simple practical problems.

KEY STAGES IN THE DRAMA

1. The teacher gathers the children round her. *I am going to pretend to be somebody who has got a problem and needs help.*
2. The teacher picks up the doll in a shawl: someone who is worried about looking after a baby.
3. The teacher puts the baby down: *What did you notice about the woman with the baby?*
4. She tells them more about her situation: she has to look after this baby for the day; she has never looked after a baby before; she has brought a bag of things she thinks will help her – perhaps they know something about babies?
5. The teacher begins to take things out of her big bag – sorting activity. The objects are placed into boxes marked 'yes' and 'no' and 'need to find out'.
6. The teacher thanks them for their help and promises to write to them.

Roles for Children	not specific
Role for Teacher	Inexperienced person left to look after a baby
The props/role signifiers	Doll

Other props: Bag of items for baby, some appropriate, some clearly not

Assessment, Recording and Reporting	
Attainment (reference to level descriptions) **knowledge, understanding and skills**	**PUPILS' RESPONSE –** Evidence
Progression (reference to level descriptions) **gains in knowledge, understanding and skills**	

STEP THREE: DEVELOPING POSSIBILITIES OF MORE COMPLEX CONTEXT – 'GOLDILOCKS'

Background and resources

This drama was designed for nursery or reception, but has been used also with older children. It is designed to set up more than one specific role and for the children to become writers. The learning objective is to look at parent/child relationships and 'being naughty', including punishment and saying sorry (from the personal and social learning outcomes of the SCAA document 1995).

In this approach to the story the teacher extends the demands on the children by taking two roles with opposing views. This is important in that, if the roles are played credibly, the children are faced with two justifiable positions, where both have points in their favour. It will teach the children to look carefully and weigh up evidence and counter-claims in order to learn how to help to resolve the conflicts.

Teacher in Role: Goldilocks's father or mother and Goldilocks. (The drama is described using Goldilocks's father throughout but the role could as easily be her mother.) The children do not have a specific role for themselves, as in the later dramas in Parts II and III, but they are being moved more towards role by being identified as 'people who know about children'.

The following resources are needed:

- hats for TiRs
- the letter from the Bears.

The stages of the drama

Stage 1. Contracting A key part of any drama is the *contracting*, where the teacher outlines how the rules apply, what she will be doing and what will be required of the children. The teacher out of role (OoR) says, *I have two parts in this story. One is a little girl and the other is a man, who is the first person you will meet. I want you to notice everything about him and tell me what you notice about him, how you think he is feeling, anything he is holding. When I am the man I will wear this hat and when I am the little girl that hat.* She shows two appropriate hats as the role signifiers. They are worn when in role and taken off when stopping to discuss with the children OoR.

Stage 2. Teacher in Role She moves away from the seat and tells the children that when she returns to it she will be the man they are going to meet. *I do not want you to talk to him but just look at him and tell me when I stop being him what you notice about him.*

She then takes the seat again wearing the hat as Goldilocks's Dad. He is carrying a letter. He signals being very worried and sits looking at the letter and reading it to himself silently. He sighs and looks very unhappy. He talks to himself about it very quietly but audibly enough for the children to hear. *How could she do this . . . She shouldn't have been out. I told her not to go into the wood on her own. She is very naughty. What am I going to do about her? What am I going to do about this (the letter)? I'll have to talk to her about it. She'll have to be punished.*

Stage 3. Teacher out of role She then gets up from the seat, takes off the hat and goes OoR. *What about him? What did you find out by looking?*

She listens to their speculations and welcomes and honours what they say, getting them to tell her all about him as though she did not know what happened.

Then she moves the drama on by saying, *He is coming back now and you can talk to him and ask questions and find out whether you were right. So what might you ask him?*

She listens to the questions and makes no answer to them but begins to think through what she might say. She checks. *So you are ready to ask him those things?*

We have been challenged here about the advisability of setting young children up to meet a stranger and encouraging them to talk to him or her. There is a truth in this but there are other elements:

- The children are in a large group and their role may be children, or they may be adults. This is not defined.
- In the fiction they approach *him* and not vice versa.
- They know, because of the two worlds in operation – fiction and reality – that, as their teacher has set this up *and* is negotiating with them out of role to talk to him, it is likely to be safe.
- If the children raised this issue – and in our doing this drama over many years they never have – we must accept their caution and tell them to go and tell someone they know before talking further to him (or suspend the drama because they must not talk and must go away from him), in other words to get permission. It would be easy to ask whom they would tell and set up that meeting, thus allowing the man to be given approval and then continuing the drama if the children were happy. Clearly any teacher who still feels that this is a bad model must not use it.

Stage 4. Moving back into role Putting on the hat again and sitting back on the chair, TiR in Goldilocks's Dad answers the questions and gives a clear idea of Goldilocks having been naughty in going to somebody's house and getting into trouble.

He can read the letter out to them and ask their advice. He makes clear he does not know what she did in the house or who the people are.

The role-play will do three things:

- give the children an opportunity to talk with Goldilocks's Dad 'as if' it were happening now. The 'as if' factor is the basis of drama that children come to school understanding
- give the teacher a chance to sow seeds of information to build towards the

children meeting Goldilocks: e.g. *I lost my wife three years ago when Goldilocks was four. We both miss her,* or *I don't have lots of time to spend with her because we have been very busy at the shop.*

- raise questions to put the children in a position of responsibility to sort out the problems the two roles are presenting: e.g. *Goldilocks is being naughty. How do I stop her? I have not been a very good father. I am told you are people who know about children. What should I do?*

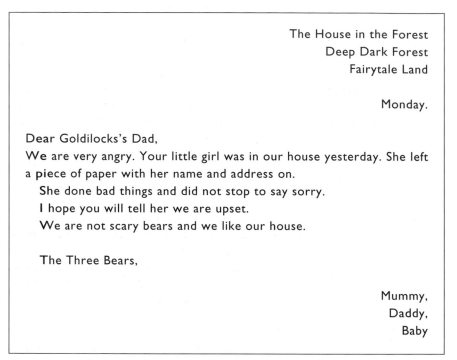

> The House in the Forest
> Deep Dark Forest
> Fairytale Land
>
> Monday.
>
> Dear Goldilocks's Dad,
> We are very angry. Your little girl was in our house yesterday. She left a piece of paper with her name and address on.
>   She done bad things and did not stop to say sorry.
>   I hope you will tell her we are upset.
>   We are not scary bears and we like our house.
>
>   The Three Bears,
>
> Mummy,
> Daddy,
> Baby

If the children offer that they know what she did at the house, Dad says, *So the rumour has already been spread. Everybody knows what she did except me, and you are all talking about it. What do I do?*

Dad can raise the issue of punishment: *What should I say to her? Should she be punished? Will you speak to her for me?*

If children suggest smacking her, we take a position as TiR that this is something we do not do. In this way as teacher you plan out corporal punishment as a solution. See an account of such an event in Ideas 6.

Stage 5. Shift from one role to another Dad exits to go look for Goldilocks, leaving them with a responsibility: *Can you help me find her? If she comes this way down the forest track, will you keep her here till I get back? I'm going to have a look back towards our house.*

Stage 6. Teacher in new role Teacher changes role by putting on the other hat. She does not need to forewarn the children in this case as they know straight away who it is. She enters as Goldilocks, who climbs on to the nearest desk or furniture as though she is climbing up a tree (or some other action that shows she is adventurous and careless). Whistling or humming to herself will help add to this image.

Initially she ignores the children as though she has not seen them and waits for the children to talk to her first. If they do not, she comes down, takes off the hat, and goes OoR in order to help them, to access them to the role. She asks, *Who do you think this little girl with the hat is? What should you do now? What do you say to her?*

When she is convinced the children can handle the situation she goes back into role and climbs back to where Goldilocks was.

She lets the dialogue develop naturally, but she begins to look unhappy 'up the tree', suddenly realising how high it is, and uncertain how to get down, in order to encourage the children to come and help her down. That makes for a good contact point and the child who comes to help has crossed that important line into the drama, has committed to the fiction and set an example for the others.

Possible directions for role-handling

There are a number of possible ways the dialogue can go here depending on how the children respond and what they raise. The teacher can help guide the directions in role by how she responds as Goldilocks and OoR by talking about Goldilocks and how they see her behaving (Figure 8).

Stage 7. Seeking help from the group At a key point when they are friends, Goldilocks asks what she should do. The drama can develop along lines the children suggest to deal with the two main issues:

- the father/daughter relationship
- the naughtiness at the Bears' house and how to make up for it. What punishment should there be for it?

Possible outcomes for the drama

First, the children can report to Dad what they have found out about the situation. There might be an issue here if they have promised Goldilocks not to tell anyone. They have to get her to allow them to speak to Dad on her behalf. They can then advise him. TiR asks what he should do about the letter and the bears.

Second, if Goldilocks and Dad have both to be present at the same time, first set out two chairs facing each other and the roles can be symbolised by putting the hats on the chairs. Then any dialogue between the two can be handled as a sort of forum theatre. (See Ideas 10.)

Teacher becomes Dad again and either the children can take the chair one at a time or all can speak for Goldilocks.

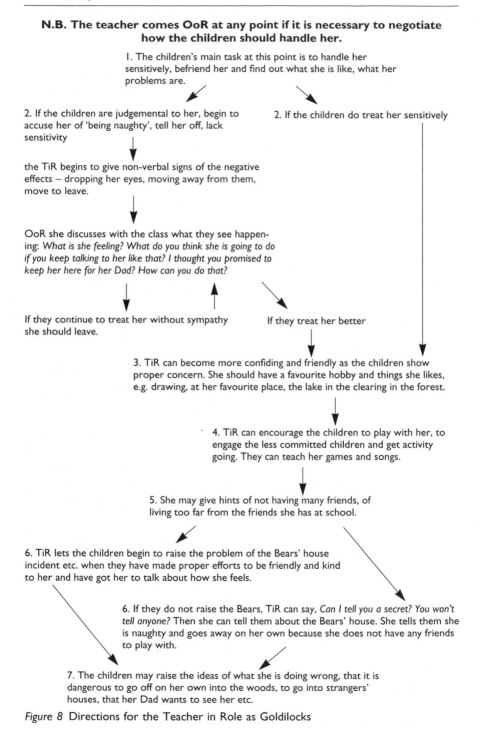

N.B. The teacher comes OoR at any point if it is necessary to negotiate how the children should handle her.

1. The children's main task at this point is to handle her sensitively, befriend her and find out what she is like, what her problems are.

2. If the children are judgemental to her, begin to accuse her of 'being naughty', tell her off, lack sensitivity

2. If the children do treat her sensitively

the TiR begins to give non-verbal signs of the negative effects – dropping her eyes, moving away from them, move to leave.

OoR she discusses with the class what they see happening: *What is she feeling? What do you think she is going to do if you keep talking to her like that? I thought you promised to keep her here for her Dad? How can you do that?*

If they continue to treat her without sympathy she should leave.

If they treat her better

3. TiR can become more confiding and friendly as the children show proper concern. She should have a favourite hobby and things she likes, e.g. drawing, at her favourite place, the lake in the clearing in the forest.

4. TiR can encourage the children to play with her, to engage the less committed children and get activity going. They can teach her games and songs.

5. She may give hints of not having many friends, of living too far from the friends she has at school.

6. TiR lets the children begin to raise the problem of the Bears' house incident etc. when they have made proper efforts to be friendly and kind to her and have got her to talk about how she feels.

6. If they do not raise the Bears, TiR can say, *Can I tell you a secret? You won't tell anyone?* Then she can tell them about the Bears' house. She tells them she is naughty and goes away on her own because she does not have any friends to play with.

7. The children may raise the ideas of what she is doing wrong, that it is dangerous to go off on her own into the woods, to go into strangers' houses, that her Dad wants to see her etc.

Figure 8 Directions for the Teacher in Role as Goldilocks

They have to handle:

- apologising to Dad
- explaining what happened and asking for his help to make up for it
- telling Dad how she feels about not having any friends, about living so far out in the country etc.

Teacher-in-role as Dad can be deliberately awkward in not understanding her point of view, and may have to be taught by the children that

- he is not listening properly
- Goldilocks is trying hard and he is not
- he has to help her as a father as well as just tell her off.

Third, if the children suggest an apology to the Bears, then that can be set up with three of the children as the Bears and teacher as Goldilocks, who does not apologise very well and has to be taught how to mean it by the children.

Or Teacher-in-role as Father Bear and the children again as Goldilocks.

Or a letter can be written.

Stage 8. A finale and pay-off for the children is important at the end. They must have a chance to see a happier Goldilocks with the children. Do they help celebrate her birthday?

They can show tableaux (see Ideas 10) of Dad and Goldilocks together containing ideas of how they spend more time together in the future.

The key aims of the drama can cover a number of the areas raised by the personal and social learning outcomes of the SCAA document 1995.

Goldilocks – PLANNING SUMMARY

LEARNING OBJECTIVES	NATIONAL CURRICULUM
to look at	**programmes of study/attainment**
• parent/child relationships, specifically the need for communication	**targets**
	The personal and social learning outcomes of the SCAA document 1995. Also, they make up their own
• the consequences of 'being naughty', including saying sorry	stories and take part in role-play with
• ideas on punishment	confidence.

KEY STAGES IN THE DRAMA

1. Contracting – the rules of the drama.
2. TiR: meeting Goldilocks's Father. He is carrying a letter.

continued . . .

3. OoR: *What about him? What did you find out by looking?*
4. Hot-seating Goldilocks's Dad. Read the letter.
5. Father exits to go look for Goldilocks, leaving them with a responsibility: *If she comes this way down the forest track, will you keep her here?*
6. TiR as Goldilocks: the challenge of a stroppy child.
7. At a key point when they are friends, Goldilocks asks what she should do. The drama can develop along lines the children suggest to deal with the two main issues: the father/daughter relationship; the naughtiness at the Bears' house and how to make up for it; what punishment there should be for it.
8. A finale and pay-off for the children – Do they help celebrate her birthday?

Roles for Children	not specific, except that Goldilocks's Dad says at some point: *I hear you know a lot about children?*	
Roles for Teacher	Goldilocks's Dad	Goldilocks
The props/role signifiers	Hat	Hat

Other props: A child's book that has been scribbled on and the letter from the Three Bears.

Assessment, Recording and Reporting	
Attainment (reference to level descriptions) knowledge, understanding and skills	**PUPILS' RESPONSE – Evidence**
Progression (reference to level descriptions) gains in knowledge, understanding and skills	

SUMMARY

- Teacher skills in taking on role can be built up gradually. Begin with brief hot-seating of a character from a story and extend to more complex interactions and structures, with greater possibilities for the children:

  - Step one: A character from story in dialogue
  - Step two: Teacher intervention to create a new story with the children
  - Step three: Developing possibilities of more complex context with the setting up of more than one specific role and the plot that then becomes possible; the children become co-writers.

- Simple dialogue can develop to become more the creation of the class's own exploratory story. Decisions are made about what to do, how to teach or in other ways help roles being handled by the teacher.

Drama and the literacy hour

In this section we examine how drama can be used in relation to the literacy hour at Key Stage One. This will take the form of an analysis of how drama can function to support and enhance the learning of the pupils in the national literacy framework. To do this we use the story 'The Billy Goats Gruff' as an example.

In the National Literacy Strategy Document (Framework for Teaching) literacy is seen as something that unites the important skills of 'reading and writing' (DfEE 1998 p. 3). The framework recognises the role of speaking and listening in the attainment of literacy skills: literacy 'also involves speaking and listening which, although they are not separately identified in the Framework, are an essential part of it' (p. 3). It goes on to underline the importance of 'Good oral work' as something that 'enhances pupils' understanding of language in both oral and written forms and of the way language can be used to communicate. It is an important part of the process through which pupils read and compose text' (p. 3).

Of course we can add to this that good oral work is a means for children to communicate how they *feel* about literature. We cannot separate children's values from their response to text nor would we want to do this. The literacy hour is not just about skill-building in a purely mechanistic fashion; it is also an opportunity for pupils to use literature to make sense of the world around them.

Drama is closely associated with the speaking and listening component of the NC. It is recognised that speaking and listening are an integral part of building literacy skills. When they are used appropriately teachers are more effective in developing the literacy of their class. The model that we are proposing in this book is for you to use drama in three distinct teaching and learning situations:

- during story hour and the literacy hour
- in focused activities in the role-play area (see Ideas 8)
- in whole-class drama lessons.

We believe that teacher role-play is the fulcrum or keystone in drama because of the nature of the speaking and listening that it generates (see Ideas 7). The use of teacher role-play within the literacy hour enables teachers to adopt language registers and styles that will not only grab the attention of the group but also model more complex language forms than might be available within the usual teacher/pupil dialogue. An example of this is the kind of language used in emotionally charged situations. The intonation, volume and non-verbal clues that can be used through teacher role-play can help the decoding and therefore the understanding of the pupils. It opens up the process to a wider range of children than simply reading the text might do, and makes available to the teacher more communicative strategies in the teaching of literacy.

Drama, in particular hot-seating (see Ideas 10), can be used in all four of the segments of the literacy hour (Figure 9). Similar opportunities for using drama are offered by the first fifteen minutes of the literacy hour and story time. This is partly because they share a similar classroom geography, with pupils sitting around you, in other words, a whole-class teacher-led activity. The familiarity of the situation for both you and the children enables you to use hot-seating without any disruption to the flow of the teaching/learning setting. The use of TiR as a means to focus and engage a large and varied ability group is undoubted. The slight rise in positive tension when 'our teacher is pretending' draws in the whole class (see Ideas 4). In proposing the use of drama in the literacy hour, we are not suggesting that it should be used every day or with every piece of text. There will be particular texts when drama will be appropriate and effective. The key factor influencing the decision to use drama in the literacy hour will be whether you want to talk about the text or engage the children in interacting with the text, through use of teacher role-play.

The strategies we are proposing open up the possibility of a dialogue not only with characters in the text but also fictional characters that are not in the text but have an interest in the events and themes of the story (for example, Goldilocks's mother or father – see Ideas 2 – or the farmer who employs Little Bo Peep – see Part II). This type of dialogue is achieved through three key drama strategies (see Ideas 10 for descriptions of these):

- TiR – specifically hot-seating
- forum theatre
- image theatre.

Planning to use drama in the literacy hour necessitates our being clear about

- how drama works in relation to the literacy hour
- which particular strategies are accessible and appropriate in the literacy hour
- the nature and quality of the text used.

Some texts will generate more accessible characters for teacher role-play and themes, issues and ideas that lend themselves to the drama way of working. There are no hard and fast rules about this: it is more a question of the potential the teacher sees in the text.

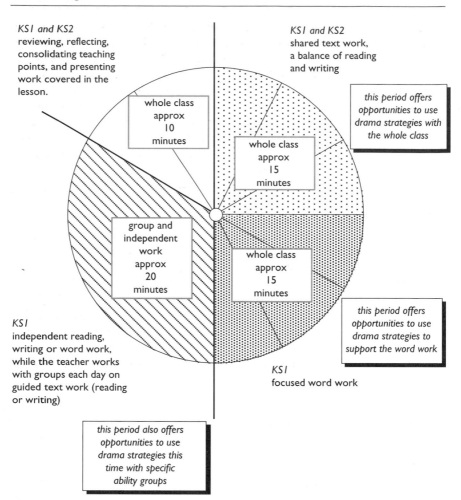

KS1 and KS2
reviewing, reflecting,
consolidating teaching
points, and presenting
work covered in the
lesson.

KS1 and KS2
shared text work,
a balance of reading
and writing

whole class
approx
10
minutes

*this period offers
opportunities to use
drama strategies with
the whole class*

whole class
approx
15
minutes

group and
independent
work
approx
20
minutes

whole class
approx
15
minutes

KS1
independent reading,
writing or word work,
while the teacher works
with groups each day on
guided text work (reading
or writing)

*this period offers
opportunities to use
drama strategies to
support the word work*

KS1
focused word work

*this period also offers
opportunities to use
drama strategies this
time with specific
ability groups*

Figure 9 Opportunities for the use of drama strategies within the literacy hour

HOW DRAMA WORKS IN RELATION TO THE LITERACY HOUR

We have chosen the story 'The Billy Goats Gruff' to illustrate how drama can be organised to run in conjunction with the literacy hour. One of the interesting things about the use of drama and traditional story is how several different dramas can be based around the same story. The reason for this is that in drama we are not locked into the original narrative. The narrative provides roles and particular events; however, the form allows us to create new events and unexpected attitudes from familiar characters. The exploration of a character through drama allows children to examine and reflect upon the attitudes of characters. It gives them the opportunity to look at the motivation behind decisions and circum-stances not necessarily revealed in the text. So, while the original story supplies us with a Troll and a confrontation with three Billy Goats, it does not tell us what happened after the Troll fell into the river. In other words, it provides a pretext to the drama and enables us to create new narrative, in a similar way to the meeting with Goldilocks's Dad. The creation of Mrs Green, a character not in the original story, allows us to use the original narrative while at the same time creating the possibility of a new one. By introducing a letter we put letters in a social context. For the class there is a real reason to decipher the letter and also the possibility of writing their own in return.

If we think of teachers partly as designers of teaching and learning contexts, the drama holds the potential to design lessons to meet the needs of the class more specifically than those defined by the NC.

For the literacy hour focus based upon 'The Billy Goats Gruff' we will meet a Troll who struggles with his reading. However, in Part II we provide a second version of this story and shift the learning to technology, at the same time not losing altogether some of the literacy elements.

Let us begin then with our literacy hour version. In order to use drama methodology in concert with the literacy hour we need to have a structure that recognises the different functions each lesson serves. Those elements of the drama that require the active participation of the class in a space will be done outside the literacy hour, whereas the more static drama strategies are perfectly accessible and appropriate to the literacy hour.

LITERACY HOUR PLANNING FOR 'THE BILLY GOATS GRUFF'

Long-term planning

One of the aims of using drama in the literacy hour is to give variety to the methodology and the content as well as contextualising the language learning (see Ideas 7). This drama was originally planned for Year One or Year Two, and therefore the desired learning outcomes can be adjusted for either year. The drama is inappropriate for reception because of the central task of writing a book. Not all the challenges and learning opportunities the drama presents can be predicted in the planning, so new content created by the class will generate new learning possibilities for you to explore.

Although we have identified literacy hour and drama sessions to highlight how different activities lend themselves to the two different structures, we have not attempted a rigid timetable within which the tasks should be done; this will depend on individual needs and organisation. The marginal boxes indicate specific references – possible, not exclusive – to elements of the National Literacy Strategy. Broadly speaking, the structure of the sessions will look like this:

Phase one   •   literacy hour sessions devoted to work on non-fiction text(s) related to looking after pets

Phase two   •   'The Billy Goats Gruff' story is introduced
            •   first drama takes place
            •   literacy hour sessions related to the text and the letter from Mrs Green

Phase three   •   literacy hour with hot-seating of Mrs Green and the warning sign she made for the Troll
            •   sessions related to warning signs, notices and labels and further hot-seating of Mrs Green

Phase four   •   literacy hour and other lessons related to making a book, *Everything You Need to Know about Trolls*
            •   second drama takes place.

Phase one

Shared text work

In the week before work on 'The Billy Goats Gruff' begins, the literacy hour will be devoted to non-fiction information books, in particular books with the theme of looking after pets. This will give the class the knowledge, skills and understanding they will need for work on making a book entitled *Everything You Need to Know about Trolls* in phase four of the work.

Phase two

Sharing the story

Read the story until the moment when the largest Billy Goat Gruff pushes the Troll into the water.

Key Question: *I wonder what became of that Troll?* List the possibilities on the board. As the question is open-ended there is no *right* answer; however, there is the opportunity to value imaginative ideas.

The class practise making the sound of the Billy Goats crossing the bridge 'Trip trap, trip trap', gradually increasing in volume. Finally the whole class make the sound of the Troll falling into the water: 'SPLASH'. All this is tape-recorded and will be used in the drama lesson. This work could be linked to work in music and provides the chance for children to use musical instruments to create the appropriate sound effects.

Repeated elements of the story

Year One Term 2 Word Level Work	Source material	
Phonological awareness Phonics and spelling To discriminate, read and spell words with initial consonant clusters, e.g. tr	The story 'The Billy Goats Gruff' trip trap, trip trap	**Focused word work**

Extension work on words that make sounds e.g. Trip trap, splash, crash etc.

Year One Term 2 Word Level Work	Source material	
Vocabulary extension New words from reading and shared experiences . . . to make collections of personal interest or significant words	The story 'The Billy Goats Gruff' e.g. Trip trap, trip trap, splash etc	**Group-independent work**

Reviewing, reflecting, consolidating teaching points and presenting work covered in the lesson.

Setting the context

First drama session

Between the two literacy lessons we have a drama lesson that links to the work the children have done on the story.

Gather the children around you and tell them that the drama is going to follow on from the work they did in the literacy hour. In the drama they are going to pretend to be the children of Newhill – Newhill is the village near the bridge where the Troll lives.

The children draw a map of the village, the school, the river, the bridge and Mrs Green's cottage near the bridge.

Move the children into a space and decide in which direction the Troll's bridge is and also point out a small cottage where Mrs Green lives. The children will meet Mrs Green later. *On their way home after school the children play on the hillside above the Troll's bridge. I want you to think of a game you would play on your way home. There are no fighting games. What other games might you play?*

Tell them to listen to the story and to freeze when they hear the sound of someone going over the bridge.

Narrate the story. *It was a beautiful summer's afternoon. The children of Newhill had finished school and were on their way home. They were playing games. Some were playing . . . others were playing . . .* Here use the suggestions they have come up with and are demonstrating.

Play the tape of the first Billy Goat Gruff crossing the bridge, 'Trip trap trip trap'. Tell the children to freeze and listen when they hear the 'Trip trap trip trap'. You may have to practise this until they understand what to do.

Continue to narrate the story: *The children carried on playing their games until they heard . . .* Again play the tape, this time the second Billy Goat Gruff crossing the bridge, 'Trip trap trip trap'.

Continue to narrate the story: *The children carried on playing their games until they heard . . .* Again, play the tape for the third Billy Goat crossing the bridge.

The children carried on playing their games until they heard . . . Play the sound of the 'SPLASH!'

The class freeze once more and you tell them you will go round and touch them on the shoulder and they can say what they think the noise was and what they think has happened to the Troll. *Has he drowned? Did he swim away?*

Stop the drama

The children sit around your chair and you tell them you are going to move the drama on to a few days later. They are going to play on the hill again and this time you are going to pretend to be somebody in the drama. You want them to listen very carefully and see if they can guess who this person is and what they want.

Take the role of someone delivering mail. As the children are playing you shout out: *There is a letter for Abid and the children of Newhill.* Show the letter and read it.

Key questions arise from this letter and they need to be discussed outside the drama because they have implications for the children's roles. They are described as 'Troll experts': it needs to be made clear what that means and that for the drama to work the whole class are going to do some work on becoming Troll experts. Also, some events have clearly taken place that are not in the original story and they need to be clarified and possible explanations put forward.

Rose Cottage
Greenfield Lane
Newhill
Tuesday 20 May

Dear Children of Newhill School,
I need your help. I have heard you know a lot about Trolls. I have a Troll in my shed. He is very wet and he is not very happy. He says he has had to leave his home under the bridge and he is very worried about the Troll eggs he was looking after. If he does not go back they will not hatch. He is afraid of the Big Billy Goat.

I have tried to help him before but he shouts at me and I am a bit frightened of him. Please can you help?

Best wishes

Mrs Green

There will be a great deal of discussion generated from this letter, and much of it will be in the form of questions that need to be asked. A possible literacy hour focus could be on identifying the questions and the statements in the letter.

The first session ends at this point and you tell them that tomorrow you will look at the letter again and have a chance to meet Mrs Green to find out more.

Phase two (continued)

Sharing the letter

The letter received in the drama becomes the focus for the text-level work. This is done by a large version of the letter being shown to the class.

Year One Term 2 Text Level Work	Source material	
Reading and comprehension To use phonological, contextual, grammatical and graphic knowledge To identify full stops and capital letters To discuss the reasons for, or causes of, incidents in stories	The letter from Mrs Green	**Shared text work**

Looking more closely at the letter

| **Focused word work** | The letter contains several words from the high-frequency list for Years One and Two. |

> Tuesday 20 May
>
> Dear Children of Newhill School,
> I need your help. I have heard you know a lot about Trolls. I have a Troll in my shed. He is very wet and he is not very happy. He says he has had to leave his home under the bridge and he is very worried about the Troll eggs he was looking after. If he does not go back they will not hatch. He is afraid of the Big Billy Goat.
> I have tried to help him before but he shouts at me and I am a bit frightened of him. Please can you help?
> Best wishes
>
> Mrs Green

Year One Term 2 Word Level Work	Source material
Word recognition, graphic knowledge and spelling	The letter from Mrs Green. High-frequency words: Tuesday, your, help, have, about, very, home, after, not, back, will
Vocabulary extension	Troll

| **Group-independent work** | The letter provides a range of teaching and learning opportunities. |

Year One Term 2 Sentence Level Work	Source material
To recognise full stops and capital letters when reading and understand how they affect the way a passage is read	The letter from Mrs Green without the full stops and capital letters. This will relate to the work the children did when they discussed the letter.

Phase three

Hot-seating Mrs Green

The class read again the large version of the letter and they devise questions for Mrs Green. Mrs Green is hot-seated (see Ideas 10): you do this with some key pieces of information in mind:

Shared text work

- Mrs Green has been aware of the Troll and his eggs for some time.
- To try and help the Troll she put up a large notice by the bridge to warn people not to cross so as not to disturb the Troll and his eggs. However, for some unknown reason the Troll pulled down the notice.
- She has heard that the children are Troll experts and she would really like their help.

OoR show some examples of warning notices and raise the question of what could have been written on the notice.

Focused word work

Year One Term 2 Sentence Level Work	Source material
New words from reading and shared experience and to make collections of personal interest or significant words and words linked to particular topics	Words associated with notices, signs: Danger Troll; Do not go near the bridge; Keep off; Don't touch.

Making warning notices, signs and labels

Time is set aside for making different kinds of warning signs, labels and notices. This could also be linked to work on non-verbal warning signs and pictorial representation of warnings – road signs etc.

Phase four

The Troll is getting worse

The class meets Mrs Green again. She tells them that the Troll is getting more and more bad-tempered. She expresses doubts about their ability to deal with him. Are they really experts?

Shared text work

Out of role tell the class they will have to make a book, *Everything You Need to Know about Trolls*. When they have completed the book they will be able to show it to Mrs Green to demonstrate their expertise.

Remind the class of the work they did on information books and looking after pets, reminding them how the book is organised, what is in the contents, what are the chapter headings and how the book is laid out.

Year One Term 2 Text Level Work	Source Material
Review of: the term's fiction and non-fiction, noting some of their differing features, e.g. layout, titles, contents pages, use of pictures, labelled diagrams	The book used in the earlier lessons on how to look after a pet.

Designing the book

Focused word work

Discuss with the children the chapter headings for the Troll book. For example:

Chapter One	What do Trolls look like?
Chapter Two	What do Trolls like to eat?
Chapter Three	What do we know about Trolls' eggs?
Chapter Four	What frightens Trolls?
Chapter Five	How do you move a Troll's eggs?
Chapter Six	How do you talk to a Troll?

Working with groups on their chapters

Work with groups on their draft chapters for the Troll book. This work can be differentiated. The less complex work will be related to what the Troll looks like and the more challenging work relating to the book.

Year One Term 2 Text Level Work	Source material
Writing composition To assemble information from own experience. E.g., . . . pets; to use simple sentences to describe, based on samples from reading	Sample non-fiction books

Writing a letter to Mrs Green

Before the class can go to meet Mrs Green they need to write a letter to her explaining that they think they would be able to help her and asking if they could come and visit her.

Shared text work

Year One Term 2 Text Level Work	Source material
Use some of the elements of known stories to structure own writing	Mrs Green's letter and other examples

Vocabulary extension work

The letter to Mrs Green and the book they have made will contain new words from their reading and shared experiences.

Focused word work

Year One Term 2 Text Level Work	Source material
New words from selected reading and shared experiences and collections of personal interest or significant words and words linked to particular topics	The chapters of the book

Second drama session

The hall or the classroom is set up as Mrs Green's cottage and her back garden with two chairs representing the door of the shed.

Talk about how to approach Mrs Green's cottage. *What sort of mood do you think she will be in? Who will knock at the door? What will you say when she answers the door? You will know when I am pretending to be Mrs Green because I will be holding these knitting needles.*

The Troll is getting more and more bad-tempered. I tried to feed him some porridge but he threw it out of the shed. I really don't know what to do. Can you tell me anything about Trolls?

Question the children about what you should feed the Troll etc. It is an opportunity to get them to tell you all they know and to read sections of their book. Ask them if they can try to talk to him because they seem to know so much. The class should have spent some time with you deciding upon what they need to take with them. The authors of each chapter will take on responsibility for different parts of the drama.

Set up the doors of the shed using two chairs, and agree that when you are the Troll you will sit on the other side of the chairs. You will come round from behind the chairs OoR to talk to the children about what the Troll says. *I want you to sit in front of the door to the shed and listen to what the Troll is saying, he doesn't know anybody is there. Listen to what he says and then we will talk about it.*

This is a good way to begin the next part of the drama as it gives the class a specific listening task. It will be short and focus their attention.

Meeting with the Troll

Sitting behind the chairs, begin to talk to yourself. *I'm hungry. I don't like porridge. Why did she bring me porridge? I want my eggs. They will be getting cold. If I could read this notice. 'D' . . . I think that's a 'D' . . .*

Reflecting on what the children have heard

The class has discovered three things:

- He is hungry.
- He is worried about his eggs.
- He is trying to read something – he cannot read very well.

Some games can be adapted to build tension in a drama, and one of these is 'the keeper of the keys'. The sign that the Troll has taken down is left by the door of the shed. The class need to retrieve it to see what it is the Troll cannot read. It is placed on the other side of the chairs. Either you or one of the children sit as if in the shed with your back to the children, while one of the children tries to get close enough to take the sign back to the class without waking the Troll. If the Troll hears a noise s/he puts a hand up or points to where the noise is coming from and the child must return before the Troll wakes up.

A similar task, only this time food is offered to the Troll by the group in charge of 'What do Trolls like to eat?'. As the Troll you may push the food back out of the shed door and say you are not hungry or you may keep it but say you are saving it for the baby Trolls.

Eventually the children will discover that the Troll cannot read the notice Mrs Green put up next to the bridge. The Troll believes it says, 'Billy Goats can cross this Bridge'. When the Troll trusts the children he will ask them to teach him what the notice says. This can be done with groups in the literacy hour group work session or with the whole class. I once worked with a class that had decided that the Troll's favourite food was a ham sandwich. The 'How do you talk to a Troll?' group told them they had to offer the sandwich on the end of a shovel because you should never get too close to a Troll that isn't eating a ham sandwich. Therefore they took into the drama a shovel and a picture of a ham sandwich!

CONCLUSION

For an alternative version of this drama see Part III. That version is not directly linked to the literacy hour and has a technology emphasis.

The National Literacy Strategy Document states that 'literacy enables children to communicate readily with others. It provides pupils with skills that give them access to the rest of the curriculum, which help them cope with everyday life and which help build self esteem' (DfEE 1998 p. 5). It is worth noting that these are the claims often made for drama: improved communication skills, building of self-esteem through successful resolution of dilemmas etc. Drama strategies provide the emergent writer and reader with a contextualisation of the signs and symbols they are struggling to make sense of. The context is a verbal and aural one, taking place before them in the present tense, 'as if' it is happening now: 'pupils become successful readers . . . learning to use a range of strategies to get at the meaning of text . . . the range of strategies can be depicted as a series of searchlights, each of which sheds light on the text. Successful readers use as many strategies as possible' (p. 3). We would suggest that drama is one of those searchlights: a way of actively engaging the children in the text as a way for them to make sense of it.

Just as it is recommended that 'they need to see the writing process being modelled by the teacher' (ibid p. 5), children are also helped by the modelling of language styles and registers through teacher role-play. They are put in the position through drama to (explain), 'to clarify and discuss . . . reasons in relation to the events in a story' (p. 8), and in this way they can see 'the way that different kinds of writing are used to serve different purposes' (p. 8).

By using drama in the literacy hour children will have an opportunity to question and in turn to be questioned (often through role) so that you may 'probe pupils' understanding, to cause them to reflect and refine their work, and to extend their ideas' (p. 8). Through drama pupils will be put in the position of

> investigating ideas: e.g. to understand, expand on or generalize about themes and structures in fiction . . . discussing and arguing: e.g. to put points of view, argue a case, justify a preference . . . listening to and responding: e.g. to stimulate and extend pupils' contributions, to discuss/evaluate their presentations.
>
> (p. 8)

SUMMARY

- It is possible to use drama within the literacy hour and alongside it.

- Hot-seating, forum theatre and still image are strategies that lend themselves to the literacy hour.
- The use of TiR adds a potent linguistic dimension to the literacy hour because it creates a kind of dialogue different from the usual teacher/pupil dialogue.
- As a teaching and learning strategy the use of TiR gains and holds the attention of pupils.

Teacher in Role

Teacher in Role (TiR) is the key to developing the educational potential of drama. However, our experience through in-service training and working with training teachers on teaching practice has indicated some resistance to using the strategy, usually by teachers who haven't had the opportunity to see it working or haven't been given a chance to try it out. They are initially put off by the word 'role'. A common response is, 'Oh, I couldn't do *role-play*, I can't *act*.'

In order to defuse the worries and fears teachers have about using role-play in their teaching, let us begin by saying something about the word 'role' and the relationship between drama in education and theatre. The confusion begins with using the same words to describe different things. The word 'role' can be used in a theatrical context to describe a written part in a scripted play, but it is used in drama in education to describe taking on a particular attitude or viewpoint, in an unscripted, improvised context where there is no audience, just the participants in the drama. It is no wonder that TiR is perceived as requiring the same kind of skills that are required to perform in front of an audience. The reality is that the TiR is much nearer to an infant teacher telling a story than to an actor in a theatrical performance.

THE STORYTELLER AND THE SOCIAL ACTOR

Now let us look at the word 'actor', beginning with the concept of the social actor. We are all aware of behaving in particular ways according to particular contexts. If we think of ourselves in the following contexts we can imagine within varying degrees differing behaviours appropriate to different situations.

at the job interview	at the wedding reception	in the staff room
at the football match	on the beach	at the school fair
at the wedding service	receiving the MBE	in the classroom

Sociologists have used the idea of a 'social actor' as a way to explain the different ways in which we behave, consciously or unconsciously, in different social contexts (see Goffman 1976). If we narrow down the social context to the primary school, it is easy as teachers to identify the variety of roles we play and witness other teachers playing. As we gain experience in our teaching we become more and more skilled at presenting different teacher roles appropriate to different situations. For example, the clearing-up-at-the-end-of-the-day teacher is not the same as the one-to-one-counselling teacher. The very-disappointed-with-your-behaviour teacher is different from the very-pleased-with-your-work teacher and the telling-a-story-to-a-small-group teacher is different from getting-the-whole-school-in-the-hall-for-assembly teacher. We slip from one teacher role to another. The changes are indicated by variation of intonation, volume, use of silence, smiles, frowns, nods and shakes of the head, pointing, raising hands in the air, clapping and putting a finger on lips – in other words a process of carefully selected signals that are sent out to the children. This selection is drawn from a range of conventions that pupils learn as they meet and interact with teachers. Inexperienced teachers watch experienced teachers at work and borrow techniques. In the borrowing the signals become part of that particular teacher's repertoire and this combines with each teacher's own social actor style. Looking at 'role' in this sociological rather than theatrical perspective shifts the emphasis away from the skills of the actor in a stage sense to the development of the teacher as social actor, that is specific semiotic skills appropriate for managing children in the classroom. TiR takes the social actor and the teacher as social actor and puts them in a fictional context.

THE TEACHER USING ROLE-PLAY

Let us now look at the distinctive features of this particular 'presentation of self'. As we have said, the teacher is using role, in the social actor sense, all the time. However, when we use TiR we are in a *negotiated fictional situation*. Unlike the social acting that takes place *in reality*, this form of social acting is clearly a pretend activity by the teacher. You are behaving 'as if' you are someone else, and therefore you need to make it clear to the children, *at all times*, that you are *pretending*. It is, in a way, the first rule of the game you are playing. They must be absolutely clear that you are pretending to be someone else, and this is usually helped by using a symbol (or role signifier), often a hat or another piece of clothing, to signal that while you are wearing it you are *in role*.

In taking on a role you will essentially take an attitude, a viewpoint. You will use your filing cabinet of social actor skills and signal or sign your point of view. All that is required is that, through the words you use and your demeanour, you demonstrate someone with a particular view of the world.

For example, you may signal to the class

- worried you – as Mrs Green (meeting the children to tell them about the Troll, see Ideas 3)

- sad you – as Goldilocks's Dad (having received the letter from the Three Bears, see Ideas 2)
- arrogant or pompous you – as the Mayor of Hamelin (telling the Pied Piper he will not be paid, see Part III).

You will use the same set of signals you would use if you were being yourself, the difference being that you have told the children about the game you are playing: you are going to pretend to be someone else and you want them to watch and listen to this person very carefully and then you will talk to them about what they have heard and seen.

THE KEY COMPONENTS OF TIR

In order to help this work, the class need to have the opportunity to talk about the person they are going to meet or to have the chance to talk about the role *during* the meeting. This means that TiR is not a teaching strategy that once you start you are locked into and cannot leave – far from it. TiR works effectively only when you shift in and out of role to stimulate then reflect upon the input. It would be more accurate to call it 'teacher in and out of role' because that is actually how it works in practice!

GOING IN AND OUT OF ROLE

A key element in good use of TiR is the regular leaving of the role to check out the understanding of the children, in much the same way as we put a story down to talk about it. It is as if you are working on two axes of dialogue (see Figure 10): each axis creates a different kind of dialogue, in role dialogue and teacher dialogue. TiR exists in the present tense and teacher OoR in past tense or sometimes in the future tense.

For example, TiR as Goldilocks's Dad

> *I am really fed up, I don't know what to do. You seem to know lots about children, can you help me?*

The conversation is taking place *as if* the event is happening *now*. When you come out of role it can be:

- in the past tense when reflecting on what the role has just said or done. Teacher out of role: *What did Goldilocks's Dad mean when he said 'You seem to know lots about children'?* or
- in the future tense when planning what to do next. Teacher out of role: *So you want to know whether he plays with her or takes her to the park? OK. Are you going to ask him that? What are you going to say?*

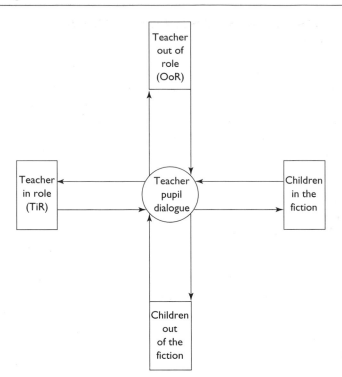

Figure 10 The two axes of dialogue

Much of teacher/pupil talk is about what has happened or what is going to happen. One of the exciting things about dialogue with TiR is that it is happening now and we are not always sure what is going to happen next, therefore producing productive tension, the expectations driving interest.

The nature of the dialogue created when Goldilocks's Dad (TiR) is asking the children for help in dealing with his naughty daughter (i.e. teacher pretending to be someone who needs help) is patently different from the dialogue of teacher asking the children what Goldilocks's father said to them (OoR). There is not only a difference of tense but also in power relationship. The power relationship between pupils and TiR can be the opposite of the one that usually exists between teacher and pupils. The teacher can become the one who doesn't know any answers. This can be very exciting for the children. You don't get too many chances to teach the teacher! It can also push the security of the teacher to the edge, and you must never let go of your professional duty to manage the behaviour of the class so that teaching and learning can take place. That is why persistently moving out of role is important, important to maintain teacher security and also the children's security. The children must never think that the teacher has abandoned them, they must always see that you are still there looking after them, managing them and in charge.

BEHAVIOUR MANAGEMENT, CONTROL AND DISCIPLINE

If I use role-play, will class discipline be threatened? Any discussion of the use of teacher role-play must make reference to one of the biggest worries teachers have about TiR, and that is whether it threatens a breakdown of discipline in the class. The simple answer is that it usually does the opposite! It can bring in the very pupils whose behaviour can be disruptive; however, there are certain key elements that need to be there if it is to be successful. These are:

- clear expectations about what is going to happen
- a serious commitment to the role by the teacher
- valuing of pupils who signal a commitment either verbally or non-verbally to the role and the fiction
- a role that will interest the children, one that deals with things they are interested in
- complete honesty with the children about when drama works and when it does not, including what is negotiable and what is not
- sanctioning those pupils who try to undermine or destroy the fiction
- moving in and out of role to discuss what is happening.

What you will notice about this list is that much of it is related to good and successful practice in teaching anyway. Clarity of expectations, clear rewards and sanctions, interesting stimulus, creating a valuing and secure environment: all these things we try to do in all lessons. The only difference here is that we are managing this distinctive drama element of the teacher shifting between fiction and reality.

Let us look more closely at each of these preconditions and see how they undermine disruptive behaviour.

Clear expectations about what is going to happen

In a moment I am going to put this chain on and pretend to be the Mayor of Hamelin. I want you to watch what I do and listen to what I say and then we'll talk about it. Is that OK? In clarifying what is going to happen and what we expect the children to do we are laying down the constraints of the teaching and learning process and in that way making it more secure for both teacher and pupil.

A serious commitment to the role by the teacher

All the gestures and words will signal that you as teacher take very seriously the game you are playing, if you don't, the children are unlikely to. When children have not seen you take on a role some of them may laugh, others will not, they will be right there in the fiction immediately. You can usually ride over the initial giggles of embarrassment from those who are struggling with this new way of working. Immediately homing in on those who show belief will help this.

Valuing of pupils who signal a commitment either verbally or non-verbally to the role and the fiction

These children, and there are always some, who very easily shift into this way of working are your biggest allies. They will through their commitment take the others with them. Plenty of positive affirmation of these children will create a positive climate and attitude to drama. Again, it is not always the children who are successful in other lessons who are the most successful or earnest in the drama.

A role that will interest the children, one that deals with things they are interested in

As with other lessons, the interest level is important to the success of the work. TiR tends to hold a broad interest level because of the range of levels at which it can be understood. A child may not understand every word of the Mayor's speech in 'The Pied Piper' – words like 'election' and 'vote' may not have much meaning – but the Mayor definitely sounds as if he is selling something and his intonation and demeanour appear to be friendly, therefore the interest level will be broad.

Complete honesty with the children about when drama works and when it does not, including what is negotiable and what is not

and

Sanctioning those pupils who try to undermine or destroy the fiction

We have put these together because it is very important that children understand, and you are going to be totally honest about the fact, that, if the class don't want drama and/or TiR to work, then it won't work. It is a group activity and there are more of them than you! If collectively they want to stop it working then it won't work. This is where TiR can be so effective. Watching, listening to and interacting with a role is very attractive to children. The earlier you can get a role into a drama the better. It may be for a very short time, but it will grab the attention of the children and immediately generate questions and problems that need to be solved. As with all teaching and learning situations, disruptive behaviour needs to be dealt with, and good teachers and good schools have policies and consistent approaches to deal with poor behaviour. Drama should be dealt with using the same approach, making clear what kind of behaviour helps it work and valuing the behaviour that achieves this.

Moving in and out of role to discuss what is happening

Going into role may be for very short periods of time – ten seconds, thirty seconds or a minute. This is particularly important in the early stages of meeting a role. The role's attitude can be clarified, you can check out the children's understanding and remain secure in using the strategy. Children do not have a problem with this because the shifting in and out of fictional worlds (metaxis) is something they are able to do easily and can be observed in their own social role play (see Ideas 1 – social role-play). The other dimension to this is teacher security. It is very difficult to sustain a role for long periods of time, and in fact it can be confusing for the children. Both you and the children need to reflect upon what has happened, what was said, how it appeared. This checking out of understanding, reflecting upon possible consequences and making decisions about where to go next are essential strands to successful and rewarding drama for children. They need to feel they are part of narrative creation and the OoR discussion and decision-making are part of this. Again you feel more secure as a teacher when you regularly return to being teacher from TiR, and it underlines the fact for the class that you haven't gone away. As one child once said to a student, *It's as if the teacher is at the door watching, ready to come back in and talk about what happened.*

SELECTIVITY AND ROLE-PLAY

The essence of taking on a role is the selection of words, intonation and non-verbal signals in order to indicate the kind of role we want to present. We must carefully select what we wish to say and how we wish to present ourselves in a role. We must also select the symbols we wish to use to support the teacher role-play. Let us look in more detail at two roles and examine the selectivity that goes into their presentation. First, Goldilocks's Dad (at the beginning of the drama) (see Ideas 2).

- **role signifier**: a flat cap
- **context indicator**: a chair which represents 'somewhere to sit down on a path in the forest'
- **attitude teacher wishes to present**: a sad father; a father disappointed in his daughter; a father who can't control his daughter and needs the help of people who know about naughty children
- **non-verbal clues**: sad face; sighs; looks at letter from Bears – looks sad; looks at torn reading book – looks sad

- **verbal clues**: *what am I going to do with her? And now I've got this letter*
- **role commitment**: Non-verbal and verbal signals demonstrate total commitment to the role and therefore the drama. In other words the presentation of Goldilocks's Dad remains consistent and is broken only by moving OoR and back to being teacher. This is signalled by taking off the hat, putting down the book and the letter, standing up and moving away from the chair.

The other example is the Mayor of Hamelin when he meets the angry townspeople.

- **role signifier**: chain of office
- **context indicator**: a chair behind a desk
- **attitude teacher wishes to present**: *I understand your problems; I am a caring Mayor; It is all under control; I have plans in hand*
- **non-verbal clues**: understanding looks; nodding with sympathy; shaking of the head with disappointment
- **verbal clues**: agreeing with all the townspeople say; informing them help is on its way
- **role commitment**: non-verbal and verbal signals demonstrate total commitment to the role and therefore the drama. The return to teacher is signalled by taking off the chain and coming from behind the desk.

TIR AND THEATRE

It is clear from what has been said that TiR is *not* about giving a performance. However, there is no doubt that TiR *borrows* from theatre. It does this in several ways:

- the use of role – verbal and non-verbal communication
- the use of props
- the setting of a context
- the use of tension.

The use of role – signalling an attitude not a character

TiR borrows from theatre but in a minimalist fashion. Although in role you behave *as if* you were someone else, it is done in a low-key fashion and without shifting into presenting *character*. The presentation of a character, as in a stage performance, will often involve using a different voice or accent or a change in body shape or the way in which you walk or move. This adoption of character becomes redundant in the use of TiR because the contexts in which the children meet the role have been explained and negotiated. This is quite different from the actor on the stage. She has to assume that the audience is seeing the play for the first time and therefore needs a great deal of information as quickly as possible, and some of the audience may be sitting thirty metres away! The physical distance between us affects the kinds of signals we choose to send in order to communicate effectively with each other.

As teachers we can relate to this when we think of leading assemblies compared to working with the children around us in the literacy hour. When using TiR you will have discussed with the class and will continue to discuss and clarify what is happening throughout the drama. This kind of dialogue, and negotiation of understanding, enables the adoption of role to be much closer to social role interaction than to performance. If it is too theatrical, too much like a performance in front of an audience in a theatre, then it will lose its credibility with the class. Just as someone behaving theatrically in real life can be disconcerting and unnerving, so can a teacher who begins to perform, in a theatrical sense, when using TiR. The children will stop believing and they are less likely to become engaged in the drama. They may even feel embarrassed because the behaviour will feel inappropriate and the embarrassment may generate pushing the role away rather than engaging with it. The nearer the *social actor* rather than the *theatrical actor*, the more engaging and beguiling the role will be.

It is sometimes very useful to give the children a chance to be the role themselves. In drama there often is a need for the class to take on the role they have been talking to, through the use of forum theatre (see Ideas 10) for example. In order for them to feel able to do this they must feel they can be themselves talking for the role. If they see you demonstrate the role as yourself they will model their behaviour on this approach.

The use of props

Again, this is borrowed from theatre but in a minimalist fashion. The prop acts as a signifier; it tells the children when you are in and out of role. It can be a hat for Cindy and Morrella or a bandaged sling in Humpty Dumpty. In 'The Pied Piper' the pipe signifies the Pied Piper and the Mayor's chain the Mayor. When placed on a chair they can represent either of the roles in conversation using forum theatre (see Part III for full descriptions of the dramas).

The setting of a context

A sense of place can be created verbally through narration and by the use of chairs, desks and teacher's table. Again the emphasis is on using the minimum required to take us to the situation of the drama. This can be done by verbal location out of the drama: *These two chairs are going to be the stone entrance to the mountain where the Pied Piper has led the children.* Or it can be done by the teacher OoR: *This bench will be the bridge where the Troll lives, and I want you to find a space on one side of the bridge and listen to me begin to tell the story. 'All the children of*

Newhill were playing on the hill above the river. When they looked down they could see the bridge where the Troll lived . . .'

The use of tension

Tension is an essential ingredient in performance: it can be created through the use of lighting, sound effects and music as well as what the audience see and hear. In drama in education a TiR can also create tension. This can be done by:

- what the children know and the role 'does not'
- what is said
- what is not said
- surprise
- the use of silence
- a sudden change of mood.

THE RELATIONSHIP BETWEEN ROLE STATUS AND LEARNING INTENTION

In choosing a role you need to be clear about what learning you wish to take place. Different types of role will produce different kinds of response from children and these responses will open up different learning possibilities. One way to categorise roles is to look at their status or power position. We can therefore divide the roles into high status, equal status and low status.

High status

The high-status role can be the most attractive role because it is most like a teacher, but it can be the most difficult to manage for the same reason. Unfortunately it is most like a teacher without being a teacher, rather like when inexperienced students struggle to manage a class because the pupils don't perceive them as proper teachers. The temptation for the children is to use the safety of the fiction to destroy the role, sometimes known as 'Let's kill the king!'. In 'The Pied Piper' the Mayor is a powerful role, and his incompetence will generate a good deal of criticism from the children in role as the people of Hamelin. This can be productive as long as it is channelled into articulating the issues for the people. The Pied Piper is also high-status and powerful and in order for some authenticity to be maintained his power must be agreed and contracted with the class, like this: *Remember, the Pied Piper is very powerful, he can use magic and will use it unless we are very careful. We must not upset him, is that agreed? We cannot destroy him, is that agreed? Our drama will not work unless we agree these things.*

In this way we can use the power of the role to generate productive dialogue, that is dialogue where learning takes place. The problem with high-status roles is they are very like being teacher, and that is their weakness. Role-play gives us the opportunity to be something not teacher-like, and that is when role can create a different and more productive kind of dialogue.

Equal status

More easily managed is a role of equal status. In this role the teacher is able to give information, ask advice, intercede to support and to warn against pitfalls and danger. The power to make decisions within the fiction is with the pupils and, while the role of equal status will offer advice and support, it is not the role's job to tell the pupils what they should do.

For example, see the use in Ideas 2 of the Goldilocks role who works very much on a par with the children, except that they know more about her than she thinks: that gives them status and an investment in the drama.

Low status

This kind of role is often most engaging for young children because, unlike their usual power relationship with their teacher, this inverts the status and they are faced with someone 'who does not know' and usually needs their help. All of the victim roles in our example dramas are like this.

HOW TIR OPERATES

Demands of TiR	Implications for the children
You are in the drama with the children.	You demonstrate the demand to take the work seriously.
You must make clear the fact you are 'in role' by using role signifiers.	The children feel secure because expectations and the conventions are made concrete – particularly important with young children.
You must be willing to accept the possibility of new responses.	The children define and decide, they see their ideas made possible, their decisions acted upon.
You must plan carefully the viewpoint of the role and select language and status of the role.	The resulting authenticity draws the children into forms of teacher/pupil dialogue not possible in the usual teacher/pupil relationship.
You must structure the role to challenge the children's ideas; this can mean taking up viewpoints that are deliberately wrong or controversial.	The children have the opportunity to disagree and challenge the viewpoint of the TiR – in this way they can explore ideas with no blame attached to them.

continued . . .

Demands of TiR	Implications for the children
You must be prepared to take the role of 'the one who does not know'.	The children's status is enhanced and they have the captivating experience of teaching the teacher.
You should be able to demonstrate a change of attitude.	Pupils experience successfully shifting opinion through their actions and arguments.
You can create tension through the use of secrecy, reluctance to speak, revealing something new, blocking ideas, applying pressure, challenging thinking, suggesting possibilities, i.e. 'depending upon'.	Because interaction with the TiR takes place in the 'present tense', children do not know what is going to happen next – this adds to the potency of the process.
You can manage the behaviour of the children from within the role.	Children respond because the control is coming from within the fictional context – something they have invested in with their ideas.
You can give them tasks without appearing to be teacher-oriented.	The need to speak, listen, read and write can be greater because of the demand of the fiction.

SUMMARY

- Using TiR does not require the ability to 'act' in a theatre and performance sense.
- TiR demands being yourself but with a particular attitude or viewpoint.
- Moving in and out of role is important to effective use of TiR. It maintains teacher and pupil security while at the same time creating the opportunity for pupils to reflect on what has happened and for teachers to assess the children's understanding.
- TiR is supported by several devices which are borrowed from theatre and these need to be considered when planning to use a role. They are:
  - careful choice of the words used, particularly in the first meeting with a role
  - a conscious decision about the non-verbal signals that will support the attitude being demonstrated
  - props or role signifiers
  - the deliberate creation of tension at appropriate moments.

Moving children into role

'Mantle of the Expert'

WHAT ARE WE TRYING TO DO WHEN WE PUT CHILDREN INTO ROLE?

Drama is not about the teacher taking roles and the children remaining as themselves. It is always the case, even when the children appear to have no defined role, as with the class when they meet Goldilocks and her Dad (Ideas 2), that they are shifting into fiction. This means that they begin to talk and behave in ways that fit the fiction, to take action and adopt attitudes which are not real. It is a very short step to giving them specified roles where what is required from them is clearly part of the fiction. Then we are asking them not to become someone else, not to act in a theatrical way, but to take up a new viewpoint, to look at the situation in a different way. Compare this to what we have said about the teacher taking on role in Ideas 4. We most often ask the children to look at the drama situation as though they are adults. This is the power of the 'as if' mode of drama.

There are a number of key objectives that can be achieved by deliberately putting children into role within a drama. We aim:

- *to give them a* viewpoint *from which to approach the learning embodied in the drama.* Giving them a role makes them think of that viewpoint more than if they were just to remain themselves. For example, if they are dealing with Max (see Ideas 2) as parents rather than as themselves they start with having to think 'parent-view', to consider what a parent would think of Max's behaviour rather than as a child and that helps them to think not simply of what a child would want. The 'parent-view' is not a particular parent but parent in a more general sense. When they are acting as a group role the different 'parent-views' of different children can surface. The contrasting views, the resulting conflict, debate and consideration can help them to come to a more informed idea of 'parent' too, thus providing breadth of viewpoint.
- *to promote language learning by putting them into a position that makes particular demands on speaking and listening*

- *to help them explore a particular content.* For example if they are foresters designing a trail for the public they have to take up a 'forester-view'. They have to pool their understandings about what they know of the forest and the work done in it into the role and the decision-making. This is where we can introduce learning related directly to the curriculum.
- *to protect them.* A role can provide distance from the subject matter because they are taking on a fictional position. The distance helps them look at controversial or difficult material with no threat.
- *to raise their status.* Children will learn more effectively if they are given status within the learning process, and one way of doing that is to give them roles with adult powers, not to keep them as children. A corollary to this is that you must take a role of lesser authority at times, though never relinquishing the responsibility of teacher overall (see Ideas 4).
- *to produce group cohesion.* To do this we tend to give the children a whole group role. In such a role they are required to work together, support each other.
- *to promote communication skills and social health deriving from developing inter-personal skills.* The children have to think through different viewpoints that there might be within a group and come to a position where, even if they disagree, they negotiate a compromise or agree to differ. This must happen so that they can act as a whole group to tackle the issues facing them.
- *to develop the children's skills in handling drama*, to operate seriously, which is the key demand of the role, to behave as a convincing 'parent' or 'forester' or other role would. This happens in pretend play.

WHAT SORT OF ROLE BEST PROMOTES THESE OBJECTIVES?

The examples given above to illustrate the objectives are taken from the particular type of role known as 'Mantle of the Expert', originated by Dorothy Heathcote. In this the children are given a role, usually a recognisable professional one and task-based, e.g. archaeologist, forester, party-organiser, farmer, town councillor, clothes designer. They can even be given fictitious expert roles, e.g. Troll experts in 'The Billy Goats Gruff' (see Part III); but even an invented one must be analogous to a real expertise. The Troll experts are like experts on any creature, so the children can offer areas they might be expert in – food, health, behaviour.

The expertise can also be more generalised, e.g. as 'people who know about settling quarrels', 'people who help children with problems' so that it ties in with general qualities the children can bring to the work. All of these roles enable the children to bring a particular viewpoint to the situation, usually one of problem-solver.

The viewpoint can be used to base the whole drama, e.g. children as forestry experts planning a visitors' centre for the forest they work in. It can also be used to take them to a drama the focus of which is not the expertise itself. They might be faced with an incident, letter, a teacher role who takes them into a drama development that uses their expertise but is not their usual job, e.g. the foresters who find a lost child in the forest and have to deal with him or her (see 'Hansel and Gretel', Part III). The connection is that the foresters 'care' for the forest but then have to apply that caring in a different way.

CAN 'MANTLE OF THE EXPERT' BE USED WITH EARLY YEARS CHILDREN?

Are children of this age not too young to take on roles as experts? Are they able to act as adults and to take on responsibility?

It is by playing at and imitating adult roles that children begin the process of learning what the world requires of them. See the section on play in Ideas 1. They adopt all sorts of roles in their play where they approximate to adult behaviour, choosing to take on roles such as mums and dads, doctors, astronauts, farmers etc. If we utilise this natural predisposition in school and make them feel able to take on roles and responsibility, children will accept the challenge and even stretch themselves as much as possible to do so. As a result they learn beyond what we might expect of them. How can we help them do this?

'SUPERHELPERS'

One example of a 'Mantle of the Expert' role for infants is 'Superhelpers'. The aim is to put the children in role as an agency who are *experts at helping people who have problems*, i.e. to be required to model and behave at all times supportively and positively towards people with problems. The initial setting up of this role itself could take two half-hour sessions. It can be separate or it can be the lead in session two directly to one of the fuller dramas to which it relates.

Contracting with the children

Gather the children on the carpet as at story time and discuss what sort of things they do to help other people. Define the nature of helping and then go on to consider the nature of 'Superhelpers', people who are very good at helping. *What does helping mean? How can you help people when they have problems? What sorts of talk do you use when you help people? How do you have to treat them?*

Here it is important to use questioning to help them understand what the role involves, to build belief in the role. *In the story we are going to do you are going to be a group of people who help other people when they bring their problems to you. They are called 'Superhelpers'. I think you'd be good at that.*

It is important that Superhelpers are not magic, do not have magic powers. Stress that the 'super' part of the name is about being very good at the job, not being like Superman or Superwoman.

Tests for Superhelpers

Give the children a chance to try out the Superhelpers' role. Provide two roles with problems for them to tackle; the first is a trial of observation, the nature of helping and also whether they can do drama, i.e. pretend with you.

The lost teddy bear

Stand up, saying, *When I sit down again I am going to be a little girl/boy. See if you can see what her or his problem is.*

Deliberately and in full view of the children 'hide' a small teddy bear under something suitable nearby. Then sit down in the chair looking very sad and wait for the children to talk to you. If they do not, begin to talk to yourself to prompt them: *I'm not very happy. . . .* Develop the dialogue along the lines of the 'lost' bear, how much it means to you etc. The children offer to find it. Let them. At the end as the TiR you honour and upgrade their work saying, *Oh, thanks very much. I didn't know where he was. I wouldn't have been able to sleep tonight without him.*

If the children are not responsive at any point in this, there is no problem; you can go OoR and talk to them about the girl or boy and ask what they should do. This gives them a chance to build confidence in dealing with the situation and gives them permission to speak to her if they feel unsure. In addition you can go OoR if necessary to help them learn how to tackle the drama, for example to help them see the need to pretend to search for the bear rather than just go directly to where they know the bear was put. That is all part of the pretend or fiction of drama.

The children will learn the rules of drama quickly if they helped to relate them to their own pretend play.

The boy who has fallen out with his Mum

The second problem role is more challenging, demanding more attention, listening and questioning on the children's part. It can follow immediately on from 'the lost bear' or can be tried on another occasion. The work benefits from being grown slowly. (The role is a 'boy' because it was originally designed by a male. It could be a girl.)

You did very well in helping find that bear and make that girl or boy feel better and showed all the skills of Superhelpers. Do you think you can help a little boy with a more difficult problem?

I'll be the boy who has a problem. When I come in as him to sit in the chair, just look at how he is. Do not speak to him. Then when I stop being the boy tell me what you notice about him.

Get up, go a few steps away and come back with an angry face and body signals, carrying a television listings magazine as a role signifier. (A role signifier is the object or piece of clothing the role always has to show the children that the teacher is in role.)

Stamp your foot and sit grumpily in the chair. Behave angrily, muttering, *She'll be sorry . . . It's not fair . . . It's my room . . .* and angrily leaf through the magazine etc.

Come OoR to discuss: *What did you notice about him? . . . I wonder what's wrong . . . What would you like to ask him? How will you talk to him?*

Back in role, answer the questions as the boy. Gradually 'he' tells about a row with Mum over not tidying his room that has led to a ban on watching television.

Then the children have to advise him on what to do.

If necessary, Mum (TiR2) comes to talk to them too. The use of more than one TiR is an important idea for the children to get used to (see Ideas 2, Step 3). 'Mum' has a different role signifier, perhaps a coat.

The outcome will be that the children sort the problem by giving advice to the boy and/or Mum. Praise their skill as Superhelpers. Then move on to setting up Superhelpers for the first full drama. Again this can follow straight on or be introduced on another occasion.

Setting up the Superhelper Agency

Discuss with the children how to set up the 'Superhelper' Agency offices they work from. They work in teams. Each group has its own area. *What does it look like? What happens there? How would you get to know about people who have problems?*

Establish the classroom as the offices, with labels on the various areas they decide it has or you decide they need – a table where letters are opened, a telephone area, an interview area, a place to write to clients etc.

In addition, to add importance to the enterprise, a logo or sign can be put up and used on notepaper. Figure 11 is an example.

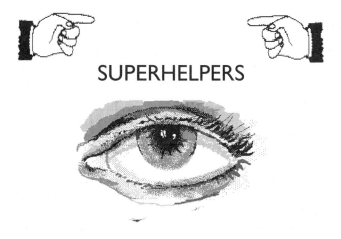

Figure 11 Superhelpers' logo

Running the Agency offices

Starting on the carpet, greet the children as at the beginning of the day's work and set up a possible agenda for the day. Then they go to their work places. The children begin to play. Some answer telephones, some open letters, some write up their notes on the problems just solved. Help them by interventions that focus their play most productively. The children must be encouraged to be serious and make it 'look real'. You have a very important task in modelling and encouraging them. Circulate as manager of the Agency, fully accepting the 'reality' of the activities, picking up a 'phone' or miming opening letters, talking to the Super-helpers about what they are doing, writing notes about what a Superhelper tells you etc., always treating them as *adults*, who know what they are doing. They are the experts and must be made to feel so.

The playing in the office will help the children build belief in their role by giving them some ownership over the place and actions. It also helps the less confident children begin to feel part of the play; they might begin to try a bit of role here where they might not feel able to contribute as fully when the whole group are questioning together.

Then introduce the first request for help that leads into a full drama (or finish and save that for next session).

Long-term use of Superhelpers

Using Superhelpers can be an extended experience. It is a whole-group role for the children which can be used and become stronger over several full dramas. Over a term or a year they can tackle the series of problems that a range of characters (TiR) seek help about. At the same time the children become more skilled and knowledgeable about how to handle this role, and more expert in it.

See Part II later in the book, where a series of full dramas will show how Superhelpers have to face the problems based on five traditional stories:

- 'Jill and the Beanstalk': a dishonest boy
- 'Mr Wolf Makes Mistakes': learning what they know about behaviour by teaching an adult how to behave properly
- 'Sleeping Beauty': helping someone who feels an outsider
- 'Little Bo Peep': helping someone who is misunderstood
- 'Cinderella': helping a family who do not talk to each other properly

Let us look in more detail at the nature of the 'Mantle of the Expert' role. It is capable of operating at two levels: full and modified.

FULL 'MANTLE OF THE EXPERT'

Dorothy Heathcote developed the method as a way of teaching the whole curriculum. Children are put in charge of running an enterprise where they need to work in a number of curriculum areas. The enterprise is chosen from different types of enterprise that offer different approaches to the learning – see below. The role of experts for the children needs to be of interest and one to which the children can bring at least some vestigial knowledge (from books, television or their own direct experiences). Time, as much as half a term, is spent building up the knowledge of the role so that the expertise becomes more real. The children must earn the label of expert rather than just wearing it for the purpose of the drama. Therefore the children learn the skills and the knowledge over a period of time so that they do as far as possible have the content knowledge needed for the expertise. The roles come from different domains according to the teaching that the role is to make possible; they are functional roles and based on tasks. The role is designed to access aspects of the curriculum that are required, for example:

Type of enterprise	Role	Curriculum areas
ecological	Foresters who are anxious that no one should get into the dangerous areas of the forest	geography, maths, English, science
service	Employees of a company that organises parties	English, design
manufacturing	Employees of a clothing factory	maths, design and technology
research	People writing a book on Trolls and their ways	all subjects but with an emphasis on science and English

(For fuller accounts of Dorothy Heathcote's 'Mantle of the Expert' method see Bolton 1992 and Heathcote and Bolton 1995.)

MODIFIED 'MANTLE OF THE EXPERT'

It can be difficult with the age group we are concerned with to follow the fully developed model of the 'Mantle of the Expert' as Dorothy Heathcote has run it. This is because it

- requires a slow building of the expertise which does not easily fit within the school framework and its restraints
- tends to apply to older children.

Generally, if we are using the expert approach for one short drama, we have taken the model as developed by Dorothy Heathcote and modified it to make it more easily accessible within limited time. In the adapted version, the level of expertise stays more at the early stages of the full version. The expertise is pretended more and based on things already known. No demand is made upon the children that would reveal any lack of ability or undermine belief in themselves. Roles are chosen so that children can assume expertise. For example, as expert party-organisers even the youngest children bring knowledge and ideas they can put together and use to help them feel *expert*, (see 'Sleeping Beauty' Part II).

This does not mean that the children are never given tasks where they have to do further research, to learn within the context of the drama and also to take on further learning in the classroom outside of the drama. That is one of the purposes of drama, to provide *the need to know*.

However, as indicated above, the Superhelpers concept can allow development over a longer period, building up the expertise, especially if they tackle different problems over a number of dramas using the same role for themselves.

QUALITIES OF THE 'MANTLE OF THE EXPERT' ROLE

'Mantle of the Expert' enables children to	Examples based on 'Jill and the Beanstalk' (Part II)
do work arising from *context*	A gardener asks for help to clear a big weed from his garden
contribute what they can and it will be used	The children offer ways of getting rid of the weed and later ideas to help Jack
work at different *pace* and *level* legitimately	Some offer ideas, some support and follow; some talk from the start, others later
'run things'	Children tackle calming Jack's mother, suggest how to get rid of the beanstalk, find a way of getting Jack out of the dungeon
carry *responsibility*	Children decide what to do about the Giant's losses and Jack's stealing
see the results of their actions *quickly*	Children take decisions about the beanstalk, how to get Jack back etc. acted on then and there
look behind product *to perceive process*	Children reflect on how we make these decisions, what are the best courses of action, the reasons for deciding
move from talk in action to *illustration, calculation and recording*	Children discuss what to do with 'weed', measure it, act to tackle it

'Mantle of the Expert' enables children to	Examples based on 'Jill and the Beanstalk' (Part II)
have to communicate with each other	Discuss suggestions within the whole group
make subtle use of communication, especially the non-verbal	Jack's mother's anger at the invasion of her garden is verbal and non-verbal – children have to use both to deal with her
move away from competition and to the valuing of each person's contribution	All the group tackle the same problem and the group must act together

DEMANDS ON THE TEACHER

You usually take a role as one of this group of experts or its co-ordinator and thus can model the qualities of commitment to the role and ask questions. You can make points to help the children clarify and believe in the role. You must move to a position of letting them take some of the responsibility.

You have to be able to	Examples from 'Jill and the Beanstalk'
avoid/withhold telling	You must not tell them how to handle Jack's stealing.
tolerate apparent *confusion*	If the children are unsure then try to help *them* make things clearer.
value each child's contributions	The children suggest chopping down the beanstalk, poisoning it, letting it stay . . . Look at all of the suggestions with the children and see what fits best. Make them look at the consequences of each.
select *when to give information*	If the children are giving clear signals that they see the Giant as bad, because they think all giants are, then give evidence of this Giant as different from that.
put to use the children's *logic*	They have to think through the choices they are making, give reasons etc.
utilise the *tasks* not *plot* to maintain the dramatic *tension*	Set up for the children to have to deal with the 'weed', to find out why Jack has not come home etc.
encourage *interaction*	Children must share differences of idea.
feed in and demand relevant *vocabulary*	Language can vary from that related to destroying the 'weed' to that about whether Jack is right to steal from the Giant.

In both levels of 'Mantle of the Expert', the expert focus is chosen because the children can bring knowledge to the role and the expertise is based on common understanding gleaned from what they have seen and experienced.

What are the advantages of putting children in such a role? 'Mantle of the Expert' can contribute in various ways.

LANGUAGE, LEARNING AND COMMUNICATION

'Mantle of the Expert' uses contexts where, to meet the challenges, the children have to use language to

- listen actively in order to understand and be able to make decisions
- manage the situation and develop the story, e.g. to negotiate, question, hypothesise, define, compromise, reason, explain, narrate
- define the technical and non-technical relating to the expertise, e.g. to list the species of trees they are working on and the ways they can be felled when diseased
- manage the teacher role(s) you challenge them with to calm, probe, confront, support.
- provide answers to problems knowing the consequences of actions.

Such demands will address the key skills required for Speaking and Listening at Key State One in the NC and more:

> Pupils should be encouraged to listen with growing attention and concentration, to respond appropriately and effectively to what they have heard, and to ask and answer questions that clarify their understanding and indicate thoughtfulness about the matter under discussion. They should use talk to develop their thinking and extend their ideas in the light of discussion. They should be encouraged to relate their contributions in a discussion to what has gone before, taking different views into account.
>
> (DfEE 1995 2b p. 4)

WHAT QUALITIES DO WE WANT TO DEVELOP IN CHILDREN?

Teachers often define the qualities they want to develop in their children along these lines: independence, co-operation, perseverance, responsibility, curiosity. Interestingly these are the words that often come up within National Curriculum objectives. How do we achieve them? What is the context that they will be engendered in? The 'Mantle of the Expert' role provides status for the children because it demands judgement and decision in the learning process; the challenges that come with the increased responsibility make it possible for these qualities to be demanded in a way that the usual teacher/taught relationship makes difficult. In 'Mantle of the Expert' the children must take responsibility. In the normal classroom relationship they can avoid that by constantly shifting responsibility to the teacher. How many of us get children constantly wanting their work approved? In this work we refuse to let them do that and they learn to take the responsibility.

Not only teachers want to see these skills in the children. Later they will be the main requirements of work. There are many skills required by children from a very early stage right through life. Here is such a list:

commitment	interpersonal skills	oral communication
enthusiasm	leadership	organising
initiative	motivation	teamwork

These qualities are often listed as being important to employers, but very little attention has been paid to incorporating them in the curriculum.

We need to, and can, begin to develop all of these skills early in life. 'Mantle of the Expert' provides the forum that demands these skills because the children are treated as adults who are capable of showing them. They have to work together to solve the problems facing the experts that they have become.

TACKLING THE SPIRITUAL, MORAL, SOCIAL AND CULTURAL (SMSC) CURRICULUM SAFELY THROUGH 'MANTLE OF THE EXPERT'

The SMSC curriculum deals with difficult issues the children themselves know about or need to be aware of. In order to work in these areas children need protection. The 'Mantle of the Expert' role can give them that because the drama is based on fiction, which is a distancing agent; the fiction is aided in this distancing further by giving children the role that builds authenticity by coming at the problems indirectly.

The expert role protects them because they are always approaching the problem from outside; they are helping someone else (usually the problem is embodied in the teacher role). By virtue of the way the 'expert' type of role operates (thinker, adviser, seeker out and understander, problem-solver), they can view it more coolly and thoughtfully than if they took on roles directly concerned with the problem focus, for example if they were the thief or the victim. This enables 'Mantle of the Expert' to be a key way of helping children approach the sensitive or controversial subjects that SMSC involves. It provides access to the subject but at the same time what Dorothy Heathcote calls a 'cool strip' to protect them from directly experiencing the events. The type of behaviours demanded by the profession they adopt helps to distance the children emotionally from difficult situations. For example, if they are experts in child behaviour advising a head teacher on how to tackle bullying, they investigate, question, sift and make decisions, but are not involved directly (and riskily) as the offenders or the victims.

See the list of dramas earlier in this section and the issues that they can raise related to the SMSC curriculum.

SUMMARY

- The purpose of role for the children includes providing the context base so necessary for the early years curriculum.
- The use of the 'Mantle of the Expert' role for young children does not mean a separate, individual role for each child, as in a play, but requires building belief in a corporate role.
- The 'Mantle of the Expert' role puts demands on both teacher and children.
- 'Mantle of the Expert' can make learning possible in a variety of areas when problems thrown up by the drama are tackled.

Story and drama for the Spiritual, Moral, Social and Cultural (SMSC) curriculum – including Citizenship

One of the key aims for all pupils, but particularly for children in the early years, is their personal and social development. Government has highlighted this. In Circular 1/94 it was noted that insufficient attention has been explicitly given to spiritual, moral and cultural aspects of pupils' development, and there can be little doubt that this observation led to its high profile in the subsequent inspection process. The Spiritual, Moral, Social and Cultural (SMSC) education of pupils is one of the four areas identified for inspection under the 1992 Education (Schools) Act, and its importance in the inspection process is reflected in that it forms a major section of the report and is included in the Main Findings and therefore in the Summary Report for Parents.

What is SMSC development and how can drama contribute? Let us start where going to school makes a significant demand on young children.

SOCIAL DEVELOPMENT

> the extent to which the school encourages pupils to relate positively to others and prepares them to become citizens who can participate fully in society.
> (OFSTED 1996 p. 3)

Drama is powerful in the way it can help to introduce a young child to the world, as the Cox Committee commented in its account of drama: 'it is one of the key ways in which children can gain an understanding of themselves and of others' (DES 1989 Chap. 8 par. 6). The basis of this power is that it faces the participants with the necessity to take account of what others think, feel and say because it involves the child having to work with others, to play at life issues with them dramatically. That in its turn requires them to know more about themselves, to think about what they are, believe in and aim for.

Drama is an important method to help induct even our youngest children in the nursery into the proper ways of dealing with each other. The basic patterns are set early, and if we are to help children's development to be positive we must be intervening most productively with the youngest children.

Living with other people – an example from the nursery

When young children are beginning the process of dealing with others we often see individuals operating in ways which show self-assertion and very little consideration of proper negotiation – the words get left out. It is the physical that dominates. This can at some times be quite subtle and at other times move towards violence, particularly with boys. The problem of difficult behaviour in young boys in nursery and reception is a growing one, judging by our contacts with schools.

Here is a detailed example of one boy we observed in a nursery trying to impose his will upon another. The behaviour is answered with a physical response because other skills are either not there or not used. It concerned two boys of about three years old, Colin and Tim, with two girls of the same age group, Belinda and Ellen, present. (Spoken words are indicated, as close to the original as possible, by using italics.)

At 9.30 a.m. Belinda is talking to the very quiet Ellen, *Let's read a book*. Ellen, who has been in the 'share a book' area since the beginning of the morning, is passive and says nothing, but Belinda carries on as if she is getting co-operation: an example of subtle, coercive, oral and physical negotiation.

Colin arrives and proceeds to establish himself in the space by putting a bean bag near Belinda and Ellen. Belinda observes, *You do not need a big bean bag*, but Colin quietly ignores her and settles himself on it, seemingly to listen to them.

Tim arrives bringing a second bean bag and plonks it down, almost on to Colin's, in the process disturbing everyone and particularly Colin.

Tim proceeds to sit on his bag in a way that begins to push Colin off his, to the point that Colin has to get up. Tim then lies proprietorially across both bags.

Colin looks at him and then pushes himself back on to his bag, forcing Tim to sit upright. Tim resists strongly and tries to get Colin off again. In asserting his rights Colin hits Tim on the head with a book. Tim, *hurt* in two senses of the word, gets up rubbing his head. *I can't stay (play?) here. I'll tell on you.*

Colin looks at him and seems distressed by the reaction – guilt? fear of 'being told on'? He says, *You coming to my house?* Tim, *No.* Are they friends who visit or is this simply a conciliatory gesture?

Tim looks out of the area for an adult, sees none and seems about to go, but he lingers. Both boys come together and end up bouncing on the bean bags – are they friends now? They look at the Christmas tree together. An adult comes their way and, now fully five minutes after the event Tim 'shops' Colin to the teacher: *He hit me with a book.* The adult tells Colin off and sides with Tim.

There is a mixture of motivations and attitudes in the behaviour of the two boys here. They are struggling to deal with what each one wants for himself, with what the other wants, with what is right and how to best resolve issues. How can we encourage children to talk, to negotiate, to seek help, to think through what they want and what are the needs of others?

How can school best help in that process? What is needed here? 'A satisfactory curriculum for under-fives will provide the foundations of spiritual and moral education by helping to foster values such as honesty, fairness and respect' (OFSTED 1996 p. 3).

Using drama to develop interactional skills

When children are involved in a drama they are *playing* very seriously with the ideas within the fiction. There is evidence from research that sociodramatic play, even when carried out by children on their own, has a positive effect on children's behaviour and social skills:

> After studying thirty-seven four and five year olds during pretend and non-pretend play . . . Jennifer Connolly and her colleagues . . . reported finding more positive and less negative affect during social pretend play than during non pretend social activities such as putting puzzles together or playing a bowling game. Social pretend play was characterised by longer duration, larger play groups and an increased reciprocity or social exchange. In social pretend play children also attempted to influence the ongoing social inter-action and they complied more with other children's directives than children in the non pretend play group.
>
> (Singer and Singer 1990 pp. 69–70)

We would maintain that drama set up in the way we are describing in this book will have even more of a positive effect. Why?

The teacher intervenes to encourage understanding of rules and social skills

Unlike some other school activities, for example painting, writing, reading a book, a child cannot do drama on his or her own. Drama is a social activity and makes demands upon the social skills of the children: they must learn to listen to each other, hold on to an idea, compromise and co-operate. They learn through meeting roles in a variety of fictional social contexts that different social skills are required in different social settings. Responsibility needs to be taken either individually and collectively. Of all the teaching methodologies drama is often cited as the one which develops group skills. These skills don't just happen because the lesson is a drama lesson: teachers are confronted by the need to make explicit the skills required by the class. The demand on teachers to structure the lesson is absolutely paramount, and part of the structuring is being clear about the behavioural expectations in order for the drama to work. Each step of the drama needs to be planned and explained to the class. Each task needs to be specific and the rules of the game reiterated to bolster the security of the class and the individual within the class and, not least, to maintain teacher security. Pushing the desks back and using play as a way to learn is very exciting for the children. It feels like 'fun', but it is also demanding in social awareness. For example, when at the beginning of the 'Billy Goats Gruff' drama (see Part III) the teacher tells the children they are going to pretend to be the children of Newhill on their way home from school, she asks them what games they play. Part of the purpose of this is to get the children actively involved in the drama, part of it is to get them to use their own ideas and bring these ideas to the drama. The children must negotiate and carry out the games productively. Should a child suggest a game that is inappropriate because it is too robust or dangerous given the space in which you are working, it must be made clear that it is inappropriate for the drama and they must choose another game.

If you get the class to make a still image of the children playing games and tell them, *The picture will come to life when I begin the story and will freeze when you hear a big splash from the river*, you have embedded another control in the structure. The children will need to listen to the story and listen for the splash. It is this kind of attention to the detail of the social situation, particularly early on in a drama that is crucial to its success. Social skills are learnt through the carrying out of the tasks and through the teacher making clear expectations of what children need to do to make the drama work.

MORAL DEVELOPMENT

'Moral development is concerned with the extent to which the school teaches the principles which distinguish right from wrong, including respect for other people, truth, justice and property' (OFSTED 1996 p. 3). Alongside pastoral systems which reward good behaviour and sanction unacceptable and anti-social behaviour lie sets of values that are embedded in particular moral positions. There are opportunities within the curriculum to promote moral development. Drama very often puts pupils in a position of confronting particular ethical principles and personal values. The distinct advantage that drama has in this process is its fictional base. This enables pupils to look at dilemmas and try out solutions without the consequences that real life brings to the situation. It takes place in a 'no-penalty area': therefore the children can experience safely the consequences of their actions and learn from them. Your role is to structure the teaching so that they can consider these things and see and experience through drama the implications of their decisions.

The teacher creates the focus for right thinking

In many of the example dramas in this book we set fictional contexts where the TiR is the focus of the work, and that role exemplifies someone who has done or suffered something that might be wrong (e.g. see 'Goldilocks' in Ideas 2). The children are deliberately put in a position to sort it out. This is a key way of helping them learn ways of negotiating, to understand the nature of the social situation and approach it with positive models rather than negative ones. When faced with the teacher role in action rather than only reading or being told a set of behaviours from a story, they are able to question, challenge, see responses from the role and understand more about the situation and the morality involved.

For example, working on 'Goldilocks', four nursery children are faced with Goldilocks's Dad (TiR) asking them what he should do with his daughter. One boy suggests smacking her. Dad (TiR) challenges this idea by simply saying, *I couldn't do that. I don't smack her. Do children stop being naughty when you smack them?* Boy: *No, but they cry.*

This helps the three-year-old to think about what is the reason for the smacking; he has to face someone within the drama who does not believe in smacking. This begins the process of dialogue about what we think is right.

Our role as teachers is 'to induct them into an understanding of the moral life . . . they will seek to provide them with frameworks for judgement and structures to sustain creative thought' (Winston 1998 p. 90). We can do this properly only 'if we are conscious and aware of our values; are willing to be open about them and justify them; and – most importantly – critically scrutinise them in practice, then we approach our teaching reflectively, maturely and with intellectual integrity' (p. 84). So there is the need for us to examine our own values and be clear about what we are doing.

The children are working as one community

When you use drama as the tool for the social and moral development of children, you are basing the work within *the positive moral framework* represented by the way the drama works. There are values built in to the structures and methods – accepting order, turn taking, reasoning properly – and the children become part of that value system. For drama is about setting the children up in a role position which requires them to work as one unit, as a community to help each other in order to help someone else. See Ideas 5 on 'Mantle of the Expert' roles and the way they demand collaborative responsibility from the children. The watchwords of the community, the collaborative role, are that all members of the community must

- care for each other
- be respected
- listen carefully to each other
- have the right to put forward their ideas
- help others, particularly those who are victims
- try to solve problems together
- uphold justice and fairness
- understand and operate by democratic values.

These are the givens that present children with a model of behaviour and thinking that inherently lends itself to contributing to the SMSC curriculum. Schools tackling this key area of education often find it difficult to teach it without being accused of bland relativism on the one hand or narrow indoctrination on the other.

Drama offers an alternative way of looking at, modelling and examining social, cultural and moral values. It involves the children in concrete (fictional) situations where they see examples of the operation of the world and can be helped to build their own moral and social code within the given framework outlined above.

The basis of the activity in all of the dramas is *caring thinking*, the sort of proper link between the cognitive and affective modes that SMSC as a whole requires. The result is adherence to values such as cherishing, maintaining, preserving, appreciating. It fosters good habits of thinking: thinking with care, thinking responsibly, thinking reasonably, thinking creatively, showing empathy, sympathy, considering what 'ought to be'.

Moral education – what are we teaching?

We need to lead children towards the moral life, to lead them towards asking the prime moral question as Aristotle saw it, 'What sort of person am I to become?' (quoted from MacIntyre, *After Virtue* in Winston 1998 p. 19). To think about how I am and what I need to be, I have to think about what happens to me and how I handle it. The reflective mode is one we all need to learn in order to know ourselves.

Drama is a key way to help children develop self-reflection, a central feature of a moral life. Dropping OoR to consider what is happening gives us the best possible reflective mode. Let's look at how this can work in the 'Goldilocks' drama (Ideas 2). When faced with Goldilocks (TiR) after hearing how worried her Dad is, children can be quite negative towards her, often attacking her: *You're in trouble. We've seen your Dad. He's looking for you.* They see Goldilocks draw back from them, giving many non-verbal signals of being threatened to the point of leaving. When I am the TiR and this happens, I drop OoR and ask them to describe how they think she is feeling and why. *How should we handle a child who is feeling guilty about what she's done?* They have to learn how their actions and speech impinge on another person, to think through what they want to achieve with Goldilocks and how best to achieve that. This is learning immediately about how we are and how we ought to be. The values are made explicit in a concrete way.

Drama provides contexts for trying out and examining how to behave. The distinguished philosopher and educationalist Matthew Lipman proposes the importance of being active in developing ethical attitudes:

> We cannot expect children to be considerate if we do not give them opportunities to learn what 'being considerate' is through allowing them to

practice engaging in such conduct . . . Rather than talking about considerateness, caring or any other moral virtue, it follows that the teacher's role is to set up situations in which children can actively partake of such experiences as will reveal to them what considerateness, caring and other moral characteristics are in the light of their own experience.

(Lipman et al. 1980 p. 173)

Lipman is aware that influence over attitudes and behaviour really happens only when the children very powerfully engage with the issues. He is not specifically talking about drama but his words resonate so strongly with what drama does.

To consider how we use the traditional stories, look at the dramas in Parts II and III, pp. 161 and 199 and the examples elsewhere (e.g. the range of situations indicated in Ideas 11). They give specific embodiment to concepts that children have to come to terms with in their everyday life: desires, values, intentions, feelings, community, judgements, rationality, attitudes, dispositions, beliefs.

We aim to get the children to examine judiciously all values, including our own, so that they can understand the decisions and choices that they have to make in the drama and make them collectively. We do this through giving them a range of specific examples. What impact does this have on the moral development? Joe Winston defines the process thus: 'Hence Bakhtin's belief that it is through becoming increasingly responsive to the particularities of individual cases that we become moral, not through our adoption of a set of pre-ordained moral maxims' (Winston 1998 p. 27). Bakhtin saw the power of novels, of story, as a way of providing this experience of individual moral situations or cases.

Moral education and stories

Can stories on their own be morally uplifting and give children the way forward? This is a difficult question. You have to do more than simply provide stories, even if they have a moral. You have to take the stories and set them up in such a way that children can scrutinise them closely and test out the ideas in them. This is necessary because many traditional stories that we use all the time are often not clear in their moral standpoint. At the end of the story of Goldilocks it might be claimed that it seems moral that the girl appears to have had a fright as the result of her escapades. However, she has not had to think about the consequences of entering someone else's house alone, of eating someone else's porridge, of breaking a chair. We do not know as she runs off whether she has learned anything. The drama (see Ideas 2) puts the children in a position to look at the girl's actions and the consequences of the actions, and includes consideration of how her parent might react and how the parent should approach dealing with the girl. The complexity of moral interaction is immediately opened up for the children to explore.

This is what drama has done for societies through the ages, as Joe Winston writes in his very interesting book *Drama, Narrative and Moral Education*. He sees the role of drama as setting up a myth or traditional story as problematic, so that the children can engage with it and re-create it, rather than simply be dictated to by it.

How do the dramas end? Rather than always looking for the happy ending, the false and facile outcome, dramas can let children consider more than one possible outcome, to illustrate their chosen ending, to consider the best and worse case scenarios. This way children can have influence over outcomes and can get a pay-off which is instructive in itself.

SPIRITUAL DEVELOPMENT

Spiritual development 'indicates pupils' developing competence in knowledge and insight into values and beliefs, and enables them to reflect upon aspects of their own lives' (OFSTED 1996 p. 2).

Much of what we have said earlier, particularly about moral development, is promoting this very knowledge and insight.

The role of religious education is probably the most easily recognised in this process, but spiritual development is not confined to that area and other subjects will present the opportunity for pupils to reflect upon the purpose and meaning of life. Drama through story often takes an analogous view of these matters . See 'The King of Spring' in Part III, where the nature of our relationship to nature is the focus.

When using traditional story you cannot avoid sets of values that differ from our own: for example, the Pied Piper believes that punishing parents by taking their children to reap revenge on the Mayor is a perfectly legitimate action. Meeting someone with a different set of values and trying to persuade them of another point of view is an activity that parallels considering different religions and their belief systems. How does someone convince someone else that their view is wrong? Should we do this or when should we do this?

CULTURAL DEVELOPMENT

Cultural development 'relates to the extent to which the school provides opportunities for pupils to appreciate their own cultural traditions and the diversity and richness of other cultures' (OFSTED 1996 p. 3). The stories we use are part of a cultural tradition. Stories from many cultures can be used (see Winston 1998). In addition drama is context-based in the sense that each drama is set in a particular time, place and social context. The cultural diversity will depend upon the particular context the drama brings and also the cultural diversity the pupils bring. Their culture will be reflected in the decisions they make within the drama, and it is the role of the teacher to plan opportunities for children to make decisions so that their ownership of the drama is genuine.

WHAT CAN DRAMA AND STORY DO FOR THE CHILDREN IN THE SMSC CURRICULUM?

The embodiment of experience within a fiction can promote learning in the following ways:

- *spiritual* The youngest children can begin to build up understanding of the values, beliefs, ideas that surround them through particular focusing of the fiction.
- *moral* Children can be faced with choices to be made within a specific context that can then be reflected on to help them understand the nature of moral action.
- *social* Pupils cannot do drama alone, unlike many tasks in school. Drama work is based on interaction and can explore how children must begin to communicate with and negotiate with others. It can introduce the rules of society and their operations.
- *cultural* What beliefs, values, customs do we want to embody in the drama? Young children can meet people from other cultures. They can explore the myths and stories of their own and other cultures.

Drama's great contribution to SMSC is to combine the elements of *values*, *thinking* and *feeling* within a specific context and to enable the human situation to be fully explored.

Many of the dramas in this book highlight key concepts for the SMSC curriculum that children should understand: family relationships, lies, truth, honesty, loyalty, authority, responsibility etc.

THE TEACHING OF CITIZENSHIP

If we are developing the children within the community framework we outline above and for the SMSC objectives we have examined, then surely it is applic- able to use the framework for implementing the Citizenship curriculum as put forward in the Crick Report of 1998. That very important report answered those who might relate Citizenship to the older child only as follows:

> Some might regard the whole of primary school education as pre-citizenship, certainly pre-political; but this is mistaken. Children are already forming through learning and discussion, concepts of fairness, and attitudes to law, to rules, to decision-making, to authority, to their local environment and social responsibility etc. . . . all this can be encouraged, guided and built upon.
>
> (QCA 1998 pp. 11–12)

The strands of that curriculum cover social and moral responsibility, community involvement and political literacy. We can see that the requirements outlined for Key Stage One in the report relate very closely to all that we are maintaining; drama is even mentioned as a key approach:

Skills
- Express and justify orally a personal opinion relevant to an issue.
- Use imagination when considering the experience of others.
- Reflect on issues of social and moral concern, presented in different ways such as through story, drama, pictures, poetry and real life incidents.
- Take part in a simple debate and vote on an issue.

Knowledge and understanding
- See how the concept of fairness can be applied in a reasoned and reflective way to their lives.
- Understand the language used to describe feelings.
- Know about the nature and basis of rules that affect their lives.

(QCA 1998 p. 46)

These are requirements we have already been identifying as central to the sense of community created by drama and may be promoted by tackling the problems it sets up.

The Report also recommends examining controversial issues which it says will enhance children's

- willingness and empathy to perceive and understand the interests, beliefs and viewpoints of others;
- willingness and ability to apply reasoning skills to problems and to value a respect for truth and evidence in forming or holding opinions;
- willingness and ability to participate in decision-making and to value freedom, to choose between alternatives, and to value fairness as a basis for making and judging decisions.

(QCA 1998 10.6 p. 57)

Drama is particularly useful for helping look at the more controversial areas in Citizenship because of the protection that operating within a fiction gives to both teacher and taught. See the Ideas 5 section 'Tackling the Spiritual, Moral, Social and Cultural (SMSC) curriculum safely'.

The Secretary of State for Education said at the time of publication of the Crick Report that 'We aim at no less than a change in the political culture of this country both nationally and locally: for people to think of themselves as active citizens, willing, able and equipped to have an influence in public life and with the critical capacities to weigh evidence before speaking and acting' (QCA 1998 1.5 p. 7). The children who learn within a drama community are working towards that very end.

SUMMARY

- We need to define what we mean by the Spiritual, Moral, Social and Cultural curriculum.
- The social curriculum is the central focus of much important learning in early years.
- Young children need to learn how to handle adults and other children.
- Because of its essential development of community, drama can develop children's social skills.
- Drama is a powerful way to open up the Spiritual, Moral, Social and Cultural curriculum including Citizenship.
- The values frameworks found in traditional story can be productively explored through drama.
- Do we consider sufficiently the role of the teacher in modelling, challenging and helping children to develop their own codes and attitudes?

Drama and language development

Much of the book up to now has shown that drama and language have a very powerful relationship. To help us see how this works, let us begin by looking at the way the National Curriculum (NC) links the two.

Drama is not a separate subject in the NC, though many teachers would argue that it should be, particularly in secondary schools, where often it is timetabled and operates separately in spite of NC pressures. This is a testimony to those schools' belief in its educative importance as a subject. However, drama is still a significant force as it has been placed within English, a core subject, in the NC and features at all key stages. As it is part of a core subject, all pupils are entitled to work in drama, but many do not receive it.

DRAMA IN THE NC

It is useful to trace the history of drama within the NC. An essential reference point for all teachers wanting to use drama is the report of the first committee on English for the NC. The Cox Committee report was written in 1989 as a precursor to the NC for English. Chapter 8 of the report was unequivocal in identifying how central drama can be: 'Drama . . . deals with fundamental questions of language, interpretation and meaning . . . Drama makes an important contribution towards the overall aims of English . . . Drama is not simply a subject, but also – more importantly – a method' (DES 1989 chap. 8 par. 3, 4, 6). It defined the power of drama in developing language: 'Drama – including role play – is central in developing all major aspects of English in the Primary School because: it gives children the chance to practise varieties of language in different situations and to use a variety of functions of language which it is otherwise more difficult to practise: questioning, challenging, complaining, etc.' (chap. 8 par. 5).

We can see these opportunities arise for early years children if they work as Superhelpers (see Ideas 5) where they face problems and have to ask questions delicately, forcefully or cannily in order to find out what is really going on. Drama provides a focused context where they have to face up to those doing wrong and challenge their power, or have to complain to authority on behalf of someone who is afraid or too weak to do it themselves. Cox continues: 'it helps children to make sense of different situations and different points of view in role play and simulation, by allowing them to act out situations and formulate things in their own words' (chap. 8 par. 5).

In a drama like 'The Pied Piper' (see Part III) pupils have to take on the roles of the people of Hamelin in order to explore their situation, to understand why the Piper takes the action he does, to examine the ideas of fairness and justice. Cox further defines the function of drama: 'it helps children to evaluate choices or dilemmas, to develop the logic of different situations, to make decisions that can be put into practice, tested and reflected upon' (chap. 8 par. 5). All of the dramas require teachers to build in some decisions and choices for the children, at the same time being clear about the choices they hold on to as teachers.

If the children are to persuade, influence or advise the roles taken on by the teacher, they are forced to think what the role's view of the world is: 'it accustoms children to take account of audience and purpose in undertaking activity' (chap. 8 par. 5). For example, failure to be friendly to Goldilocks (see Ideas 2) means that she will not listen to them. If they act like her Dad and try to tell her off or discipline her then she will walk out and they are faced with having to stop that happening. They have to see the consequences of what they say, the effects on the person in order to achieve what they promise Dad they will do.

Why have the claims by Cox about the power of drama never been fully acted on in the implementation of the NC? Classroom drama is most certainly not provided by all schools regularly for all children, yet the opportunity is still there because the place of drama in English has remained firm, supported by feedback to the Dearing Committee when the English Orders were being revised: 'Some respondents felt that there was too little reference to drama. As a result the references to drama have been made more consistent in the programmes of study for speaking and listening in all key stages' (SCAA 1994 p. 16). It was not just teachers and educationalists who supported drama's place in Dearing's consultation: 'Both parents and employers believe that drama, including debate and discussion, has an important role to play in developing children's inter-personal skills, communication skills and confidence' (p. 57).

These pressures have ensured a strong place for drama in the NC for English. For Key Stage One 'Speaking and Listening' we find 'imaginative play and drama' as part of the range of purposes: 'Pupils should be encouraged to participate in drama activities, improvisation and performances of varying kinds, using language appropriate to a role or situation. They should be given opportunities to respond to drama they have watched, as well as that in which they have participated' (DfEE 1995 1d p. 4).

On occasions where the children face an authority figure like the King or Queen in 'Sleeping Beauty' (see Part II), appropriate formal language is required. They have to use appropriate professional language and approaches when they are Superhelpers. They are usually in role as adults in the dramas. All of these viewpoints are chosen, when planning a drama, in order to create the context for practising the language the NC requires, and the results can be outstanding.

As we write this, consultation is taking place for the review of the NC in England, and the published proposals in the 'consultation materials' contain even more references to drama, suggesting the greater recognition of the importance of that subject: 'Teachers can improve boys' achievement in English . . . teachers should ensure that boys' ability in spoken language is recognised and channelled purposefully, e.g. through drama and work in role' (DfEE/QCA 1999 p. 9). If the proposals are adopted, the entry under Key Stage One 'Range' becomes more detailed:

> 4. The range of drama activities should include:
> a)   working in role;
> b)   presenting drama and stories to others, e.g. telling a story through tableaux or using a narrator;
> c)   responding to performances.
>
> (p. 14)

So there is more evidence of the need for all teachers to adopt these methods.

WHY IS DRAMA SO EFFECTIVE IN ACHIEVING THE OBJECTIVES IDENTIFIED IN THE NC DOCUMENTS?

The currency of learning through drama is language: not just oracy but also non-verbal communication. This has several positive implications for anyone using drama. In the first place, many children find the need to write or to read inhibiting because of their own developmental stage in these skills. Research has shown that the language used in drama lessons is often closer to the language used by children in the playground (Parsons et al. 1984). This means that children who may feel challenged by the kind of discourse encountered in the more formal classroom situation may not feel these inhibitions in the drama lesson. Research has borne out the efficacy of drama in language development:

> When Smilansky discovered that children living in extreme poverty do not engage in sociodramatic play, she decided to train teachers to intervene. She found that when the children are taught the basic techniques for sociodramatic play, they make significant improvement in oral language, including fluency, increased sentence length, and the use of more parts of speech.
>
> (Wagner 1998 p. 42)

Language is one of the most powerful learning areas for very young children, and it is useful to have a medium that bridges the physical and oral for them (see the story of Colin and Tim in Ideas 6). For young children bring highly developed skills in the reading of non-verbal signals and can feel very comfortable in a medium where the teacher is helping them to understand the situation by letting them use and read a whole range of signals, not only the words they are least familiar with.

One of the key features of drama is the contextualisation of language. Language in a drama exists within the fictional context created. This may be the language of a town square meeting, filled with rhetoric and electioneering promises (see 'The Pied Piper', Part III), or the language used to describe the mountain prison where the townsfolk work to persuade the Piper to release his captives.

Language is put in a concrete context because we are using actual space, time and symbols. Two chairs may represent the door through which the villagers must pass in order to meet the Queen but the physical act of moving through them and into the throne room is a representation of the need for a particular kind of language and behaviour. This is much more accessible to children than a theoretical discussion of how 'we would behave if we met a Queen. We are doing it and watching others do it; not only that, our teacher is taking it as seriously as we are and modelling the kind of behaviour and language we would expect in this situation.' Listening skills become crucial, active listening can be practised when a genuine, albeit fictional, purpose is generated. Language specific to particular purposes, language formal and informal, language in context, all these opportunities can be presented within dramas.

We know how pretend play is important for language development in the very young child (see Ideas 1). By using drama in our teaching we are tapping into the methods children already understand as a way of learning: 'Vygotsky suggests that at a certain stage in the pre-school child's development he progresses from thinking solely in terms of what is present in his perceptual field to thinking beyond what is immediately present' (Bolton 1979 p. 20). Thus the child has the capacity to create meaning through play. Language has to meet the challenges that play provides. Drama is based on sociodramatic play (see Ideas 1) and has the same creative capacity for language demand and development.

FACTORS FOR LANGUAGE DEVELOPMENT

What circumstances do you need to provide to help the child? Three factors have often been identified as vital for language development:

- the opportunity for imaginative play
- dialogue with an empathetic adult
- an enabling environment.

Drama combines and reinforces all of them for, as we have already discussed, drama is based on 'imaginative play'.

It can offer the greatest variety of adults for the child to engage with since the empathetic teacher using drama can adopt a huge number of roles to suit particular learning, authority figures, good and bad, victims, go-betweens, adults both clever and foolish, people who know and those who think they know but clearly don't. The children have the best fun sorting all of these out.

As for 'an enabling environment', what is more effective than the imaginary, negotiated environment of drama? There are no limits to where we can be in drama: in a forest, a palace, the Giant's land in the sky, any of the places that our traditional stories take us. The children can be asked to describe the place, to share what they see in their mind's eye, and again language work comes to the fore.

Hence the language possibilities for the young child are enormous. Figure 12 (based on Neelands 1992 p. 22) is a diagrammatic summary of how language is generated through drama.

New context is created through the drama

New fictional roles and viewpoints are established

New relationships develop and operate in the drama

New language demands are made by the drama situation

Language demands are tackled in role (and out of role)

Language development is the result

Figure 12 How does drama work in challenging language?

THE NATURE OF THE LANGUAGE EXPERIENCE

The result of using drama that involves the children is that they have a shared experience with you, which is the basis of the dialogue that takes place. This helps them talk more naturally because it is not the abstracted, hypothetical, 'talk-about' type of language that most classroom talk consists of, a language which is hard to become involved with the younger you are. A vital part of this is the fact that the experience involves *being and doing and thinking and feeling* at one and the same time. Most dramas engage the children in the affective, in feeling about the situation. This is not some indulgent, emotional outpouring but a controlled response to the events and roles. It is also vital that the drama is stopped at these moments in order to reflect on what the moment means.

When the children are depicted as missing in 'The Pied Piper' (see Part III), a class can empathise with the parents they are representing. The drama can then be stopped to consider what these feelings mean and what to do about them. The language to describe the situation will be the fuller and more developed because of the feeling dimension.

Finally the result of all this is that the language has purpose and belongs to the children as they help to create the situation. They are using language to act and not only on the receiving end. The created situation is important even though it is built on a fiction. For the children it can feel real, it can be powerful and the demands of language and the growth can be consequently the more significant.

WHAT ARE THE KEY ISSUES TO REMEMBER IN ORDER TO ACHIEVE SIGNIFICANT LANGUAGE DEVELOPMENT THROUGH DRAMA?

Talking – moving away from teacher talk to dialogue

Developing children's language depends on you, the teacher, using your own language most effectively. It is testing on you, a learning experience for you. You must bear in mind how you are operating as you use language.

It is the experiential drama mode that seems to be most effective here in enabling teachers to influence language development. Parsons and her collaborators found in their research that

> The evidence from children engaged in presentational drama was that once groups blocked out a scene and rehearsals began, it was difficult for the teacher to bring about radical change . . . On the other hand, evidence from classes involved in experiential drama seemed to indicate that from a position *within* the drama (teacher-in-role), the teacher was able to intervene with considerable effect.
>
> (Parsons et al. 1984)

Therefore, it is important to use role yourself as it is the only way to change the relationship with the pupils from the normal teacher/pupil perspective: teacher as the one with the answers, pupil as the ignorant one. If, conversely, the pupils can begin to see themselves as having answers, if they see that you (in role) are the one needing answers, needing their help, then they are more likely to use language more effectively because they feel more in control, more ready to voice ideas and take risks. They are given power to find out and make decisions when they are Superhelpers (Ideas 5) and teacher roles are coming to them for help.

You must strive for authenticity in dialogue. That means not expecting children always to talk the same as adults; one pupil identified the lack of communication in the classroom thus: 'Sometimes I think children have a different language to adults and adults have a different language to children, because sometimes they don't understand. When they don't understand they just think we're talking a lot of rubbish, so they just leave us.'

So you must be able to listen more attentively, to ask for further clarification from the child when you do not understand, just as reading a child's writing demands interpretative approaches when it is not quite what adults might write.

You must expect pupils to be serious and to listen properly, and must do so yourself. For authentic dialogue is when attention is being paid, when all of the participants are learning how to learn off each other: teacher from pupil, pupil from teacher, pupil from pupil. There must be no points-scoring but intention to hear the other properly, to respect what is said and agree or disagree properly.

You must use what Dorothy Heathcote calls a 'subtle tongue' and be seeking to intrigue, to hook the listeners in, to be providing interest, holding back from too much telling, pretending not to know the answers even if you do know them. You must hint and suggest so that children can achieve what Adam Phillips calls the second stage of learning, 'when each student, consciously or unconsciously makes something of their own out of it all; finds the bits they can use, the bits that make personal sense' (Phillips 1998)

Examples of this can be seen in TiR responses like: Cinderella's Dad: *Don't tell my wife the real reason why you have come to our house* (see Parts II and III, pp. 161 and 199). This raises expectations about the wife and at the same time involves the children by requiring secrecy. It hooks them in.

Another level of language is reached through OoR reflection on what is happening in the drama. For example non-verbal signals given in the drama can be looked at: *I wonder why Goldilocks's Dad went so quiet when you told him off for not playing more with her?* (see Ideas 2). This requires the children to observe, interpret and draw conclusions.

Listening – the undervalued skill

A key gain is the training in listening. Drama must involve skills training in speaking and *listening*, particularly how to concentrate for the latter. There has been too little thought about how listening can be made most active and valuable in the classroom. It is too often assumed that children

- know how to listen
- value listening properly.

We must make these requirements more explicit in our teaching so that children understand them. We must acknowledge that in the limited time in any class-room situation there will never be enough time for everyone in a class to speak. We must provide opportunity for as many to contribute as possible, ensure equality of opportunity. However, we must also help children see that there can be a virtue in not speaking, that listening is a positive activity. That will help particularly the most and least vociferous. The former have to be taught to hold back, to realise they must give opinions but selectively. The latter lack confidence and, if they see their thinking as being valued, they may decide to share thoughts at least sometimes.

Do we all put too much emphasis on talking as the index of success? Do we have to speak in order to achieve? Children can learn to be involved even if they do not get an opportunity to speak. We can give clear signs of the value of thinking, for example simply saying, *Who was thinking the same thing as X just said?*, which values that some of the non-speakers were also at that point. Thinking is active participation as long as we have a chance to reflect on that thinking. We need to promote thinking and monitor it, to honour the importance of silence and pay attention to it.

How does it work? In drama children are wanting to listen and therefore learning to listen. When they are not sure how the Troll will respond in the 'Billy Goats Gruff' drama (see Part III) they pay attention and hold their breath. Even though they know it is their teacher who will reply, they are concerned because they want to believe in the Troll, the Troll they want to believe in is scary and the response is a tantalising unknown.

Drama – space and listening

It is important to consider how to use the geography of the drama space in promoting successful speaking and listening.

Because drama is not based at desks, we need to think clearly about the use of space very carefully.

Decisions have to be made when to

- gather children round you
- use a circle
- use sub-groups – unlikely with the youngest children

and how to

- group children when setting up a hot-seating or forum theatre (see Ideas 10)
- make sure all children can be seen, heard and reached by you to draw them in.

These organisational issues can influence the success of dialogue. For example, one teacher set up her class in a big circle in order to discuss the questions to put to a role. She placed herself at and behind one side of the circle and thought she could see everyone. However, a video of the work revealed that

- children immediately to her sides did not get the same attention as ones opposite

- the circle of over thirty children was too big for children to hear each other well so there was repetition of suggestions by different children and the necessity for her to repeat what children were saying in a loud voice. That slowed the whole process down far too much.
- some children became inattentive because of the inadequacy of involvement.

On that occasion a much tighter grouping was needed.

SUMMARY

- Drama provides the context for learning to speak and listen and significantly develop verbal and non-verbal language for all children.
- Drama can help fulfil all attainment targets of the NC for English.
- The key agents for successful language development include:

    - appropriate use of TiR
    - setting up the context for language learning using play
    - granting of status to the children and their ideas
    - giving proper attention to listening
    - using space effectively to help all the above.

Using drama in the nursery and reception classes

The purpose of this section is to consider the application of the methods outlined in this book with particular reference to the youngest children in the school system. There are many examples and references that relate to working with this age group in the text as a whole (the whole of Ideas 2 could relate directly) and many of the other examples are easily adaptable,

Here we want to summarise how we see the relevance of the method and make particular recommendations for these children.

A PRODUCTIVE SPACE?

The traditional space for drama to take place in early years teaching has been the role-play or theme corner. This learning area has a lineage that can be traced back through 'the home corner', limited to one physical context, and before that the 'Wendy House', the embedded sexist assumption being that this was an area where only 'Wendy' and her 'sisters' would want to play! We now have a situation where the idea of a theme corner liberates the choice of context in which structured and social role-play can take place. Not only can a variety of contexts from 'a pizza restaurant' to 'an igloo' be constructed but also these theme areas can be linked to the current teaching and learning. Teachers who work in nurseries will have noticed, as we did during our research, that, despite the dedication of a specific area to the generation of social role-play, in the eyes of the children this kind of activity is not limited to the space defined by the teacher. In the minds of the children the climbing frame can be a house or castle or a rocket, the sand pit a kitchen, the water play area the sea and, as for the space in the playground, it can represent anywhere, at any time, where they can be anybody.

The general view is that the theme corner is the most appropriate area for productive social role-play. We would like to challenge this view. By 'productive' we mean successful learning with desirable educational outcomes. In fact from our observations the theme corner without teacher supports those children, usually boys, who negotiate through physical intimidation and aggressive behaviour. The implements and tools put into the theme corner are often used for purposes for which they were not intended.

The central problem is that too often children find themselves in the theme corner left to their own devices. What is required is for the teacher to manage the learning, to focus the children's ideas and challenge their thinking. The aim of our work in the nursery was to study the relationship between play and drama, to define the conditions for useful adult intervention and to explore the adult's use of role-play to enhance children's' learning, particularly social learning. Initially we observed and worked with the children in the theme corner but we found that the array of tools, implements and objects put in by the teacher to create a realistic 'set' often got in the way of the human interaction we saw as being central to what we were trying to teach. In other words the theme corner worked well as a means to produce 'activities' often in parallel or isolated play, and this raises the question whether free play encourages and reinforces unacceptable dominance behaviour and allows stereotypical patterns of behaviour to develop unchallenged.

Recent research has backed up our reservations about the way role-play is used in the early years. Bennett, Wood and Rogers's (1996) research into the use of play in reception classes identified two problems when they looked specifically at social role-play:

- Teachers' intentions in using role-play in the theme corner are often not realised.
- Teachers are reluctant to intervene in the children's use of role-play in that area.

The researchers found that there is often a discrepancy between what teachers intend in setting up for role-play and what children actually do. They reported a number of case studies. In one case the teacher set up a shop to enable the children to

> learn how to co-operate, negotiate, take responsibility and improve their language skills. She had already observed some of the children's play and was dissatisfied with what was happening: 'I have watched them play in their shop before and they tend not to play buying and selling. They don't tend to communicate very well. They do burglaries or they have guard dogs and they spend most of their time . . . away from the shop chasing robbers.'
>
> (Bennett et al. 1996 p. 110)

In our own research in a nursery we have seen similar turning of role-play areas to more violent and anti-social play. This is noticeable when there is no adult monitoring; the most common form of role-play area, the home corner, produced behaviour such as a boy vacuuming the walls in a very aggressive manner. On another occasion all of the moveable objects were thrown into a box that was put into the area to see if the children would use it in an imaginative way. On yet another occasion two boys simply chased each other round 'a castle' and the nature of the carefully constructed area led to no play related to its form.

There is also evidence that if there is too much reliance in the theme corner on the content doing the education, if it is too much of a 'set', in the theatrical sense, where there is great effort to include objects, clothes etc., it does not necessarily lead to the development of play. Rather it can produce the same play activity over and over and can limit the children. In one instance, one of our students carrying out research videotaped a number of children playing in a home corner in a reception class. Examining the results, he came to the conclusion

> that the processes of making tea, playing babies, packing a 'going away' bag etc. involved the children in selecting objects relevant to the activity. Throughout the three sessions . . . the symbol use appeared to be routine in nature, implying a stagnant environment . . . The limiting of experience this created was evident in the segmented and often repetitive nature of the play.
>
> (Underwood 1995 p. 48)

Furthermore, he observed that when new pretend play possibilities, not allowed for in the setting, arose, they were restricted by the environment: 'the context of the theme corner was "designed" to be that of a home environment and therefore the children's "hospital" play faltered' (ibid. p. 48).

So what should be done? Teachers clearly need to be involving themselves in role-play. Bennett et al. found, even in the light of unsatisfactory outcomes, that teachers are reluctant to intervene 'on the grounds that it might "inhibit" children' (Bennett et al. 1996 p. 40).

Our belief is that children need adult intervention to direct and model behaviour if we are to achieve educational objectives. Bennett et al.'s conclusions were similar: 'Where intentions [for learning in play] were realised, the activities often involved adult participation' (p. 118). Our intention in this book is to suggest ways to set up role-play involving adults because the research evidence from Bennett is that 'teachers are reluctant to intervene because they are unsure about how, and for what purpose, they might intervene' (p. 41).

THE USE OF ADULT INTERVENTION WITH SMALL-GROUP TEACHING

I was working in a nursery class that had allocated one corner of the classroom as a 'home corner', and their usual way of working was for the children to play in there without teacher intervention. My plan was to negotiate with them that I would join in their play as someone who needed some help. I observed each group playing and then intervened as someone who was doing some shopping for an old gentleman who was too ill to go to the shops. My problem was I didn't know what he usually bought, and could they help me make a shopping list? The responses from the groups were very different.

Group One dressed up as soon as they got into the home corner. They then began 'parallel play'. They were cooking, looking after the baby in the pram and making cups of tea. When I came in and told them I needed help making a shopping list for the little old man, who was not well enough to go to the shops, they joined in, making suggestions and watching me write down their ideas. After a while Aneela left the group and moved a desk into a space, she came back and said she had made a shop and we could go and buy the things for the little old man.

The play moved away from the theme corner and turned to a variety of mime shopping activities. We took turns in being the shopkeeper, and then it was time for the next group.

Group Two were not interested in dressing up, and I started the drama sitting round the table in the home corner and making the shopping list. Again there was a great deal of interest when I wrote down their ideas; from sitting down all the children would stand and lean over me to watch the process of making a list. One of the children, Sunita, suggested I buy a book for him to read and then proceeded to go to the library area and get a book. She was followed by the rest of the group doing the same, and I said how much I thought the little old man would enjoy the books. Again the drama moved away from the home corner area to a space where two chairs could be put up to make a bed. I took the role of the little old man and the children came to visit me and read to me. Of course, they could not read, but, because this was drama and they knew the stories, they pretended to read. They got the clues of what to say from the pictures and what they remembered of their teacher telling the stories. I told them how much better I was feeling since they came to read to me, and the 'play' ended.

If we look at what had happened in those two examples, we see that the intervention of the teacher focuses the experience for the children by using their ideas to create a new context or situation. The play moves away from the home corner to a new situation, the shop and the little old man's house. Each one of these puts the dialogue in a particular context. The shopping and the reading are set in a social context and crucially both activities move away from the theme corner to a space where the shopping play and the reading play can take place.

Another example of productive social role-play away from the theme corner happened when I was working with nursery children on the theme of what were appropriate clothes to wear for different weather conditions. The theme corner was an igloo made of white shoe boxes. I had planned to go into role away from the theme corner as a man about to go on holiday and then move the drama to the igloo to show the same man staying in an igloo, but with inappropriate clothes for the weather conditions. The children watched me pack my holiday clothes, swimming trunks, snorkel, bucket and spade etc. I showed them a picture of where I was going – a picture of snow and someone skiing. There was no response from the children, they just watched with bemused expressions on their faces. I moved the drama on to a week later. We sat in the igloo and I complained about how cold I was, still very little response. Then Ben suggested I made a fire, and I asked him what I should use. He suggested some wood, and we moved away from the igloo and began miming breaking off pieces of wood and building a fire. The drama became how to light a fire, and various suggestions were made, including *You need a magnifying glass*. The drama suddenly became focused, active and interesting for the children – away from all the props and fixtures and fittings of the theme corner.

In adopting this style of teaching through drama, we came to the conclusion that moving away from the theme corner to the carpet area and carefully selecting only those objects and symbols that are essential to the drama generated a more productive dialogue with the children. This minimalist approach creates a context in which the children are focused upon the issue as presented and managed by the teacher, who moves in and out of role as appropriate to the learning.

We are not arguing against the use of theme corners, but we need to be clear and aware of the kind of learning that takes place there. The role of the teacher may be as an observer or as teacher playing alongside the children and is crucial to the quality of learning. It may be necessary to move away from the theme corner if we want to focus upon learning that is related to how we treat each other, the kind of social learning through modelling behaviour that drama in education is so good at looking at.

Why is drama so relevant to the youngest children?

THE IMPORTANCE OF DRAMA FOR SOCIAL TRAINING

One key area for the use of drama with the youngest children in school is to help with the social training. That after all is the central focus of learning when they first join a nursery unit or reception class. Our ideas on this stem from the research work carried out in nursery. Our observations of the sociodramatic play and other activities of nursery-age children was revealing.

There was noticeable evidence of the need for the sort of social development identified by the SCAA (see SCAA 1995). For most children attending nursery (and for some children in reception class), it is the first time they have left home and the first time that they have been with so many children having to share not only resources but an adult's attention. The social skills they require are not developed, and many of their early attempts at socialising are based on their previous experiences and on trial and error.

The importance of drama and language development

There is more and more evidence of the crucial importance of good talk, dialogue, in the development of language abilities in the early years. For example, as reported on the BBC in 1998, Dr Sally Ward from Manchester believes that the way in which parents talk to their babies between the ages of nine to 13 months, plays a crucial role in helping them develop this link between the sounds of words and their meaning.

She and her colleague, Deidre Birkett, set up a study in Manchester with 140 nine month old babies, and their parents. Half were given advice on how best to talk to their babies, the other half were left to their own devices.

After seven years Dr Ward set up a series of tests for the children in her study to measure their language and intelligence. As she had expected, the children who had received the baby-talk programme did better in their language ability tests.

But with the results of the intelligence tests she was in for a surprise. They showed that on average the same children were over a year ahead in general intelligence!

(BBC 1998)

The maintenance of productive dialogue as a means to sustain this development is essential and drama provides the kind of interactive discourse around an issue that motivates the children to talk with purpose, and more importantly on topics they care about and can have a direct effect over their outcome.

Physical negotiation

The nursery child often displays a lack of skills of verbal negotiation. This is replaced by physical negotiation, sometimes quite subtle and at other times moving towards violence. See the extended example of the behaviour of two boys in Ideas 6. Other nursery specialists have observed the same tendency: 'The majority of children who enter our nursery school do so with either absent or inadequate verbalisation of their needs and wishes; instead they express their feelings by means of gestures, actions, temper tantrums and other affective outbursts' (Phillips 1998 p. 41).

Peer power negotiation and play

Other interesting observations we made included the point that in pairings one of the pair took the leadership role while the other followed. In particular the leader would decide on the activities chosen while the other child would merely follow the leader to the activity. Rose would lead Gemma because she did all the talking and dominated in choosing where to go. She moved as she wished, often pushing or pulling Gemma gently but definitely in the direction she wanted, at other times simply walking off with no warning, Gemma rushing to keep up. She never gave reasons and she never asked Gemma what she wanted. Gemma never asserted what she wanted either.

The ability to negotiate verbally was lacking for many of the children; non-verbal signals predominated and usually involved harassing such as pushing, hitting etc. Some children such as Katie would often watch others playing and seemed to want to join in but lacked the social skills to do so. On many occasions children would refuse other children entry to their play. That could be done by single words, by blocking them physically or by turning away.

Play tended to follow the expected pattern of some children playing alone, others playing alongside with little real interaction. Frequently boys played alongside other boys and girls played alongside girls; rarely did the genders mix.

WHY USE DRAMA?

Drama can provide contexts to help children develop the verbal skills they need. It picks up on the children's natural pretend play skills, their ability to learn through sociodramatic play. Singer and Singer (1990 pp. 133–7) pick out three areas to show the benefits of sociodramatic play:

- 50% increase in actual spontaneous verbal output;
- corresponding increase in social interaction;
- a significant improvement across a range of cognitive skills after 'training' in imaginative play.

From our observations of what nursery children seemed to need, we could see that drama could be a useful approach to help children learn how to negotiate, to consider conflict and its resolution and to come to see that aggression was not the way to resolve issues. Drama could address these areas and help children learn to

- respect others
- take turns
- share fairly
- behave appropriately
- develop a sense of right and wrong.

Let us look at how using 'Goldilocks' makes the right sort of demands on the children (see Ideas 2). The children have to tell her that she is doing wrong (behave appropriately) and that her Dad wants to speak to her. They point out what will happen if she goes off on her own (point out the difference between right and wrong). She is not easy to get down off the furniture and is cheeky to the children. The teacher will have to come OoR in order to negotiate with the children the best and most effective strategies to get Goldilocks to behave (asking questions about why things happen).

In one session a group of nursery children taught Goldilocks how to play hide and seek. What was interesting was one child aged three was able to pretend to play the game as if it was really happening. They were using the rather small carpeted area and it was patently obvious to him that those hiding could be seen.

However, in order to pretend play the game he had to imagine that the children could not be seen and he wandered about musing, 'I wonder where everyone is?' This sense of the willing suspension of disbelief at the age of three illuminates the power of drama as a teaching tool. If the children have contracted into the drama, they can enjoy the possibilities of being anywhere, in any time, with any one that the teacher or children choose to be. Characters in stories can become roles the teacher adopts in order to enable the children to open up a dialogue with and to help out (see Ideas 2).

In this section we want to illustrate the power of adult-initiated drama. Drama offers challenges for the children to face and they have to work collaboratively. In fact the essentially social nature of the dramatic event is unique in motivating children to have to and want to communicate, to negotiate with adults and, very importantly, with the other children.

What is required?

First, the challenge for nursery teaching is to allocate adult time to the role-play area or a clear space. Unfortunately, role-play is often the very activity not given adult input because children are believed to be able to do it for themselves. The necessity of a planned adult input is what we recommend.

Second, the work needs to be properly structured if the children are to find real choice: 'children need clear frameworks within which to exercise their choice, and to be taught the necessary skills and strategies for carrying out and reviewing their activities and experiences' (Bennett et al. 1996 p. 122). The drama work we offer provides both of these.

USING THE MATERIAL IN THIS BOOK

'Goldilocks' (Ideas 2) is usable as it is, and it shows the way that some of our other example dramas could be adapted for younger children. 'Goldilocks' works by using the two key roles to meet the children and dialogue with them. A summary structure is:

- Meet TiR 1, Dad.
- Accept responsibility to keep Goldilocks there if she comes.
- Meet TiR 2, Goldilocks.
- Play games with the children.
- Challenge children to sort out the problem of what Goldilocks has done.

We can see a very similar structure in the drama 'Baby Bear Did It' (Part III):

- Watch TiR as Baby Bear.
- Meet TiR Goldilocks – accept responsibility to keep Baby Bear.
- Meet TiR as Baby Bear – play fishing with him.

- Challenge to sort out what Baby Bear has done and reconcile Goldilocks being blamed. For a full description of these dramas see Part III and Ideas 2.

How might we look at using this approach to adapt other material in the book? Here is a way which one of the more complex dramas for older Key Stage One children might be broken down. For the full structure of 'Sleeping Beauty' for older children see Part II.

'Sleeping Beauty'

Meet TiRI: The Queen

With a group of four or six nursery children: *In our story you will be visiting a Queen.*

Set up the Palace hall first. *Will there be a throne? What will it look like? How should we behave when we visit the Queen?*

Visit the Queen. The Queen announces the Fifth Birthday Party for HRH the Princess. She says, *I would like you to come to her party and I want it to be a big surprise so will you set it up for her?*

OoR: Discuss with the children: *What makes a good party?*

Meet TiR2: The Bad Fairy

Play activity for the children: The children are set to preparing for the party. In pairs they decorate, then bring in food and/or other activities they see as important.

As this is going on, teacher moves out of the way and then reappears carrying a book labelled 'spell book'. As the Bad Fairy she mutters, *All this trouble for such a silly little girl. I'll make sure she doesn't have a good party,* and then exits.

OoR: *Who is that? What did she say? Should we find out who she is? Will you tackle her if she comes in again?*

Re-enter TiR2

The children speak to her; she is very reluctant to talk and says, *You are on her side . . . that spoilt little girl.* It must transpire that she is never invited to the parties and she is going to make sure that Princess never enjoys another party. The children have to tackle her themselves *or* they go to the Queen.

It depends how much you want to do. Of course this could happen over two or three sessions, but if you want only twenty minutes or so, so that other nursery children get a chance, you will slim it down.

The dramas not designed for the youngest children are usually capable of adaptation by taking key TiR entries and using them separately with a small group of children. Also see the lists of possible role entries in Ideas 11: Story Starters.

SUMMARY

- Is the use of drama in the home corner or theme corner or role-play area as effective as is thought?
- Appropriate adult intervention is essential to ensure educational advantage.
- Drama is effective in stimulating language and social development for very young children because it is a form they are familiar with.
- We indicate the material in the book that is designed for these children, and the adaptability of the other drama work offered in the book.

Drama and special needs

One of the key demands on teachers is having to plan work appropriate for the range of abilities they face in an average class.

One of the most appealing aspects of using drama is its capacity to engage children across the ability range. The dramas we offer in this book will work for children of all abilities. If a child will agree to the rules of drama, then s/he can achieve. Drama differentiates by outcomes not in the planning, although the teaching approach can be varied to enable the access of children who make special demands. In this section we consider how it is that drama can be used to access all children and look at how it relates to a number of types of special need.

CHILDREN WITH LEARNING DIFFICULTIES

Drama often provides a medium for children with learning difficulties to find a voice and the accompanying confidence because it functions by

- creating a context for learning
- using both verbal and non-verbal communication and not relying upon reading and writing, but potentially providing stimulus for those activities
- working through elements of play and game.

Here are examples of these happening as evidence of what drama can do to enable children to participate.

THE EFFECT OF NON-VERBAL COMMUNICATION

In a class of Year One children that I was going to work with there was a boy, Paul, with learning difficulties particularly centred on language. The class teacher pointed out that he would not understand much of what I would be doing with the class.

As preparation for three sessions with the class I used the preliminary work setting up Superhelpers (see Ideas 5). I gathered them round me on the carpet in the classroom. I discussed what helping people meant. Paul sat and listened to the discussion and made some contributions which were difficult to relate to but at least we talked. I then set up the first teacher role of the little boy who had lost his teddy bear. During the search for the bear, he pointed to the place where it was and was clearly aware of what was going on, but was frustrated at the 'pretend' search. At times he seemed not to be tuned in and his attention wandered. At other times he was looking and commenting, nodding or shaking his head.

His most notable involvement and contribution came with the second test role, the boy who had fallen out with his mother. He sat fascinated when I came in as the boy and showed how grumpy and unhappy I was, which was all done non-verbally.

As the children adopted their Superhelper role and began to find out what was at the root of the problem, Paul paid closest attention as they advised the boy how to apologise to his mother if he wanted to be allowed to watch television. Suddenly he said to the TiR, *And you must not stamp your foot.*

TiR as Boy, *What?* Paul, *You stamped your foot.* TiR as Boy, *When?* Paul, *When you came in.* TiR as Boy, *What do you mean?* Paul, *Like this.*

He got up and stood crossly with arms folded, his face grumpy, as I had when I first came in as the boy, and then he very deliberately stamped his foot, as I had done.

TiR as Boy, *Oh, did I?* Paul, *Yes, and she won't like it if you do that!* TiR as Boy, *Oh, right, I see. She wouldn't like that.* Paul, *And she won't let you watch telly.* The rest of the children sat and watched carefully through this and supported Paul very strongly, something I suspect did not happen in that way very often.

When we moved on to the fuller drama, Paul again had various levels of involvement and certainly needed a helper to support him within the more linguistically challenging stages. Using helpers with such children is vital within drama as within other activities.

Another example of this involved Craig, a Year Two child who had recently suffered severe emotional trauma and whose behaviour had become attention-seeking and disruptive in the classroom. We had been working on the drama 'Cinderella', and Craig had been shouting out and dominant during the early stages of the drama. He was committed to the work and enjoyed the setting up of the Superhelpers' office and the setting up of the party, although his concentration on any one activity was short.

At one point in the drama Morella, Cindy's stepsister (TiR), comes in and says quite aggressively, *Where is she? She's in deep trouble 'cause she hasn't done her jobs properly! Our Mam is going to shout at her.*

Craig's reaction was very defiant: he took two steps forward and confronted Morella, he told her she was lazy and she should help her sister. She told him she couldn't because she would get her clothes dirty and her hands would not be soft and smooth if she had to scrub the floor. This attitude generated more indignation not only from Craig but now from the rest of the class. The nature of the dialogue was in the form of the pupils explaining the unfairness of the situation, an imagined context generating real emotional engagement. Craig's usual role of special needs behavioural difficulties was replaced with class leader and spokesperson. He *knew* about injustice, and owing to his own emotional difficulties was allegedly sometimes the perpetrator of it. However, the drama gave him the opportunity to play the role of the prosecution and referee, roles he was not often able to perform. He was in reality more likely to be the perpetrator and defendant. In this way drama gave him a voice and a status he had not often had the opportunity to enjoy.

PLAY AND GAME

One way of involving children with severe learning difficulties is making sure that the play and game elements of a drama are used effectively. An example of this involved a Year One girl, Melanie, with severe difficulties, who was helped to participate in 'Jill and the Beanstalk' (see Part II) by being given a responsibility in the drama context within a game format.

At this point in the drama the Superhelpers were in the Giant's Castle trying to get Jack out of the dungeon in which he was locked. The key, an important symbolic prop, was hanging near where the Giant was imagined to be asleep. The student teacher who was running the drama suggested that children, one pair at a time, try to get the key without making any noise. A very serious game is thus being used as part of the context. After three volunteer pairs were brought back for not being quiet enough, Melanie was sent off with another girl to try. The tension was high, reinforced by the previous 'failed' tries, and the concentration on the face of Melanie was apparent as she crept very carefully towards the key. The student did not call this pair back for making a noise at any point and thus let them win by getting the key. They brought it back and were clearly delighted at their success. The other children were appreciative of them.

Melanie was not very interested in the rest of the drama but kept repeating her taking of the key, fetching it from whoever had it, finding a separate space and acting out the event. Even when she did not have the key she did elaborate mimes of unlocking a door. In addition she kept muttering about the key to other children and students in the room. This was a very significant moment for her and was not to be relinquished.

The main element in the involvement of these two children is the power of the non-verbal, a way of communicating that is always available in drama although not often utilised in other classroom activities. In addition, with Melanie, the strong tension of game-playing was also significant.

THE OUTSIDERS

Often we are faced with children who are not good mixers or communicators. One such was Darren. When I began working with his Year Two class he seemed very uncertain about drama or me or both, and refused to come with the others. Instead he sat out, very close to his teacher.

This was not a problem, and if I had been working on my own I would have allowed him to do the same unless many children had wanted to follow his example. Here the others were used to him being peripheral and did not let that affect them.

However, it is interesting that as the first session progressed Darren showed greater and greater interest in what was happening in the drama and first came to sit or work at the edges of things, but by the beginning of session two he was sitting right by the chair of a key role and offering advice in a forum theatre set up, although he was not willing to take the role on and sit in the chair as other children did.

The attraction of the developing story lured Darren in. Drama can be operated with the whole group working together so that no one is put on the spot unless they opt to be. This meant that he could hide and gradually in his own time he could feel more secure.

THE HIDDEN AGENDA

Occasionally we are faced with an unpredictable situation in drama. Miriam sat with the rest of her reception class ready to do drama. This was the first time we had met, and her class teacher sat away from the class ready to observe her children working with another teacher. I started the drama by saying I was going to move away from the chair and when I came back I would be pretending to be somebody who needed their help. I moved away from the class and picked up a large doll in a shawl and a shopping bag full of appropriate and inappropriate things for looking after a baby (see Ideas 2). I sat down with the doll and started to rock it and then confided in the children that I'd never had to do this before. I was looking after a baby for the day. I asked them if they knew anything about babies. Some said they did, and then I asked them if they would help me sort out the things I needed for the day. Quite suddenly Miriam stood up and let out an almighty yell. 'NO!' she screamed and ran over to her class teacher and buried her head in her lap. The teacher reassured me and the class and said everything would be all right and she would stay with her for the rest of the lesson.

After we had finished the lesson the teacher told me that Miriam had had a new baby brother arrive the week before and, from being the only one, she was now having to share time with her Mum and Dad. When I had asked for the children to help me, the last thing she wanted to do was play that game. The fiction was one she did not want to be involved with, and interestingly enough when I observed her later that day she played on her own looking after a doll in the home corner. On her own she had complete control of the situation and was able to act it out on her terms. We do not always know what luggage the children bring into a drama, and while children will usually use it to make sense of their world there are occasions when the fiction is not one they want be part of because it is too close or the wrong time for them to look at it. We are patently *not* there for therapeutic purposes, that is not our role. While we must recognise the power of the medium we are using we must also not forget that the central function of the work we do is for specific educational purposes.

OTHER SPECIAL NEEDS

Severe learning difficulties

It is not our intention to deal with all of the issues relating to drama in the special school situation, but drama functions there very effectively. In fact we advocate not having special dramas for such situations but applying good teaching to the structures we are offering. Music can add important shared dimensions to the dramas, like singing as we climb the beanstalk in 'Jill and the Beanstalk'. The inclusion of play and group-building or group-making activities (for example, making the monarch's throne room using large soft shapes and decorating it with paper flowers the group has made earlier) before introducing the monarch can help build belief and create a more tactile environment, and the efforts of the participants will increase their commitment. Being in a wheelchair does not prevent a child from becoming the monarch's guard, nor does it diminish the importance of the role.

Mobility

I once worked on a programme linking a Year Six class with a class of children with severe learning difficulties. Some of the pupils were in wheelchairs and the drama, which was based on the *Beowulf* epic tale, required them to take a test of stealth. The test was based upon the 'Keeper of the Keys' game and required each of Beowulf's warriors to remove a set of keys from the guard (who was blindfolded) without the guard hearing. All the group lay in a circle around the guard, including those who had been in wheelchairs. It began as an individual task, but it became obvious that in order for the special needs children to achieve the task it had to become a group task. The irony of this was that, as a group task with the special needs child being slid along the polished floor, it became more effective. The blindfolded guard couldn't tell from where the intruders were coming as other children set up decoys and distractions so as to achieve success.

THE PROBLEMS DRAMA FACES IN THE CLASSROOM

Behavioural difficulties

Throughout this book we stress one very important requirement for drama to work: that is, the need for children to contract in. If they cannot accept the rules, if they cannot be contracted and re-contracted at key times to believe in the fiction, to accept the underlying democracy of the procedures etc, then a class or a child is not ready for drama and a teacher is best not doing drama, in the case of a class, or isolating the child, if it is an individual.

When working on 'Goldilocks' (see Ideas 2) with a mixed reception/Year One class I had contracted that I was going into role as a man they needed to look at and tell me about when I sat down. As I took my seat, Sunil and David at the front said, 'Hello, Mr Toye.'

I got up, went OoR and re-negotiated that I was going to be someone else and not Mr Toye for our story and tried again. Again I was met with a similar challenge and other children told the two of them off, *But he's told you he's not Mr Toye. They're just being silly, Mr Toye*, which, of course was the truth. I therefore asked them to sit on one side of the room *until you want to join in the story*. They must not be allowed to prevent the drama for the rest of the class. I did give them the opportunity to rejoin, but, although they did go along with the work, they never really committed to it.

John and the alien drama

From the moment John walked into the drama studio it was clear he was not happy. The class had walked up from their school to the drama studio at the college, a walk of about fifteen minutes. Most of them had never visited the college before, and the sight of a dozen trainee teachers sitting around the room must have been quite intimidating. On top of this, John, according to his teacher, had *not had a good day*. Having taken his coat off, he slid across the floor and crashed into some of the other children. He was not helped by the fact that he was about to work with a teacher he had not worked with before. Right at the beginning I told the children to have a good stare at the teachers who were observing the lesson and then we could forget about them. The drama was about a space journey and, like most dramas, the early part of the lesson was spent contracting how it would work. We talked about what would be on the spaceship going on a mission that would take a long time, maybe even years. During this discussion Frank suggested nuclear bazookas. *There are no nuclear bazookas on this mission*, I told them. They looked quite disappointed, but I knew weapons needed to be planned out of the drama, otherwise it would disintegrate into the kind of 'zap the alien' drama that is unproductive and too easy. They were going to have to negotiate solutions; it was to be a peaceful mission. This was a non-negotiable rule!

As we continued the planning of the spaceship, John either made suggestions to make the class laugh or annoyed the person next to him by poking them. I told John that for drama to work we have to take it seriously and if he didn't want to do the drama with us he could sit and watch until he was ready to join in and work hard to make the drama work. He said he didn't want to do it, and I found a chair for him to watch.

In the next section of the drama the class got to work on drawing their computer consoles, the tools they used and the special things they would take with them to remind them of home. I noticed that John had come off his chair and was lying on the floor looking at one of the pictures being drawn. I asked the child if she wouldn't mind if John help her colour it in and she said that was OK. He worked away and I told him what a good job he was making of it.

For the next part of the drama he was on the edge of it watching, in that safe part of the drama where nobody is looking at you or making any demands upon you except to listen and watch the events unfold. The class met the alien and gave him a tour of the spaceship. The drama progressed until they demanded to see the planet's leader to ask permission to take some samples back to Earth. I didn't want to take the role of the leader as it is too much like a teacher. I wanted a role of less authority. I asked for a volunteer to be the planet leader – all they would be required to do would be to sit and listen to the astronauts as they put their case. They wouldn't have to speak if they didn't want to. They could be a very aloof leader who didn't have to speak to these humans if they didn't want to. John put his hand up. We spent some time setting up his throne room. We rolled paper and taped it on to the back of the chair and he asked if he could have a crown so we made one. John sat in his throne and during the negotiations he said little while I questioned the astronauts on why they wanted the other planet's plants and minerals. Then suddenly he leaned forward and spoke: *What will you give us for our rocks and plants?* Money, they said, *lots of money. I don't want your money, it's no good here.*

I suggested to him that perhaps we could keep one of the astronauts in return for the rocks and plants. He smiled. *Can I choose?* I said, *You are the leader, of course.*

We stopped the drama to consider the implications of this. John had moved from the role of disrupter to leader of the aliens. Why? It seems to me that drama is no different from any other lesson in school. The rules of the game must be made explicit. The consequences of actions must be rewarded when positive and supportive of the drama, and sanctions must be clear and applied consistently when the work is being destroyed. Drama is social, you cannot do it on your own. It therefore requires the willing suspension of disbelief of the class. They must agree to try and make it work and if they can't then they can watch the others or, if they continue to disrupt, the same sanctions that would apply to a child getting in the way of the learning of other children must apply. John was drawn into the drama because it was boring not being in it. The active nature of drama is an enticement, the content must of course appeal, but that is true of any lesson. If the opportunity to play a pivotal role occurs then, as teacher, you will grab it for the disruptive child. In drama there are lots of opportunities for symbolic roles who do not have to say or do very much, but symbolise their power. Often drama is attractive for the disruptive child as it is much more accessible than other forms of learning and they will respond to it more positively. If they have a good experience in drama, they want it to work again and will work for it.

The child who is not used to pretend play

An example of a child who found drama difficult was seen in a group of four children working with me on 'Goldilocks' in a nursery. Rose was very wary of drama and seemed unsure of how to respond to the pretend element, especially with teacher taking a role. She was tentative and this can clearly be seen on a video of the work. Her face goes through a range of emotions, sometimes quite anxious, as when Goldilocks (TiR) was upset at two of the four children telling her off for having disobeyed her Dad. Rose was unsure how to react: she showed signs that she believed Goldilocks to be really upset. I believe that she was unsure of the fictional nature of the work, despite teacher going OoR and the clear evidence that a bearded man could not really be Goldilocks. Her nursery teachers gave some very interesting evidence that she seldom played in this way on her own or with other children and that she was 'a very serious little girl'.

There will be a minority of children who come to school without the skills developed from play, for whom pretend play is a strange world. The evidence is that they will have difficulty with learning, not just with drama.

The 'academic' child who finds drama an unusual challenge

Drama requires some academically able children to operate in ways they are not used to. Speaking and listening predominate rather than the *ostensibly* more academic world of reading and writing. If they find that the classroom games that they have learned to win at are not available and they are unable to succeed in the usual way, this 'failure' can provoke a negative response to drama. A colleague of mine had two children in her class who were very successful in the usual classroom situation but would seek to undermine the drama lessons by not taking them seriously. This kind of behaviour generates a great deal of resentment from the rest of the class who enjoy their drama lessons. This is often the most effective control strategy. As their peers make explicit their impatience, the children are more likely to conform. In the case of my colleague the two children conformed by taking a low profile in the drama lessons, but the inability to adjust completely and become effective in an alternative learning style remained.

Hearing-impaired and sight-impaired children

Drama can be very powerful for all children and, with careful consideration of the needs of children with hearing or sight impairment, the dramas we offer can be used. Often hearing-impaired children have special aids and thought must be given to the accessibility of the microphone to the teacher leading the drama but also to how other voices in the class are heard. This is no different from the challenge of speaking and listening and of general discussion in the classroom outside of drama.

Sight impairment can be a barrier to the subtle use of non-verbal communication by the TiR, but again this is about the same issues that arise with other classroom tasks and teaching.

SUMMARY

- Drama, like many arts subjects, can be differentiated by outcome and therefore has an all-inclusive dimension to it. The key is to plan activities and use stimuli that will capture the interest and attention of the group.
- Drama can give a voice to children who have learning difficulties because it is a group endeavour and a single significant contribution can be as important as many ideas. Part of the function of the teacher is to use contributions in a way that will challenge the group and value the contributor.
- The currency of drama is language (verbal and non-verbal); this means that many children who struggle with reading and writing are liberated by the wider range of communicative forms in drama.

Planning and structuring for drama

It is not our intention in this section to look at the issue of designing and planning new dramas from 'scratch'. We do not think that this process is realistic for busy teachers who are struggling to manage the delivery of an overloaded curriculum. Planning a successful drama requires ingredients that are not usually available to classroom teachers: quality time, collaboration with experienced colleagues and the opportunity to trial the dramas with groups of children and then modify the plans. It is a central function of this book to provide tried and tested dramas and beginnings of dramas so that teachers may concentrate on the successful delivery of the teaching and learning process. Out of these experiences should emerge the kind of skills that will generate the confidence to adapt and re-design dramas for particular needs.

Planning begins with the curriculum to which the pupils are entitled, and drama relates to the NC at several points. First, drama operates through English, in particular AT 1, Speaking and Listening. However, much of the work generated will create a real need for reading and writing. It is because talk is the currency of drama that, whenever drama strategies are used, you will be meeting some of the Programmes of Study for English and at the same time creating opportunities for assessing Speaking and Listening skills (see Ideas 7 and Ideas 12).

The second planning consideration in relation to drama is the content knowledge of the drama itself. If, for example, the content knowledge within the drama is historical, then the children will learn about the particular history content of the drama. Alongside this they may also have the chance to practise particular historical skills. (The NC lists these as 'Key elements': 'range and depth of historical knowledge, chronology, interpretations of history, historical enquiry, chronology and organisation and communication', that is, the ability to communicate an awareness of history in a variety of ways.)

Finally, there are the personal and social aspects of a drama. No drama can be value-free. In drama children are usually dealing with someone who needs help or advice. This means that children will often be confronted by attitudes and actions they may or may not agree with. The resolving of dilemmas through active engagement with the people involved engages children and enables them to look at their own values through the prism of a fiction. The opportunity to engage with someone who is modelling social behaviour and to have the chance to be actively involved in offering solutions to problems within the safety of a drama is central to effective personal and social education (see Ideas 6).

Drama is social, you cannot do it on your own. The skills developed in using the art form are transferable to other group situations. There is no doubt that when a class use drama regularly the social health of the class improves.

So, when planning for drama you will meet desired learning outcomes at several levels simultaneously: some will be met whenever drama is used as a way to teach and learn (soft objectives) and others will be specific to the particular drama being used (hard objectives). We would like to illustrate this by relating three of the dramas in this book to these three learning areas (Figure 13). Another consideration in planning is the range of techniques or conventions we might regularly need to use.

	The Pied Piper	The Billy Goats Gruff	Goldilocks
English – speaking and listening	Pupils are given the opportunity to talk for a given purpose and to an intended audience, i.e. meeting the Mayor.	Through the story pupils read language with recognisable repetitive patterns and rhythm.	Pupils are given the opportunity to develop and clarify ideas, predict outcomes and discuss possibilities.
Content knowledge	Pupils learn about bread-making in preparation for the tableaux work about 'rats' and 'vermin'.	Pupils learn about information books and how they function as a means to inform children in the care of pets.	Pupils learn about letters as a means of communication, the way they are structured (address, signed by the sender etc.).
Personal and social education	The central themes of justice, fairness and retribution as a method of punishment are examined through the drama.	The pupils have to meet and negotiate with a role who is 'difficult to talk to' and unhappy, they learn about how to communicate successfully with such a person.	The pupils have to deal with a 'naughty' child and to explain the difference between right and wrong and asking grown-ups for permission to do something.

Figure 13 Types of learning in three dramas

CONVENTIONS USED IN OUR DRAMAS

These are only some of the strategies available to the teacher using drama. For further information on these techniques look at *Structuring Drama Work* by Jonothan Neelands (Cambridge University Press, 1990). As children get older the kind of strategies that are appropriate will change and the demands that can be put on them, for even the simple strategies, can be increased. A teacher can use a wider variety of techniques.

Teacher in role

For a discussion of teacher in role see Ideas 4.

Dramatic playing and occupational mime

It is a good idea to give young children a chance to 'play' early on in a drama, for example as the children of Newhill in 'The Billy Goats Gruff', as the Super-helpers working in the office or as the children teaching Goldilocks some games. These games usually involve some mime of a task or tasks their role requires them to do. This is known as occupational mime and enables the children to be 'actively' involved at an early stage, something that is particularly important for younger children.

Hot-seating

Hot-seating takes place when you take on a role and answer questions from the class while you are in role. This is indicated when you take your place on the 'hot-seating' chair. To come out of role move away from the chair and talk to the children as teacher again.

Here are some things to remember about hot-seating:

*   Be clear about what your point of view is. Don't make it up as you go along.
*   Ask the children what questions they want to ask *before* you sit down, so that you have some idea of what you have to deal with.
*   Regularly interrupt your in-role contributions by moving out of role, talking about what the role said, clarifying and stimulating more questions.

Tableau or still image

A tableau is a *still* picture of a *key moment* in time frozen. It is usually in groups but can be a whole-class image. For young children the cultural link is a photograph or picture from a storybook.

Tableau should be used sparingly with young children, as they find it difficult to stay still for too long! But it can be used as a way to focus their attention and is very effective to draw the class together (even more so in conjunction with a

Polaroid or digital camera – the results can be used for class displays of drama work in action). It is also useful as a way to begin and end dramatic playing/ occupational mime.

Progression in use of tableau

1   For younger or inexperienced children start with 'Freeze Frame'. Explain to the children that while they are doing an occupational mime you will clap your hands or shout *Freeze* and they must all stand absolutely still so that you can see their activities at that moment.

2   When children understand the stillness idea, they can be asked for a 'tableau' to be made by them of a moment from their mime. *Do it as if I had taken a photograph of it.*

3   When they understand more about how tableau can summarise ideas, they can be asked to choose the moment that is the most interesting or most sums up what the activity is about.

4   Later still they will be able to think of a composite tableau where they can assemble different stages of an activity into one picture

5   Develop further by incorporating the idea that tableau can show different attitudes and relationships of people in a situation.

6   Introduce the idea of a sequence of events described by a series of tableaux.

7   As children are more experienced in drama, try thought-tracking those in the tableau for information, reactions, feelings.

8   When children are more experienced, you can use tableau to introduce the idea of group play-making, short 'improvisations'.

However, group improvisation and short presentations can be the scourge of the drama lesson. There is an all-too-familiar scene with older children in the classroom or school hall, a small group of children acting out their little play. The participants are enjoying themselves immensely, while the rest of the class gradually lose interest and the teacher stands there on the horns of a dilemma, either to bring the play to a close, prematurely as far as the participants are con-cerned, and not before time in the view of the rest of the class, or to let it ramble on, unfocused and unconstrained.

The structured use of still image can enable the children to build their drama skills. They begin with a still image and then add one movement or gesture to the picture: this will assign more information to the picture. From this point they create a picture of the final moment, again adding one gesture each to the picture. When these have been devised, a link picture can be made to join the two events. In this way children learn to build a presentation by strictly editing and thinking carefully about each gesture they decide to incorporate. In the same way these pictures with gestures can be further enhanced by one word or phrase for each participant. Silence or no verbal response allied to a gesture is of course an effective alternative. In this way children can build their performance skills.

A good example of this is the introduction of group presentations. But this needs to be done in a structured fashion if it is to be successful.

Thought-tracking

If you want to access the children's thoughts in a still image or at a specific time in a role-play, you can go around the group touching them on the shoulder and asking them to speak the thoughts of the people they are pretending to be. Of course, you need to tell them it doesn't matter if they cannot think of anything to say as this makes the exercise more relaxed. Thought-tracking also enables you to assess children's confidence in speaking in front of the others.

Forum theatre

We have adapted forum theatre from the version proposed by Augusto Boal (Boal 1979, 1992) and others. In his idea a short scene involving a problem is played out by a group of people and the audience has the chance to intervene, stop the action and take over the key role in order to attempt to solve the problem. This forms the basis for discussion and debate.

In our version forum theatre is also used to help the children explore possible solutions to a problem. Instead of necessarily working out a scene, they take part in an improvised confrontation where there is a problem. It is usually a dialogue between two people. The physical arrangement of the children and TiR enables the children to take on one role and the TiR the other. This is shown in Figure 14, an example from the 'Pied Piper' drama. The teacher, OoR, sets up the space as above. One child sits in the chair representing the Pied Piper. The child begins the role play but the other children can stop the improvisation and take over the role by sitting in the chair when they have something to say. In this way the TiR as the Mayor can have a conversation with the whole class as the Pied Piper, represented by one child at a time.

Progression in forum theatre

1   The younger or more inexperienced children should begin by having no individual take the seat but, as in Figure 14, all can speak as the role, therefore having a collective or composite role. Initially they put up their hands to speak. If they disagree then OoR the different views are discussed and a decision is made as to the line to take.
2   Two or three volunteers can take the chair and help each other by assuming the composite role.
3   One volunteer takes the chair and the rest of the class listen. They brief the representative and anyone can stop the dialogue at any point to suggest ideas or put points to the representative. They cannot talk directly to the TiR. They must talk through the representative, who can also stop the role-play

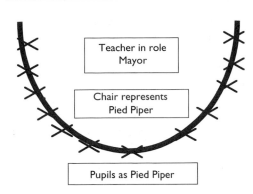

The use of forum theatre enables the teacher in role to have a one-to-one conversation with another role. It achieves this while at the same time facilitating all the class to take part in a structured and manageable fashion.

Figure 14 Forum theatre

at any time to consult the class. The representative is therefore never solo but all the class have to take responsibility for the drama.

4 The swapping in of other members of the class as described in the forum section above is the next stage.

5 Children can take both roles, with the teacher as facilitator, in order to have responsibility to see both points of view.

In 4 and 5 the teacher must ensure that the children understand the needs of the role(s). The teacher must also ensure that the children do not stop the role-play and swap roles every few seconds just because they want to get into the limelight.

THE ELEMENTS OF A DRAMA

Another major consideration in planning drama is that of lesson structure. As well as thinking about how it relates to the curriculum, the drama must be structured in such a way as to contain the ingredients that will help it work as a drama. There would appear to be several elements that need to be considered in all dramas, and missing any one of these can lead to a diminishing of its effectiveness.

Material and stimulus

The first consideration is one which applies to planning for all teaching, and that is the appropriateness of the material used. Appropriateness is essentially gauged by the interest level and how far the pupils can bring their own experience to the stimulus. The immediate impact of the starting point is also important: a bright and colourful picture, a dramatic piece of text or meeting a TiR who grabs the pupils' interest. The last stimulus is distinctive to drama and therefore has the added advantage of being unusual as a stimulus. It is always a good idea to plan the meeting of role very early in the drama as this has the effect of drawing the class into the fiction very quickly and as a whole class.

A clear learning objective

If your learning objective is 'to examine issues of justice and fairness through a story about someone who breaks a promise' you have a clear focus for the learning. With a clear focus you are able to frame your questions and present unequivocal attitudes in the roles you present. It is important to maintain consistency in the learning objective so that the class are not confused by too many ideas and learning objectives.

Contexts – framing time and place

Each situation the children meet will be carefully structured for particular purposes. The place and time of events will generate questions, tensions and interest.

Roles – teacher and children

The roles for the teacher will challenge the children's ideas and stimulate them to want to know more. The roles for the children will enable them to be bound together as a group looking at a problem. They will be roles that will make clear their status and their viewpoint, usually a position of power to sort things out.

The focus

The focus is a planned event within the context that engages the children's interest and stimulates their desire to unravel the problem and resolve the issues.

Key moments

Planned moments to enlist the curiosity of the class and motivate them are structured into the drama. Information is often held back so that it can be discovered by the children. Roles are set up and then presented in a way that is unexpected.

A USEFUL FRAMEWORK FOR PLANNING A DRAMA

Sometimes it is useful to use the same framework and adapt it for several dramas without having to plan a new drama from scratch. In using the same pattern of events the children become familiar with the structure and feel secure in its framework. This can be used with nursery rhyme characters, for instance: the roles are familiar, only the dilemma changes. Often these dramas undermine the original view of the main character – Humpty Dumpty as foolish or Little Bo Peep as irresponsible. The following table shows two different dramas, 'Humpty Dumpty' and 'Little Bo Peep', which use the same structure but different learning objectives. Full versions of these are given in Part II.

Try our dramas, but you can also take them and use the structures applied to different material and for different learning. The children will help you develop your skills and, if you listen closely, offer important learning for you as to how drama can be what one teacher called 'the only way of teaching that has an electric effect'.

Strategy	Event – Humpty Dumpty	Event – Little Bo Peep
Introduction – pictures of nursery rhymes turning them into stories	Collective storytelling with the class: Jack and Jill, Humpty Dumpty	Collective storytelling with the class: Mary had a Little Lamb – show a picture of a shepherd with some sheep and a sheepdog
Collective drawing setting up the community roles	Humpty was sitting on a castle wall. What did the castle look like? Draw the rooms in the castle – whole class	Little Bo Peep lived in the country. Each year – a show with stalls and a sheepdog trial. Draw a plan of the show ground
Setting the children's roles	Who worked in the castle? What jobs did they do? occupational mime	What jobs needed to be done?
TiR giving information	TiR as the chief servant – information 'the King is having a big party for everyone'	TiR as the organiser. The sheep pen needs to be built for the competition
Still image to occupational mime	Group work or still image – jobs that needed doing – look at these – bring to life – occupational mime	Group work or still image – jobs that needed doing – look at these – bring to life – occupational mime
TiR giving information (two roles in Bo Peep)	TiR – chief servant – news of accident – Humpty has been hurt – what happened?	TiR brings cups in, tells the children about last year's winner Farmer George – see him arrive with his dog 'Shep'. Teacher changes role to George the farmer. George checks that the pen is strong enough. Very worried about Bo Peep. Asks the children to find out where she is

continued . . .

Strategy	Event – Humpty Dumpty	Event – Little Bo Peep
Teacher OoR reflecting on events	OoR – questions for the King's men – what did they see?	What was Farmer George like? What sort of mood was he in? Where might Bo Peep be? If they met Bo Peep's Mum, what would they ask?
TiR and children receive information to make sense of	Children question the three King's men – put together the evidence	Children receive information about what Bo Peep has been doing in a phone call (no TiR)
TiR adopting an attitude	Servants meet King – he's very angry with Humpty climbing on walls – doesn't want him at the party	They take the information back to Farmer George. Farmer George is very angry with Bo Peep
OoR reflecting	Reflect on how they feel about the attitude of the King	Reflect on how they feel about what Farmer George has said
TiR other side of the story	Meet Humpty – hear his side of the story – he was rescuing the King's cat	Meet Bo Peep – she has been to the vet with a lamb
OoR reflecting	What does the King need to know? How shall we tell him?	OoR reflect on how they feel about what has happened. Was Bo Peep right to leave the sheep and take the lamb to the vet?
Children explaining	Tell the King what really happened – King is not so angry but says that people who are ill can't go to parties	Tell Farmer George what has happened. 'What do you think I should do with Bo Peep? Should I sack her?'
Children devising a solution	Children have to design a party for children who can't walk – who are in wheel chairs – what games can they devise – they take their plans to the King	He tells them he will need help to bring the sheep down from the mountain – he gives them a test of stealth (Grandmother's footsteps) – the children show they can help
The resolution – the children winning	Conclusion – the party photo album – groups make different pictures to show how they can help Humpty enjoy the party	Conclusion – the children show pictures of them getting the sheep down from the mountain and the results of the sheepdog trial

SUMMARY

- If this way of working is new to you, use tried and tested dramas rather than trying to plan from scratch. As you gain in confidence make adjustments to the drama to suit your needs and the children's needs.
- Planning for drama works at several levels:
    - delivery of the NC – in particular the speaking and listening elements
    - generating a stimulus for other areas of English, e.g. reading and writing
    - content knowledge of other subjects when drama is being used in a cross-curricular way, e.g. history or geography
    - an opportunity to practise skills associated with other subjects, e.g. history or geography
- Drama uses a range of strategies, some more accessible to early years teaching than others. These include TiR, hot-seating, forum theatre and tableaux or still image.
- Progression will occur in the use of the medium by the children as their experience grows. It is possible to plan in progression in use of still image by gradually increasing the complexity of the tasks.
- Planning must take account of the interest level of the children and this in turn will help define the stimulus used.
- Planning can be similar in structure for different dramas.
- Planned assessment opportunities can be structured into the drama.

Developing drama from story starters

This section of the book offers a way of starting dramas based on traditional stories. The ideas offered can be used as simple story-time role-play moments or developed further as dramas. We also give pointers as to how to develop the ideas further and how to think through the planning from the initial role stimulus that is given here.

THE RELATIONSHIP BETWEEN DRAMA AND STORY

Drama can be and often is used to act out a story, and that approach has its place. However, such work is limiting in several ways. Firstly in story we all know what is going to happen, and that makes it impossible to provide decision-making opportunities for children if we are re-enacting the narrative. Second, the number of roles the children can take on is often limited by the number of characters in the story. Teachers are then forced to have the class acting all of the characters as the story is narrated and there is no real communal interaction, or the class work in small groups, thus creating problems of class management and a lack of focus for the work. If individuals take the main roles then there are problems creating enough roles for everybody. This is usually compensated for by crowd scenes where most children are much less involved.

Therefore we are *not* dramatising the stories but seeking to achieve key learning objectives in work based on the story. We focus on significant events in it or before or after it; therefore our 'Sleeping Beauty' drama in Part II selects from the given story when the Princess is having her seventh birthday party at which the Bad Fairy is intending to harm her. 'The Pied Piper' (Part III) takes as its focus the consequences of the story when the class, in role as the parents of the lost children, have to face the Pied Piper and negotiate with him.

We slice through the story and explore the ideas arising at a significant point. We are not primarily concerned with sticking to the story as given.

STORY AND STEREOTYPING

Most traditional stories work by using stereotype, and beginning with stereotype is not in itself a bad thing. There are useful truths in stereotype. Children can identify the roles and understand them. The characters are often representatives: Mother, the Wolf, the obedient daughter in 'Little Red Riding Hood'.

As educators, however, it is vital that we move beyond and challenge stereotype, to help children see other possibilities. In the 'Story Starters' later in this chapter roles often reverse the normal view of the character, e.g. the Wolf who is running away from Little Red Riding Hood or, in Part II, Jill as the sister who is the heroine, rescuing her feckless brother in 'Jill and the Beanstalk'.

Allied to this is the need to avoid *the pantomime view* of the stories. Most of the stories have been caricatured through pantomime and it is important for us to refresh them. Thus in our 'Cinderella' we have avoided using names like 'Ugly Sisters' or having the mother seen as a crude pantomime Dame. She can be cruel to Cinderella and more authentic in that behaviour if she is credible and serious. To produce a 'Dame' would be to invite laughter and undermine the drama.

WHAT IF THE CHILDREN KNOW THE STORY?

As most of our dramas are based on well-known stories, it is important that the way the drama unfolds takes account of the fact that the children might know it. In fact it is better if the drama is set up to capitalise on children's knowledge. There will be opportunities to reinforce their feeling of contributing and having some ownership. That in turn promotes commitment on their part.

For example, when children meet Goldilocks's Dad (see Ideas 2), they do not know who he is at first, but he mentions her name when reading the letter. Most children will react to that and say, *we know what she did*. Dad can react in role to accept that information and reinforce the 'now' nature of the drama. He can say, *So the rumour has already been spread. Everybody knows what she did except me, and you are all talking about it. Tell me what she did. . . . Oh my goodness, that is terrible. I told her not to go in the wood, and certainly never to go into strangers' houses. What do I do?*

The children sometimes desperately just want to replicate the original story and talk about it in a way that stops the drama from moving on. If a child should say, *That isn't what happened to Little Red Riding Hood*, or *The Wolf did not say that*, step OoR and explain that *we are not doing the 'Little Red Riding Hood' story, we are making our own new story from it, so new things can happen. Is that all right? It's very good that you know the story so well.*

In our experience this is rare if you negotiate at the beginning that you are expecting them to help you make a new story . . . and if in that introduction you *do not mention* the story the drama is based on. Then their expectations are not raised.

In some of our dramas the children never recognise the original story. Our drama 'Sleeping Beauty', in Part II is like that. An advantage of this is the possibility of doing literacy work by reading the original and comparing it to the story created by the drama.

THE THINKING PROCESS

The planning in its simplest form involves you in deciding what event or situation from the story provides the most potential for the learning intention. Then you *frame* the drama to put the children in at that point, giving them a particular viewpoint from which to approach it. For example, the first issue in planning 'Sleeping Beauty' was to decide how the children should meet the Bad Fairy and discover that she is planning to harm Sleeping Beauty.

Then you plan back to where it is best to start with the children to get them to that most challenging moment, meeting that most challenging TiR and seeing it from a viewpoint that engages them directly with the issues.

For example, in 'Sleeping Beauty' the starting point is giving the children the role of party-organisers. We do this because we need a reason for the children to be in the Palace, to have an interest and investment in the situation of the threatened princess. With this role the children can be active having to get the contract from the King and begin setting up the party, doing all those activities. The Bad Fairy can then enter when the children do not know her, do not expect to meet a dangerous person and the tension can be produced. See the 'Sleeping Beauty' drama in Part II.

Handling the role for the teacher

You need to keep a number of objectives in mind when setting up roles for the story work:

- getting away from being dictated to by narrative. See above
- helping the children see that there is more than one viewpoint
- varying the role for the teacher – like a teacher or not like a teacher?
- deciding what control is possible from within the role and when will it be necessary to step out of role to organise or reflect.

The following are examples of roles for you (the teacher) (see Ideas 4).

- *authority* (high status) – king, father, manager
- *opposer role* (high status) – someone who sets out to be in opposition to the children, whom the children will not like, for example the stepsister 1 in the 'Cinderella' starter later in this chapter
- *a middle-ranking role* (equal status) – one who goes between the authority

figure and the children's role, e.g. the Chief Servant of the Beast in 'Beauty and the Beast' (see later)

- *a role similar to the children's* (equal status) – one of the workers, one of the townsfolk who does not trust the Mayor
- *one who does not know* (low status) – who needs the children's help and needs them to answer the problems, like Goldilocks's Dad
- *a victim role* (low status) – who needs help, like Cinderella.

In practice roles are more complex and combine more than one type of role. For example Cinderella's father, who is in theory in authority, does not know what to do and is a victim of his wife and other daughter. Therefore the role is overall low status.

A role must produce proper focus, through creating challenge, tension and providing a problem. It must introduce productive tension. This means the setting up of those moments which the children are not expecting, that catch their interest and face them with problems to solve, decisions to make. See 'The key moment later' in the examples below. There can be a number of key moments that provide challenge and decision-making for children in a drama, depending on the length and complexity of the structure.

It is important to frequently go out of role, into real time, to reflect on the fictional time and events. At chosen stages of the drama stop to check the children understand and to find what ideas they have and particularly to discuss issues, clarify meaning or consider what to do.

STORY STARTERS: A RANGE OF TEACHER ROLES AND CONTEXTS BASED ON TRADITIONAL STORIES

There follow a number of beginnings of ideas for different teacher in role opportunities relating to traditional stories. They were created by ourselves and by practising teachers we have worked with. They can be:

- used in this limited form as a one-off hot-seating stimulus (see Ideas 10), as simple but challenging speaking and listening problem-solving ideas for twenty to thirty minutes' oral work
- developed more fully into a drama using the suggested planning models above or in Ideas 10.

These beginnings are presented in a standard format:

The learning intention

This indicates a possible focus for the learning but clearly can be more specifically focused depending on what you do with the idea. For example in the first one below there are two possible key areas, e.g. you might want to highlight 'favouritism' and help the class examine how parents should be careful to handle children fairly. Each of the starters could be used for a more specific curriculum area.

The contact role

This is the teacher role (TiR) which sets up the central issue for the children. There are implications in most of the starters that another TiR will be used later, e.g. in 'Jack and the Beanstalk (1)' (see pp. 134 and 135) where Jack wants the children to explain to his Mum the cow swap for beans.

The context

This gives the basic frame or situation with hints on how to handle the role and build in constraints and challenges.

The key moment later

This indicates a possible development idea later in the drama that could be an objective for further planning. Of course this does not have to be used if you want to keep the work simple. Other challenges or tension makers could be used instead.

Stories covered

Beauty and the Beast
The Billy Goats Gruff
Cinderella
Goldilocks
Jack and Jill
Jack and the Beanstalk
Little Bo Peep
Little Boy Blue
Little Miss Muffet
The Little Red Hen

Little Red Riding Hood
The Pied Piper
Pinocchio
Rumpelstiltskin
Snow White
Three Blind Mice
The Three Little Pigs
The Ugly Duckling
The Wolf and Seven Kids

CHOOSING DIFFERENT TIR APPROACHES FOR DIFFERENT PUPIL RESPONSES

You can create different focuses for a drama depending on the responses you seek from the class and the learning intention you are setting. Even the same learning can be approached in different ways by varying the choice of situation and roles.

You need to choose roles with a clear idea of *the response you want to evoke* and craft them carefully to generate that specific outcome.

Here are four different roles for the teacher, based on the story 'Cinderella', that create different responses and thus a different way into the learning for the children. In each case do not tell the class that this has anything to do with the story of Cinderella. Let them uncover the parallels. The learning intention is to look at fairness and favouritism.

Cinderella

She enters fed up, angry and jealous. *All they talk of is dresses and going to the ball. My Dad doesn't let me go. And you'll probably be just like them. I bet you're all going to this dance thing. I don't want to go anyway.*

Go OoR to discuss with the children. *Why is she upset?*

This is a *victim role* (see earlier for explanation of types of role) which is not likeable immediately and can challenge the children's preconceptions of Cinderella as the goody-goody; in order to help her, the children have to take trouble to get to know her.

Stepsister 1

She enters as a self-centred person. *I do like my new dress. My Mum bought it for me. My new Dad is mean. He says we spend too much but I don't take any notice of him. He's all right sometimes, especially when he gives me money.*

This is an *opposer role* displaying great selfishness that provokes dislike in the children. Their task is going to be to have to sort her out.

However, the stepsister could be introduced more like this:

Stepsister 2

She enters very quietly and with a sort of resignation. *You seem very sensible people. I bet you would agree with me that it's wrong for someone to let you down. It's really bad, isn't it, when you can't do something and it's someone else's fault. She promised to have my new dress ready for the big party and now I won't be able to go if she does not finish it. I've been downstairs and she's just sitting staring into the fire. Her Dad always lets her off and makes me forgive her.*

This is more subtle. The tone makes it sound as though she is the victim and the group would have to see beyond that to the inherent selfishness.

Stepmother

She's nothing to do with me . . . Why should my daughter do the work? I want the best for my daughter. She's going to be a lady. I didn't get where I am now by scrubbing floors. The youngest should know her place and do the work. My husband follows my rules.

This is an *opposer role* provoking the children to have to challenge an adult. They have to learn how to challenge her most effectively. Straight-on confrontation is unlikely to work as she is too powerful in the house. She might well respond to a direct challenge: *There is no problem. Why do we need your help? Cinderella's just jealous. My daughter is prettier than her. Cinderella should go live with her Mum. There is no reason for Cinderella to be jealous. My daughter spends ages helping her and playing with her.*

This is an *opposer role* who does not see the truth of the situation because of favouritism. She is manipulated by the stepsister.

SIX IDEAS FOR DRAMAS BASED ON THE SAME STORY

A strong story can produce a range of possible dramas. Here are six different ideas based on 'Sleeping Beauty'. They were suggested by practising teachers as the start of their planning for a fuller drama.

In each case you will see a beginning and a later key moment which uses TiR to focus learning. Each of the examples needs to be developed further by thinking of the other elements of planning listed above – how the children get to the key moment, how that is set up etc.

In the first four cases the children are in role as Superhelpers (see Ideas 5), and the beginning was based around someone from the story (a specific TiR) contacting them. In 5 and 6 the children have been given different roles.

1. Learning intention: To consider being left out of things.
Contact role: Father of the princess who will be Sleeping Beauty.
Context: He is worried because Sleeping Beauty's sixteenth birthday is approaching and the curse is in place. Can Superhelpers help?
Key moment later: the children discover how much the Bad Fairy resented being left out of something as important as the christening.

2. Learning intention: To consider how prejudice can be shown to people.
Contact role: A person who has been left out of the invitations to the Princess's christening approaches Superhelpers for help.
Context: We keep the person's identity anonymous at this point. It is the Bad Fairy of course. She informs the Superhelpers that she is suspicious that *it is because I have dark hair and the others all have blonde hair*.
Key moment later: Superhelpers are in the middle of trying to find out the reasons by talking to someone in the palace (the children can decide whom) when the Bad Fairy, tired of waiting for them to sort her problem, rushes in and puts the curse on.

3. Learning intention: Getting on with people you do not like.
Contact role: The Queen.

Context: She is putting together the guest list for the christening and wants help because she is inviting three of the fairies but does not want to invite the fourth and does not know how to say no. The fourth is a troublemaker who has caused trouble at a party before.

Key moment later: Either the Superhelpers have persuaded her to invite the fourth fairy and are let down by that fairy because she casts the spell even though she promised she would not, *or* they helped the Queen find a good excuse and the Bad Fairy burst in to cast the spell after she was not invited.

4. Learning intention: Learning from your mistakes.
Contact role: The King
Context: He approaches Superhelpers after the christening party when the spell has been cast and is desperate to find the Bad Fairy to find out why she did it. Can the Superhelpers help make her take the spell off?
Key moment later: The Superhelpers have to persuade the King, who believes he is always right, that not inviting the Bad Fairy was unfair.

5. Learning intention: The importance of finding the root cause of a problem.
Contact role: A horse rider.
Context: Starts after the curse has been put on. The children are foresters working in the forest. They do not know about the curse and are approached by a horse rider who is carrying a strange message telling him *to seek a palace hidden in the middle of the dense forest*. He is lost. They have to help him with maps etc.
Key moment later: The kiss fails to wake Beauty and the Prince seeks their help to find out what the problem is.

6. Learning intention: How to make someone (the King) see the importance of thinking about others as well as yourself.
Contact role: A messenger.
Context: The children are all villagers whose livelihood is spinning and selling wool and making things from the spun wool. The messenger brings a command from the King that *all spinning wheels in the kingdom are to be destroyed by the end of the week. Anyone found in possession of a spinning wheel after that time will be put to death.*
Key moment later: The villagers have to face the King about keeping their livelihoods. A further development could be that the King orders the death of a villager found to have a spinning wheel.

SUMMARY

- There are ways to develop from an initial ideas presented here to a fuller drama.
- You need to develop the role for the teacher carefully to promote tension and reflection.

- Consider the issues raised when using traditional story: narrative limitation; stereotype; what if the children know the story?
- We give a whole range of beginnings based on a number of stories.

STARTER IDEAS FOR OTHER STORIES

Beauty and the Beast

Learning intention: It is the person who matters, not how they look.
Contact role: Chief Servant to the Beast.
Context: The children are all in role as servants to this secretive person who never appears from his room except wrapped in a scarf. He is a kind master, but hardly ever seen. The Chief Servant issues the order that all mirrors should be removed from the house. Apparently the master is going to walk through the house when the servants are not there. He also spends time gazing out of one window towards the road that passes close by.
Key moment later: The servants find a crumpled letter in a waste bin written to *a young lady who passes by* saying how much he loves her.

The Billy Goats Gruff (1)

Learning intention: When should you be polite and when should you stand up for yourself?
Contact role: A scarecrow.
Context: The scarecrow has met the goats since they crossed the bridge. He did not like the goats' attitude. He thinks they should be taught to be more polite. The children have to tackle the goats and start with the youngest. Gradually they realise that the oldest has been teaching the others to stand up for themselves against the Troll.
Key moment later: Discover that the Troll has been laughed at by the others because of the way s/he looks and has decided to not let anyone near.

The Billy Goats Gruff (2)

Learning intention: Ownership and sharing.
Contact role: A child who uses this bridge.
Context: The children are expert bridge-menders who have been sent to check for the safety of this bridge. They meet a child with a broken toy sitting on the other side of it. A Troll has broken the toy and won't let him cross the bridge. The Troll refuses to let them inspect the bridge because it is his and no one else can use it, so he does not need someone to inspect it. Refuses to discuss it.
Key moment later: Discover that the Troll is driving people off the bridge because he thinks they might damage his bridge.

Cinderella (1)

Learning intention: To look at being left out and favouritism.
Contact role: Eighteen-year-old girl wandering outside hall.
Context: The children are all in role as decorators or designers employed to prepare the hall for the Great Ball *or* as villagers waiting outside the hall to see the party guests arrive. They meet the girl as she tries to see what is going on and have to find out what she wants. She says, *I'm just trying to see what all the fuss is about. I'm sorry, I didn't mean to get in the way. I'll go now. It's just a pity that's all. Makes me feel bad that . . . oh well, never mind. I expect they'll tell me about it.*
Key moment later: The villagers have to deal with what to do about the exclusion of Cinderella, especially when they discover her treatment by her stepsisters.

Cinderella (2)

Learning intention: Not judging by appearances.
Contact role: The Prince's Aide
Context: The trying on of the shoes. Looking for the person the shoe fits. The children have to help find the person.
Key moment later: (1) The children bring Cinderella but she refuses to try on the shoe as she has lost all confidence and says, *This cannot be for me.* They have to talk for her when the Prince ignores her even though she is there because he sees *only a servant.*
(2) The Prince's Aide rejects her from even trying on the shoe as she is not well-dressed and cannot speak to help herself.

Cinderella (3)

Learning intention: Privacy.
Contact role: Postman or postwoman.
Context: He or she has found a lost diary. It has information about what has happened to Cinderella, her dreadful life. Do the children read it when he or she asks them too, especially as it is marked 'private'?
Key moment later: Cinderella is very upset that they (the post person and children) have read the diary, even if they are returning it and *have not* read it. She will not listen to them initially about the Ball etc.

Cinderella (4)

Learning intention: Bullying.
Contact role: Cinderella.
Context: Children see Cinderella writing a letter to her Dad. She does not know they are there. They are briefed to watch and not talk to her. She is trying to find

the right way to tell him in the letter that she is being bullied by her stepsister. She mutters, *I hate her. She shouldn't do it . . . But Dad won't believe me* etc. to intrigue the children. She gives up writing and leaves the letter there . . . not sure whether to give it to him or not. The children can read it and will find out what is happening. Do they take it to Dad?

Key moment later: Dad does not believe stepsister could be like this. She is very nice when he is present.

Symbol: Burnt invitation card which Cinderella has to prove how she is being bullied.

Goldilocks

Learning intention: Do you tell on someone who has done wrong?
Contact role: Goldilocks.
Context: The children are in the playground when Goldilocks comes up bragging of everything she's done. *I've been in someone's house and tried their chairs when they weren't there. I tried their food as well. Only thing is, I've got a bit of a burnt tongue. Shows how brave I am. Bet you couldn't do something like that.* What should the children do when they know this? Should they tell someone, a teacher? Should they get Goldilocks to go and own up? Let them decide.

Key moment later: They discover that she has stolen Baby Bear's toy too.

Jack and Jill

Learning intention: Learning difficulties.
Contact role: Jill.
Context: Jack has wandered off after banging his head. Jill seeks help from Superhelpers (see Ideas 5). How do they find him? When they find him he cannot remember anything, can't add up or think of the right words for things.

Key moment later: Jill laughs at him and thinks he's a real dunce. Jack is very upset by this. What do the Superhelpers do?

Jack and the Beanstalk (1)

Learning intention: Facing up to someone when you have done something wrong.
Contact role: Jack.
Context: The children are gardeners (gardening pre-activities possible) and meet Jack, who is hiding away in their garden shed. He is afraid to go home, scared to tell his mother that he did not get money for the cow. Could they help him tell her about the magic properties of the beans so he can be excused?

Key moment later: Mum still threatens to throw him out and the children have to help him.

Jack and the Beanstalk (2)

Learning intention: Envy, or being afraid of owning up to having done something wrong.

Contact role: Jack's friend.

Context: The children meet Jack's friend, Jean, who has a beautiful bean and wants to share it but keeps hiding it away because she is afraid to show it as it is stolen and she is feeling guilty. *I haven't got anything . . . No, which pocket did you see me put it in? . . . Oh, I have to tell someone. Do you want to see . . . It's beautiful. You won't tell anyone?*

Key moment later: The children discover that Jack is stuck up the beanstalk and his mother had it chopped down before she realised that Jack had gone up it. Can the children persuade Jean to hand over her bean, the only one left, in order to grow another beanstalk?

Little Bo Peep (1)

Learning intention: To look at making a promise. Trusting people. Should children stick together against adults?

Contact role: Bo Peep.

Context: The children are all at the village school. They are playing many games in the school yard (activities for the children). Bo Peep comes by and stands watching the children and asking about the games. She's really bored doing what she has to do. She tells them she is Bo Peep if they ask, otherwise not. Gradually she gets them to play with her to teach her games etc.

Key moment later: She suddenly stops and asks all the children to listen. *Look, someone's coming I don't want to meet. Can you hide me and not tell him I'm here?* She hides The farmer (TiR) comes in: *Where are my sheep? Where is Little Bo Peep? She is supposed to be looking after my sheep and now she and they have disappeared. Can you help me?* OoR: What should the children in the story do?

Little Bo Peep (2)

Learning intention: Geography – using a map to find something, or what to do when you find someone has done wrong.

Contact role: Bo Peep.

Context: The children are all farm workers (preliminary activities to set this up). Bo Peep comes by crying. *I can't find my sheep. I have to tag them all so I know which ones are mine. Someone said you know about animals and could help me.* She goes to find her map, which will have clues like a broken gate marked on it. They all look at the countryside round about the field where they were and decide how they might have got out and where they might have gone.

Key moment later: While looking for the sheep the farm workers overhear sheep stealers discussing where the best place to keep the sheep might be. What to do about this?

Little Boy Blue

Learning intention: To look at responsibility and the consequences of irresponsibility. Forgiveness?
Contact role: Villager from next village.
Context: The children are all villagers who are excellent gardeners. Their village is working hard to try to win the Best Kept Village Award. Then two days before the judging, cows and sheep run through the village causing devastation. Two tableaux show the gardeners looking at their work before and after the stampede. The Villager brings news that Little Boy Blue has run away and cannot be found. The children as the villagers have to (1) decide if it is his fault and what to do about it; (2) find him.
Key moment later: Alternative ideas, with different emphases: When he is found he will not return because he is too afraid; *or* he comes slinking back to ask for forgiveness. The villagers have to deal with Boy Blue.

Little Miss Muffet

Learning intention: Phobias and bad relationships.
Contact role: Little Miss Muffet.
Context: A poster advertises 'Lost Child'. The children (Superhelpers? – see Ideas 5) help decide how to look for her.
Key moment later: Discovering her, hiding away, terrified to come out – she reveals her fear of spiders. What to do about it? Possibly a letter from Spider explaining how frightened he is of Little Miss Muffet.

The Little Red Hen

Learning intention: Sharing.
Contact role: A Farmer.
Context: He has had a letter from all his other animals complaining that the Red Hen is *a hen who takes and never gives to others*. The children plan what to say to her.
Key moment later: The children discover that the animals conveniently forget they did not help. So there has to be learning on all sides. Why do they not help her? Is she too bossy?

Little Red Riding Hood (1)

Learning intention: Always wanting to be someone else.
Contact role: Little Red Riding Hood, who has been to visit her Grandma and is suspicious that the person she has seen is not her grandma.
Context: The Wolf has locked Grandma in a cupboard and is pretending to be her because he hates being a wolf and being feared and always tries to be someone

else. The children as Superhelpers have to advise Little Red Riding Hood what to do to rescue Grandma.

Key moment later: They discover that the Wolf has low self-esteem and needs help to face up to being himself.

Little Red Riding Hood (2)

This could be a follow-up to the previous frame.

Learning intention: To punish a criminal or try to teach him?

Contact role: Grandma.

Context: This drama starts after the traditional story has finished. Grandma was tricked by the wolf and locked in the cupboard. They have caught the wolf. What should they do with it?

Key moment later: Either a wolf needing help as above or the wolf is set in his ways. He may lie that he will change but gives other signals that he will not.

Little Red Riding Hood (3)

Learning intention: Bullying.

Contact role: The Wolf; later Little Red Riding Hood.

Context: The Wolf meets the children and is very distressed. He is running away from a girl he met who is making him do things he does not want to, like run errands for her. At first he is reluctant to talk because he is ashamed of being afraid of a girl. The children have to calm him to get some sense out of him. Possibly he tells, or not, before he hears Little Red Riding Hood coming and hides. *Don't tell her I'm here. You promise?* Enter TiR as Little Red Riding Hood who is looking for the Wolf. *He won't do as he's told. He must take this basket to my Grandma's. If you don't make sure these big bullies do as you say, they get all above themselves.* Do they tell her or get rid of her?

Key moment later: Helping the Wolf stand up to Little Red Riding Hood.

Little Red Riding Hood (4)

Learning intention: Safe places and stranger danger.

Contact role: Grandma.

Context: Grandma writes to the children (as Superhelpers – see Ideas 5) to get them to advise her granddaughter how she should look after herself and avoid danger in the wood. She believes her daughter (Little Red Riding Hood's mum) takes too many risks and should keep Red at home more . . . not send her through the wood. The mother should come herself.

Key moment later: They meet Mother, who thinks Grandma fusses too much, that children have to learn independence. Children to write a set of guidelines for parents and children about where it is safe for young children to go alone, where it is safe only with permission and where parents must go with them.

Little Red Riding Hood (5)

Learning intention: Peer group pressure.
Contact role: Grandma.
Context: Grandma is being menaced by a wolf who prowls round her cottage. She seeks the children's help to get rid of him. *He tried to bite me on the hand when I went out the garden gate and then he ran away.* They meet the Wolf who pretends to be very aggressive and bold. Children are in role as Superhelpers (see Ideas 5) *or* experts about wild animals.
Key moment later: They find a painting or drawing by the Wolf which shows him all on his own and with all the other wolves pointing a finger at him. He'd really like to be friends with Grandma and wants to be a friendly wolf but the others won't let him and keep setting him dares to prove he is a good wolf – like biting her finger.

The Pied Piper

Learning intention: What is happiness? How parents treat children.
Contact role: The boy who was left behind and did not get into the Magic Mountain.
Context: Set after the end of the story. There is great sadness among the villagers of Hamelin because the children have all been taken, so they are keen for the boy to tell them what has happened and where they can find their children. However, he refuses to tell them where the mountain is. *I heard the music and it told me of the beautiful land in the mountain. You are all selfish. Your children will all be happy where they are and I am the lonely one. I want to be taken to the mountain.* Do they help the boy or seek to get the children back?
Key moment later: A child from the mountain tells the villagers that the children do not want to come back. They are all happier in the mountain. However, the villagers also find that he has lost his memory.

Pinocchio

Learning intention: To consider the importance of schooling.
Contact role: Teacher and Pinocchio's friend.
Context: The teacher comes into the staff room where all the other teachers (the children) are and tells them, *I don't know what to do with Brian today. He won't sit still in class. He keeps getting up and looking out of the window. I've never known him to be so awkward. He refuses to do any work. He says he doesn't see the point. Someone's told him there's no point. Will you talk to him?* Brian has a secret and has promised he won't tell but he's worried about the other person.
Key moment later: The teachers meet Pinocchio where he is waiting for Brian to persuade him to come with him. Pinocchio is full of how *it's better to learn out in the world; to find out how to live for yourself; you can't be a real child in school.*

Rumpelstiltskin

Learning intention: Lies and greed.
Contact role: The girl; later Rumpelstiltskin and the King.
Context: The children are the straw deliverers. Amazed at how much straw they have to keep delivering to this barn, when they have unloaded all the straw, they knock on the door at the bottom of the stairs. A girl who is locked in the room upstairs shouts through the door and tells them she needs help. She has to spin the straw into gold for the king because her foolish father, the miller, boasted she could. But she can't. What should she do? She has to keep giving this ugly old man her belongings to do the job for her or the King will kill her. She has nothing left to give him tonight and they have brought even more straw. *Can you help me?*
Key moment later: Depending on what the children suggest to do – confront the King, who is too greedy to listen; confront the father who dare not tell the King he lied; get her to tell the truth of what is happening; no one believes her? Rumpelstiltskin offers to take her first child when it is born if she wants the corn. Does she agree?

Snow White (1)

Learning intention: Jealousy and where it can lead.
Contact role: Woodcutter.
Context: Seeks help from Superhelpers – he was sent to take *this young girl and kill her in the forest. I could not do it and just left her. I do not know where she has gone and am worried in case the Queen finds out I have not done it. Is she dead? I must find her, so will you help me?*
Key moment later: The children are confronted by the Queen, who knows where Snow White is. She is disguised, carrying the poisoned apple in a box. She is looking for the Forester as well.

Snow White (2)

Learning intention: Can the children trust a stranger?
Contact role: The Queen.
Context: The children meet someone claiming to be the dwarves' ex-housekeeper who lost her job when *this other young girl arrived.* She, however, hasn't the skills and is not doing very well. Could the children help her do better? *I know she won't accept help from me but if you go to the cottage and help her, tell her how she should do all this, she might listen.*
Key moment later: The children find a letter from the Queen ordering Snow White's death. This one has two possible directions: that the woman is honest and the children have to help Snow White learn her own limitations; or, in a more complex scenario, that the children have to discover that the woman is the Queen in disguise and is trying to get them to help poison Snow White.

Snow White (3)

Learning intention: How being in a mood can put people off you.
Contact role: Grumpy.
Context: Grumpy enters stamping about, picking up bags, moving chairs as though looking for something and moaning: *I can't find anything. She tidies everything away. It was better before she came. Don't just sit there. Can you get up and find my pickaxe? I can't go to work without it. They all think she's so wonderful . . . They follow her about, do what she tells them. What's happened to them?*
Key moment later: Grumpy is approached by the Queen to get Snow White to eat the apple because she knows he hates her. The children find a letter he is writing about this and have to stop him. They have to persuade him that it is wrong to take out his moods in this way.

Snow White (4)

Learning intention: The need to be careful of strangers.
Contact role: Snow White (name should be changed, but she talks fondly of the people she works for, the seven of them).
Context: She is having a tea party for her friends at the house to show them how happy she is in her new place. There is a knock at the door and she comes back with an apple that a kind old lady has brought for her. *That is how friendly people are around here. I'll save that for my lunch tomorrow.*
Key moment later: If they do not twig and Snow White eats the apple they are sought by a desperate dwarf who has found Snow White 'dead' so that they have to find the old woman to face her with the crime and get her to reverse the poison.

Three Blind Mice (1)

Learning intention: Fear of violence.
Contact role: The farmer's daughter
Context: The mice are scared of the farmer's wife. They have been chased by her with a knife. They write a letter to the farmer's daughter and she seeks help from Superhelpers (see Ideas 5).
Key moment later: The children are confronted by the sort of pest damage caused by the mice.

Three Blind Mice (2)

Learning intention: Peer pressure or parental expectations.
Contact role: The Third Mouse.
Context: The mouse has lost his or her tail (TiR carries length of rope to represent) and s/he seeks help from the children who have been set up in role as

medical staff of a casualty department. When s/he first appears s/he stands embarrassed in the corner, won't sit down and has to be coaxed into owning up why s/he has come to casualty. S/he won't tell how it happened at first, but s/he has been leant on to knock on the farmer's door and run away by the older mice. Other mice have managed to run away unscathed but s/he got caught and had tail chopped off. How to tell mother? how to stand up to peers?

Key moment later: The children meet mother or one of the other mice who thinks Third Mouse is a wimp and should stand up for self more.

The Three Little Pigs (1)

Learning intention: Technology.
Contact role: The first pig (do not use the word 'pig').
Context: The pigs have been sent out to build their houses. The children run a building suppliers. The pigs come one at a time to buy things to build their house. If the children offer advice they ignore it.
Key moment later: The children get complaints from the first pig about materials not working because the house blew down.

The Three Little Pigs (2)

Learning intention: Fairness, justice.
Contact role: The third pig.
Context: Two of the pigs' new houses have been destroyed by someone and the third pig seeks help from Superhelpers (see Ideas 5) to find the culprit. His brothers have run away because they are so frightened and refuse to come back until the problem is sorted out. They have to stake out the third house to see what happens.
Key moment later: The wolf at first is confrontational and tries to bluff it out, but, if handled properly, he gradually reveals he is secretly guilty and unhappy at being a vandal. He does not find it easy to own up to this, though, especially as he sort of enjoys the power and reputation.

The Three Little Pigs (3)

Learning intention (related to a technology project): When someone is arrogant about their abilities and will not listen to a grown-up.
Contact role: The pig's mother.
Context: The three pigs have decided to go because they are headstrong and think they are great builders. Their Mum, who is very worried, comes to Superhelpers (see Ideas 5). *They would not listen to Dad, who is a building inspector. Could you help me by making sure the pigs know how to build a good house?*

The Three Little Pigs (4)

Learning intention: Envy of those who have.
Contact role: The pig who has had his or her stick house blown down.
Context: The children are in role as people who care for animals on a farm that is open to the public (possible pre-activities about how to look after animals properly). The pig approaches them looking for a home and is very anxious that it is 'blow-proof'. S/he will not settle down however they look after him or her because s/he really wants the wolf sorting out.
Key moment later: The wolf is jealous of all people who have homes as he does not have a permanent one.

The Three Little Pigs (5)

Learning intention: Do you trust someone who has a reputation for deceit?
Contact role: One of the pigs.
Context: The Wolf has come to him saying, *I'm all alone, homeless and hungry. I'm really good at building houses. Will you help me if I promise to be good and help you re-build your houses?* Should the pig trust him? How can he know?
Key moment later: How can they test him out?

Ugly Duckling (1)

Learning intention: Someone who is not accepted by others; discrimination.
Contact role: The 'duckling'. Here in fact the key role is a child because the animal idea is limiting.
Context: The children are all playing games in a playground and the child (TiR) comes in all wrapped up in a coat with a hat covering all her or his hair and keeps away from everyone. S/he sometimes goes to look at games but never joins in and moves away when spoken to. *You wouldn't want to play with me. They say I'm no good at anything. They say no one will want to play with me.* S/he does not mention her appearance as the key issue and avoids questions about the covered-up head. Even when it becomes the subject, s/he is very shy about saying what the difference is. They, her or his brothers and sisters, all have lovely black, brown or blonde hair and hers is bright blue, very bright blue (or she is bald).
Key moment later: How do the children get the brothers and sisters to accept the difference?

Ugly Duckling (2)

Learning intention: Prejudice; discrimination.
Contact role: A child who has seen one of the six ducklings being bullied and driven away from all the others by its mother.
Context: The children are in role as farmers (possible pre-activities to get them

into this role) and meet the child who is very upset by what he has seen. Do they interview Mother?

Key moment later: Mother won't talk about it. She is ashamed that one of her brood is not at all like the others. She denies that the sixth duckling exists.

The Wolf and Seven Kids

Learning intention: Safety and keeping safe.

Contact role: Goat Mother.

Context: The children are put in role as baby-sitters for the kids. Mother tests them and makes sure they can do the job and know all about safety etc. (see Ideas 2 and adapt ideas from 'Looking after Baby').

Key moment later: Mother has gone out and the children are organising the tending of the kids when the Wolf arrives. What do they do and how do they cope?

Assessment, recording and progression

WHY ASSESS?

Many people have questioned the role of assessment within creative activities such as drama. We have firmly concluded that not to assess and record pupils' considerable achievements in the creative domain is to fail the children. If we do not assess we are not properly reflecting what they are and what they can become. We must assess and evaluate what we do and what they do in drama, at the very least in order to be able to plan further for progression and development of the work. It is only a short step further to record and therefore to be in a position to report so that children and parents can understand what they have achieved.

The Dearing Committee, when considering assessment in the NC, summed up the need to be sensible and flexible in this area. Here is a digest of its key principles (adapted from SCAA 1993 pp. 100–4):

- The best systems integrate curriculum planning, assessment, recording and reporting.
- Records should be kept of significant progress by the child only when they are likely to serve the following purposes:
  (a) informing future planning.
  (b) informing reports to parents.
  (c) informing future teachers.
  (d) providing evidence for teacher assessment.
- Records should be useful, manageable and easy to interpret.

Drama offers opportunities for children to develop their language skills significantly, first in speaking and listening. In addition we should be considering their knowledge, attitudes and skills in using the drama form itself and in the SMSC curriculum. Drama can be a method of testing their knowledge in other subjects too.

How do we assess in speaking and listening? Dearing saw the task as the teacher's and as informal, relying on 'notes made from observation' (SCAA 1993).

We need to identify efficient methods of assessing children's achievements and recording them. Assessment will involve gathering the evidence from observation to make explicit what children know, understand and can do. This might seem a difficult task when drama is often fluid and possibly chaotic, with a class of thirty all producing a variety of behaviours.

The fact that there are more focused moments helps. When a class are gathered round hot-seating a teacher role or opting into taking turns to tackle a teacher role in forum theatre (see Ideas 10), we can have more extended opportunities to look at individual children. We must be looking to note significant interactions with children at these moments.

The other guiding rule is to select a limited number of children (say six) to be the targets for assessment in any one session.

What about the criteria to be used? The approach Dearing recommends is taken up in OFSTED inspections where assessment of speaking and listening skills is by 'lesson observation'. Unless teachers have produced audio or video recordings during drama sessions, there will be no 'product' to take away and evaluate. The implication is that assessment in this area of the curriculum is formative and demands a criterion referenced checklist. Assessment benchmarks are provided by level descriptions and, while these are often vague and generalised, they at least provide us with a starting point. Perhaps the inadequacy of these benchmarks for assessing drama is underlined by the fact that, in the 'Guidance for Inspectors', team inspectors are advised to evaluate 'pupils' ability to create imaginary characters, situations and sequences of actions as well as their skill in adapting, improvising and improving their work' (OFSTED 1998 p. 20).

This would seem to indicate that even OFSTED identifies two kinds of learning when observing drama: first, assessment of the speaking and listening elements of English and, second, knowledge of and ability to use drama skills. However, we would argue that drama offers other kinds of evidence of children's learning beyond listening and speaking and drama skills. The nature of drama enables a teacher to observe children making explicit their current knowledge, skills and understanding relating to the topic being studied, in other words their content knowledge. It also provides evidence of the social health of the group because it demands group working skills.

We must begin by looking at the NC programme of study and level descriptions for the Speaking and Listening section of the English National Curriculum (Attainment Target 1). Most of the behaviours and skills listed there are eminently visible in good drama work, and some language use can be demonstrated in drama that is not in the official levels. Why is drama so useful? We have explored the relationship of drama and language in Ideas 7.

Drama, by virtue of its creation of concrete fictions, can provide the greatest range of contexts for talk. For example if we look at the requirements in the Programme of Study for Speaking and Listening at Key Stage One we see that 'exploring, developing and clarifying ideas' is part of the range of purposes. In the fiction of a drama such as 'Goldilocks' (see Ideas 2), the children have to understand what has happened to Goldilocks and come up with ways in which she can cope with her guilt and handle her Dad. We also find that 'purpose and audience' are important. Speaking to Goldilocks and her Dad provides two very different demands. In the latter the children have to handle an anxious and confused adult. In the former they have to be careful not to be too harsh with her and to disarm her defensiveness because of her guilt so they have to 'adapt what they say to the needs of the listener' in both cases or they will not establish proper dialogue with them. Goldilocks will walk off if they are too aggressive to her.

FOUR AREAS OF LEARNING

If we accept that drama creates wonderful worlds for talk, how will we see what children are achieving? We can look at the same drama lesson as a tool to assess four distinctive areas of learning. See the list in Figure 15.

Let us begin with the assessment of the five- to seven-year-olds; we will deal with the under-fives later. We will take each area of learning described in Figure 15 separately, starting with the NC levels for Speaking and Listening.

English – speaking and listening	• increasing confidence in talking and listening • speaking clearly when developing ideas • listening carefully and responding appropriately • using more formal vocabulary and tone of voice
Content knowledge	• using information books • creating information books • posing and recording questions in writing prior to reading non-fiction to find the answers
Personal and social education	• developing self confidence • developing effective relationships with other children and adults • learning to work as part of a group • expressing a range of emotions • initiating ideas verbally, non-verbally and symbolically using drama forms
Ability to use the art form	• developing self confidence • developing effective relationships with other children and adults • learning to work as part of a group • expressing a range of emotions • initiating ideas verbally, non-verbally and symbolically using drama forms

Figure 15 Four areas of learning in the drama lesson

English – speaking and listening

Here is a sample grid that will help assess children in speaking and listening at Key Stage One:

Level One Description	Evidence from the drama
speaks audibly	
talks about matters of immediate interest	
listens to others	
usually responds appropriately	
conveys simple meanings to a range of listeners	
begins to extend ideas or accounts by providing some detail	

Level Two Description	Evidence from the drama
speaks clearly	
begins to show confidence in talking and listening	
shows confidence in talking and listening where topic interests him or her	
shows awareness of the needs of the listener by including relevant detail	
responds to the listener's questions with further information	
uses a growing vocabulary	
usually listens carefully and responds with increasing appropriateness to what others say	
beginning of awareness that in some situations a more formal vocabulary is used	
beginning of awareness that in some situations a more formal tone of voice is used	

Level Three Description	Evidence from the drama
explores and communicates ideas	
in discussion shows an understanding of the main points	
demonstrates listening actively through comments and questions	
is beginning to adapt what s/he says to the listener by varying the use of vocabulary and the level of detail	
begins to be aware of standard English	
begins to be aware of when standard English is used	

You could break the descriptions down further, giving closer definitions of what you are looking for. Using the 'Goldilocks' drama as an example (see Ideas 2) we might see the following evidence alongside the description of the assessment criteria.

Description	Evidence from the drama
contributes new idea in front of the whole class	X suggests that Dad should buy Goldilocks a climbing frame as *she likes climbing*. The first time she has spoken voluntarily in the full class
volunteers to represent the class	Y goes to speak to the Bears to prepare the way for Goldilocks to apologise: *I know you were upset about the little girl who came to your house . . .Well . . .*
listens and feeds back with no hesitation	Z hears in full what Goldilocks did in the house in order to tell her what she should say to her Dad about it. *You should not have gone into the house but breaking the chair was an accident.*

Targeting specific pupils on different occasions is much easier than trying to record the responses of the whole class in every session. A running record can be built up for all the children over a period of time, particularly cataloguing where they make significant moves, as in example X. Once a profile of children's attainment has been made, progression in their learning can be identified. Progression is seen as 'gains in knowledge skills and understanding' and will be demonstrated as pupils move to the criteria in the next level description. The closer the assessment process is to the methodology used by external assessors, the more useful the data will be. For examples of progressive demands of techniques see 'Tableau' and 'Forum' in Ideas 10.

Content knowledge

Drama does not offer only opportunities to make assessment in Speaking and Listening; there are opportunities to assess content knowledge where the content of the drama relates to specific areas of NC, for example in the use of drama to teach history.

In the 'Pied Piper' drama (see Part III) some of the key elements highlighted in the NC will be dealt with during the drama sessions. First, 'Chronology' is explored at various times in the drama, during the discussion about the initial stimulus of the Brueghel painting *Children's Games*, and when the class are making bread. Both these activities will generate common words and phrases relating to the passage of time. The second key element, 'Range and depth of historical knowledge and understanding', will be looked at through the story when aspects of the past such as the clothes people wore and the way they lived their lives are examined through the issue of the threat of vermin in the town. A third key element, 'Interpretation of history', will be demonstrated through discussion of the Brueghel painting at the beginning of the drama. It is possible to see that strands that run through particular dramas open up assessment opportunities in other subjects.

Personal and social education

See also Ideas 6. This is an area identified as being of significance to be 'reported on in full . . . with specific reference to behaviour in the section on attitudes, behaviour and personal development' (OFSTED 1998 p. 12); 'personal and social development underpins all the other areas of learning for young children. It focuses on children learning how to work, play and co-operate with others in groups beyond their family; it also promotes self-esteem and confidence' (p. 13). Much of the focus in dramas for this age group is on social and moral dilemmas, and the skills developed by the children in these dramas model the skills needed to deal with real life. Drama's affinity to children's natural social role-play means that it provides a venue to observe and develop these skills.

The following behaviour indices are applicable not only to drama but also to other activities. For example, drama gives ways of exploring some responses to adults in ways that other activities cannot because the TiR can be a range of adults and provide contexts for responses that the normal classroom does not.

Description	Evidence from the drama
The self	
is confident in a range of situations	
shows appropriate self-respect and self-esteem	
can understand and use the language to describe feelings	
controls his or her feelings properly and behaves in appropriate ways	
is able to analyse a range of feelings and shows understanding of them	
can take responsibility	
is developing self-reflection	
can express and justify a personal opinion relevant to an issue	
Others	
is able to learn from mistakes of others	
is able to establish effective relationships with other children	
is able to establish effective relationships with adults	
shows understanding of how others behave	
helps others, particularly those who are victims	
works effectively as part of a group: by leading at times or by following and supporting effectively	
is sensitive to the needs and feelings of others	
can take instruction and direction from others, adults and children	

Society	
has a good sense of the consequences of actions	
has a clear sense of what is right, what is wrong	
acts on a sense of what is right, what is wrong	
knows about the nature and basis of rules	
shows respect for truth	
shows respect for justice and fairness	
shows respect for property	
understands and operates by democratic values	
shows beginning understanding of his or her own traditions and culture	
shows respect for other cultures and can learn from them	

Monitoring children on the basis of these descriptions will give a clear idea of the social and moral health of our children. Drama is a social activity and therefore is an excellent method of diagnosing the social health of individuals and a group. It also allows children to critique and explore their values and the values of others in order to understand, absorb and build a social and moral code that is respected.

Ability to use the art form

Some of the speaking and listening skills and understanding can be unique to drama and other language and communications skills can be shown. What about these?

Description	Evidence from the drama
Use of non-verbal communication	
holds still image position effectively	
demonstrates more developed understanding of what still image can contain	

continued . . .

Description	Evidence from the drama
uses occupational mime with skill	
responds with understanding non-verbally, e.g. helps Goldilocks from the tree	
Use of role	
can relate to TiR	
commitment to the fiction	
takes on role with understanding	
supports others into role by responding appropriately	
challenges the teacher role	
takes on different type of role, e.g. more formal (see standard English in speaking and listening matrix)	

Once you are confident with assessment, it then becomes possible to identify progression in children's learning by plotting the gains in knowledge, skills and understanding, from comparisons of assessments made over time.

ASSESSING THE UNDER-FIVES

Let us now turn our attention to the assessment of the under-fives. In terms of assessment and progression the under-fives are treated as a separate key stage and the areas of learning in drama should be in concert with those described using the SCAA guidelines on Nursery Education Desirable Outcomes for Children's Learning (see SCAA 1995):

- personal and social education
- language and literacy
- physical development
- creative development

The tracking of progress of the youngest children can be achieved adapting the following grids. Section 10 inspectors are advised to give priority to language and literacy, personal and social development, particularly behaviour (see OFSTED 1998 p. 12).

Language and literacy

Recent government initiatives have highlighted the importance of language and literacy, seen as 'central to effective provision for this age group. Opportunities to develop and practise the four elements of language, i.e. speaking and listening, reading and writing, should have a high priority, with the emphasis on children learning through talk' (OFSTED 1998 p. 13). The quality of teaching in this area is judged by the extent to which teachers engage children in both planned and spontaneous conversations, which help children to listen and respond appropriately, by 'participating in children's role play, for example: taking the part of a character; supporting and extending their imagination and use of language: adding a new dimension to the story; intervening to re-focus the learning' (OFSTED 1998 p. 13).

LANGUAGE AND LITERACY	
Description	Evidence from the drama
listens attentively in small group	
listens attentively in large group	
talks in small group	
talks in large group	
uses a growing vocabulary with increasing fluency	
expresses thoughts and conveys meaning to the listener	
listens and responds to others' ideas	
takes part in role play with confidence	
initiates ideas in the drama	

Physical development

The physical development of children is often seen as the province of PE and dance, and this is reflected in the criteria indicated in the SCAA document. However, we would argue that drama offers teachers opportunities to assess the physical development of children, particularly in those periods of drama where occupational mime or improvised play is taking place.

PHYSICAL DEVELOPMENT	
Description	Evidence from the drama
moves confidently and imaginatively with increasing control and co-ordination	
shows awareness of space and others	
handles appropriate tools and objects in the drama real and imaginary	
mimes effectively and with increasing skill	

Knowledge and understanding of the world

While young children will bring their moderate factual knowledge and understanding of the world, it is in their ability to relate to others that drama provides us with rich data to assess their development. The function of drama to teach or even discover facts is of less importance than creating opportunities to know how to deal with people and their problems. It is only later in their drama experience that drama teaches knowledge about facts, and even then the priority is stimulating the finding out rather than presenting the facts themselves.

Creative development

Drama provides a wide range of experiences in story making and imaginative play. These will help to develop children's ability to express ideas and feelings in creative ways.

CREATIVE DEVELOPMENT	
Description	Evidence from the drama
responds in a variety of ways to what they see, hear, smell, touch and feel	
through imaginative play, shows an increasing ability to use imagination, to listen and to observe	
uses a widening range of media within the fiction to express ideas and to communicate feelings	
explores shape, form and space in three dimensions	

SUMMARY

- Why assess the youngest children?
- The observation of children working in drama is an extremely efficient way to make judgements about their strengths and weaknesses, their knowledge, skills and understanding.
- In Key Stage One the assessment of drama is closely related to what children know, understand and can do in terms of Speaking and Listening. These indices are laid down in the level descriptions for Attainment Target 1.
- Attainment and progression for the under-fives (and related to reception) are seen in relation to DLOs laid down in the SCAA document.
- The adaptation of SCAA personal and social targets with ideas from the SMSC curriculum provide useful levels for assessing attainment for older early years children.

Introduction to the example dramas

These dramas are more extended ones and build up children's learning in the skills, attitudes and knowledge. They all develop work to achieve the objectives of language, social skills and speaking and listening, as well as having other specific objectives to do with moral and social learning and other curriculum areas. (See hard and soft objectives defined on page 158.)

There is a variety of lengths and degrees of complexity. Within each of the two sections of dramas they are put in order of demand on the children, both in content and in complexity.

USING THE DRAMAS

The 'Superhelpers' dramas can be used individually and it is not necessary to do them in order, but they can be used as a sequence of lessons, linked by the common role of the children as Superhelpers. Thus they have a specific progression as the children become more expert in the use of that role over a number of weeks. Some of the other dramas can be adapted as Superhelpers dramas. The children take the role of Superhelpers who are approached for help by one of the key roles.

You might wish not to use the Superhelpers role at all. If so in each case, in the planning summary, we have suggested an alternative role for the children. Leave out setting them up as Superhelpers from the structure and do some work with them to build up the alternative role they have been given. 'Sleeping Beauty' has alternative starts, with the class as a company organising parties or as Superhelpers.

The dramas can each last at least two sessions of about half to three-quarters of an hour, but can be shortened or further developed. 'Baby Bear Did It' can be used for one half-hour session if you choose to stop after giving Baby Bear advice. On the other hand, 'Hansel and Gretel' was used over three separate hour-long sessions with one Year One and Year Two mixed-age class.

FLEXIBILITY IN DRAMA

All of the plans laid out here can and should be changed and adapted in their use. The outline structures given are a distillation from our use of them and will work, but we must always be awake to the opportunities for alternative development that the children offer. None of them is exactly the same each time we do them with a class, and that is the joy of drama. The more experienced you are or become the more you will understand how the children can make a good drama better by showing other potentials for its growth. At times in the plans we have laid out alternative directions that are possible, for example two routes in 'Goldilocks' towards the end (see Ideas 2). Children have taken the route of dealing with the Bears as the priority; one group offered to mend the Bears' chair as a way of Goldilocks making amends. Another group had the relationship with Dad as the focus and suggested to him that he should build her a climbing frame, because she liked climbing so much, and they helped him design it.

In 'Sleeping Beauty' there are two routes at point 17 in the plan. To illustrate how children can initiate ideas in the progress of the drama, at one point all of the Year One class were 'hiding' (i.e. pretending to hide, rather than being behind any real barriers) watching the Bad Fairy with her spell book in order to find out what she was like. It was at the point where I normally let them find her diary (point 14). I was TiR as the Bad Fairy and, as I put the spell book down in order to take the diary to write in it, at the speed of light one of the children, with no pre-planning, zipped across the floor past me, dextrously picking up the spell book, and hid again. There was a unanimous roar of approval from the class and I stood open-mouthed. Immediately I went OoR to discuss what had happened and to decide with the children what they would do as a result. I had to point out that they had revealed that they were there now with the shout and asked what they wanted to do with the book. They said they wanted to keep it to prevent the Bad Fairy from harming the Princess and spoiling the party. I agreed that that was a very good approach and suggested we go back into the drama to see what would happen now that she did not have the book and she knew they were there. They eagerly agreed. This gave me the chance to use their intervention rather than the diary.

They were very full of themselves as they waited to be called out of hiding to confront the Bad Fairy, so I ignored them, sat down very quietly and buried my head in my hands, muttering, *That is so unfair. The spell book is all I have. I'm not even very good at those. They don't work anyway and it is only that people think I can do them that makes them afraid of me. What can I do now? No one will take any notice of me and Lucy's parents will never invite me to the party.*

Then I stopped, went OoR and discussed what they had heard. The child who had taken the book felt he might even give it back if she was so upset about it. I asked if they trusted her. Some said they might like to find out more before they trusted her. They could see that there was more to this than the spell book and wanted to talk to her, which is the next part we did, having thought about how they might go about it.

Thus the children can be the playwrights with us and become even more committed to the ideas that evolve. We have to see how to use the ideas they come up with.

AIMS AND OBJECTIVES FOR THE DRAMAS

Part of the progression in work is to see how well the children become engaged, how long they can concentrate and work together and how this can be extended as they become more experienced.

We have indicated learning objectives for the dramas in the planning summary at the end of each drama. We have not specified the speaking and listening objectives in every case because all of the dramas here could be applied to key speaking and listening objectives as laid out in the NC for English, for example from Attainment Target 1 for Key Stage One:

> to talk for a range of purposes . . . imaginative play and drama . . . exploring and clarifying ideas; predicting outcomes and discussing possibilities . . . describing events . . . making simple, clear explanations of choices; giving reasons for opinions and actions.

> to consider how talk is influenced by the purpose and intended audience.

> to listen carefully and to show their understanding of what they see and hear by making relevant comments . . . to remember specific points . . . and to listen to others' response to them.

> to participate in drama activities, improvisation . . . using language appropriate to role or situation. They should be given opportunities to respond to drama . . . in which they have participated.
>
> (DfEE 1995 p. 4)

We call them *soft objectives*. Objectives which are specific to one drama in particular are *hard objectives*. They relate to other curriculum areas such as design.

For examples on the range of objectives in the SMSC curriculum see our 'levels tables' in Ideas 11.

The 'Superhelpers' role itself is designed to give children positive thinking and patterns of behaviour for moral and social development.

FORMAT

We have laid the dramas out with the stages clearly marked and with guidance in the form of

- what is done
- what is said, with the examples of what the teacher might say in and out of role *in italics*. This is *not* a script that must be spoken exactly as written here, but gives ideas of how to handle the role.
- numbers for the stages of the drama with a short note in the margin indicating the techniques being used.
- a summary of the stages with objectives and NC connections at the end of each drama. It includes the roles being used, and ideas for the role signifiers.

In the classroom you may find it easier to use the summary than to use the full scenario.

CONTRACTING

Contracting is negotiating the doing of drama before it starts. It is important to lay down the rules and conventions. We have not repeated this at the beginning of every drama. How you handle it will vary according to whether the drama you are doing is the first for the class or not. For two examples of this procedure see Ideas 2 where contracting is described more fully in Stage one of both Step two and Step three.

GENDER

Most of the teacher roles in the dramas are recorded in our writings as male. This is because the authors are both male and the dramas are described as we originally carried them out. Therefore, unless there was a reason for a role to be one gender, the roles were developed as male. However, many of them could be played as male *or* female, so it is important to recognise that our recording of the drama does not mean the roles can not be females. Here some of the roles can be either and you should play them as suits you.

Drama	Male	Female
Little Bo Peep	Farmer George	Farmer Jane
The Pied Piper	Pied Piper	Pied Piper
The Pied Piper	The Mayor	The Mayor
Jill and the Beanstalk	The Giant	The Giant
Baby Bear Did It	Baby Bear	Baby Bear
The King/Queen of Spring	The King	The Queen
Humpty Dumpty	Humpty Dumpty	Humpty Dumpty

The only exception to this is where the gender itself has learning potential. For example, Goldilocks's Dad offers the opportunity to deal with a dad who is not managing his daughter's behaviour, Mr Smith the librarian in 'Mr Wolf Makes Mistakes' is short-tempered and rather intolerant. The drama is planned so that children will successfully manage him and in so doing will have a chance to look at his attitude. The Troll is aggressive, a common trait amongst males, and yet he has to care for his eggs: this contradiction gives the opportunity for the teacher to explore with the children how to help him and gives another dimension to the male role.

However, we also take female roles, as with Goldilocks or Cinderella. In our experience if it is negotiated properly, children will easily accept male teachers taking female roles and vice versa. It is the attitude that is presented that engages the children. This in turn makes redundant the need for using costumes and make-up. In the 'as if' of drama children will easily accept male teachers taking female roles and vice versa because the focus is dealing with what they say and what they do, not what they look like.

THE FRAMES

The small numbered frames in the margins show the stages of the drama and the technique being used. The numbers correspond to the numbered planning summary at the end. Where we have used specific children's names in the teacher's speech in the dramas, you should choose appropriate children from your class to refer to and use their names. Example, from 'Little Bo Peep': *The children were busy building the sheep pen for the competition.* <u>Everton</u> *was sawing the wood,* <u>Miriam</u> *was hammering. They were all working very hard when George the farmer came in holding the cup he had won in last year's competition.*

Part II

'Mantle of the Expert' dramas

Mr Wolf Makes Mistakes

Structure outline

Set up the Superhelpers (see Ideas 5). Explain that the Superhelpers have received a letter and a video to go with it.

1 Superhelpers

Set up an area of the classroom to represent a large video screen: two chairs with a space behind could be used. In the video screen area is a table and some chairs; on the table is a notice that reads *Library – Quiet Please*.

Tell the children, *You are going to see a piece of video filmed in the local library by the security cameras. It is going to show a boy, James Wolf. Watch it and then we will talk about it.* (It is deliberately a boy here as this addresses one of the difficulties schools seem to be facing: the unsatisfactory behaviour of boys in particular.)

One of the children can hold a video handset and when you are quite still they can start the video. Go into the video area and put on a baseball cap. Pick up a book and remain still.

The video

James is reading his book. He laughs very loudly. *This is really good.*

2 TiR James Wolf

He takes out an apple from his pocket and starts eating it. *Hey, listen to this everybody . . . no, I won't shush . . . don't you want to hear the joke in this book?*
STOP THE DRAMA

Talk with the class about what they thought was going on. *What was James doing? How was he behaving? Was he enjoying himself? Where was he?*

3 OoR reflection

4 OoR preparing to meet James Wolf's Mum	Superhelpers have had a phone call from a worried mum. She wants to talk about her son, James.
5 TiR James Wolf's Mum	Key points to make: *James won't go out. He used to love going to the library. He just stays in his room. His Dad got into some trouble with the Three Little Pigs and isn't around at the moment.* She knows nothing of the library incident.
6 OoR reflection	*If you could speak to James, what would you say? What do you need to find out? I've made arrangements with his mother for him to come in. How will you talk to him, if he is as upset as she says?*
7 TiR James	Initially be very reluctant to talk about it. The children must work at getting his trust. (OoR discuss ways to do this . . . what is he interested in?)

Eventually he admits that Mr Smith the librarian has banned him from the library for making too much noise and eating an apple. |
| **8 OoR reflection** | *If you could speak to Mr Smith, what would you say? Do you want to talk to Mum first or after seeing Mr Smith? What questions have you got for Mr Smith?* |
| **9 TiR Mr Smith** | Mr Smith is very intolerant of James. *I don't want him back in the library, not if he behaves like he does. He is noisy and he has walked out without getting his books stamped. He is also very late returning them.* |
| **10 OoR challenge for the Superhelpers** | *Is Mr Smith being fair on James? Does James really understand what he should be doing?* The children must come up with a plan to help James and convince Mr Smith he should be given another chance.

Let the children win but only after they come up with a plan. |
| **Making a plan to help James** | *What are the rules of a library? Can you show James how to behave and what to do in a library? I bet you could help James by showing him how a library works and what the rules are. Could we make the library in the story here? You could be the people in the library, working and borrowing.* |

The children discuss the jobs they could do in the library to help the librarian – putting books on the shelves, stamping the books coming in. Some of them will be working in the library and some of them will be visiting the library demonstrating to James what he should do.

Set up the library with an entrance, a place to have books stamped in and out, tables and chairs and shelves of books. The rules are on a large piece of paper on the wall. Practise the library on a busy day. When the class are ready James Wolf will watch them.

11 OoR setting up the context

Right, this is the day of training James what to do. Get ready for him to come in. James is first of all going to watch what he has to do.

As James, watch the rehearsed activities in the library, making suitable comments as you see things happening that you didn't know anything about, e.g., *Why do they all talk so quietly? Why do they stamp the books? What does that sign say?*

12 TiR James watching

However, when the time comes for you to enter the library say, *I can't do it because everyone will be staring at me.*

13 TiR James has to face the challenge

Negotiate with the Superhelpers that they will carry on as normal and not stare at James, but that they can say *stop* if they see him do something wrong so that he can be helped.

OoR

Oh dear, he seems shy of coming into the library now. He doesn't like us looking at him. What can we do to help him? Can you all get on and be keeping an eye on him at the same time as pretending not to? But if you see James doing something wrong you must say 'stop' so that we can all look at what is going on and carefully help him.

This is in effect a control mechanism so that the children are actively involved in the drama while at the same time watching it from within.

Deliberately make out that you do not understand all of the rules the children have come up with and break them. This will enable the children to stop you and demonstrate to James what he should do.

14 TiR James is trained in forum theatre

Other possible contexts for further work

The training can move to other locations where James cannot seem to obey the rules: a café, the park or the playground. These can be part of a rolling drama over several sessions. All of them are concerned with teaching James Wolf how to behave in different contexts. As a result the children are able to look together at why certain rules apply in certain places and justify them to James.

Mr Wolf Makes Mistakes – PLANNING SUMMARY

LEARNING OBJECTIVES	NATIONAL CURRICULUM programmes of study/attainment targets English
• to introduce reception children to drama • to create opportunity for them to teach someone about rules • to look at the issue of rules for different contexts, i.e. the library, the café and the park	• Pupils should be given an extensive introduction to books, stories and words in print around them. • Pupils should be encouraged to participate in drama activities, improvisation . . . using language appropriate to role or situation.

KEY STAGES IN THE DRAMA

1. Contracting the drama and setting the context – the Superhelpers office.
2. TiR James Wolf – watching the video.
3. OoR reflect on what have seen.
4. OoR prepare to meet James Wolf's Mum.
5. TiR James Wolf's Mum.
6. OoR reflect on what found out.
7. TiR James Wolf.
8. OoR reflect on what found out.
9. TiR Mr Smith the librarian.
10. Making a plan to help James.
11. Setting up the library.
12. TiR James Wolf has to observe the library.
13. TiR James Wolf is shy in the library.
14. Forum theatre – training James Wolf how to behave

(Extension work – the waiter/waitress and the park keeper.)

Roles for Children	Superhelpers (or people who are training to be librarians)		
Roles for Teacher	Mrs Wolf	James Wolf	Mr Smith, the librarian
The props/role signifiers	shopping bag	baseball cap	date stamp for books

Other props: Table, books, pencil, library ticket, OHP

Assessment, Recording and Reporting	
Attainment (reference to level descriptions) knowledge, understanding and skills	PUPILS' RESPONSE – Evidence
Progression (reference to level descriptions) gains in knowledge, understanding and skills	

Little Bo Peep

Pre-drama activity

| I Picture stimulus |

Use a picture of nursery rhyme (e.g. Jack and Jill) to ask them what nursery rhymes they know. Then tell the class the nursery rhyme. Those children who are familiar with it join in, then tell them the story in prose.

| Nursery rhyme to narrative form |

Once upon a time there was a little girl called Jill who had a friend called Jack. They had a very important job to do for their Mummy. She had asked them to go and get some water from a well on the top of the hill near their house . . .

Structure outline

| 2 Contracting |

Now our drama today is going to be about a farmer called George. We are all going to be in the drama. You are going to be the Superhelpers, children who are very good at helping people and sometimes I am going to pretend to be some of the people in our drama with you. Is that OK? If you are not sure or have a question to ask we can stop and sort it out.

| Narration setting the context |

Every year in Greenrigg there was a sheepdog competition where all the farmers brought their sheepdogs and sheep to see who was the best at rounding them up and putting them into a sheep pen.

| Context picture clue |

Hold up a picture of an advert for the sheepdog trial or a similar picture.

| 3. Collective drawing whole-class activity |

Draw a field with a sheep pen in the middle and explain how a sheepdog trial works. *What other things do we need at the trial?* Possibles: refreshment tents, stalls to sell things, a bouncy castle for the children.

Take ideas from the class and put them into the picture.

Now we're going to begin our story. I am going to pretend to be someone in the story and you will know when I am pretending because I will be carrying this stick. Listen as I tell the story and you will know what to do.

4 Moving into role

Here we are now, Fly. We'll have a rest. You've done really well this morning. Finding that lost ewe and rounding her up was excellent. I'll give you a drink. There you are. I bet you'll like that. Put down a dog's bowl and come OoR.

Who do you think I am being in the story? Who is he talking to? Discuss with them.

5 OoR checking understanding

I'll be him again and you can see if you're right.

Well, you look like very helpful people. My name is George and I'm a farmer. I wonder if you could help me. Let me introduce you first. This is my sheepdog, Fly, one of the best. I'll even let you make friends and stroke her if you like, though she's a working dog and we don't normally pet her.

6 TiR

How can you show you are stroking this pretend dog?

Get some of the children to demonstrate and build them all up to doing it with care and authenticity. *Now let's see what he wants us to help with.*

OoR negotiating into the 'as if' world

Well, like I said, I've got a real job on today. We're holding a sheepdog trial and show. I think my Fly stands a good chance of winning. First time for her but she's very good. I have to get a pen made for putting the sheep in at the end. Do you think you could make it for me? I haven't got very much time because the sheep to be used for the trial have not arrived. I've got to go and find out what has happened.

7 TiR

Discuss how Superhelpers can help and what they would have to do for him. *The pen is made from wood. What shape will it be? What tools will we need to make it? Show me how you make things out of wood.*

OoR

Working with the class, get them to demonstrate sawing, hammering nails, using a screwdriver and measuring the wood.

8 Occupational mime

Moving into a space and setting children's' roles	The class decide which job they want to do and to begin work on the sheep pen. Chairs are used to represent the pen so that the class have something to focus their mime upon. STOP THE DRAMA
9 From narrative to TiR	*The children were busy building the sheep pen for the competition. Everton was sawing the wood, Miriam was hammering. They were all working very hard when George the farmer came in holding the cup he had won in last year's competition.*
TiR Farmer George	*Where is she? She should be here by now!* *(To the children) Are you building the sheep pen? Make sure it's very solid won't you. You're doing a grand job. Show me what you've done so far. I want to win this competition and see this cup, this is the one for the competition. Have any of you seen Bo Peep? She was supposed to be here by now. (Sounding quite angry) I give her a simple job to do and she can't do it! She's not as reliable as you all are. If you see her, tell her I am looking for her and I am not happy.* Move away from the children and then stop the drama to talk about it.
10 OoR reflecting on events	*What was Farmer George like? What sort of mood was he in? He was different from last time you met him. Why? Where might Bo Peep be? How do they find out where she is?* If they offer that she is looking for her sheep that is lost, accept it and add that, if it is true, it makes it all the more important they might find her to make sure she knows Farmer George is looking for her.
Preparing to meet Mrs Peep. Setting a task	*If the Superhelpers meet Bo Peep's Mum, what do they need to ask her?* *Mrs Peep is doing lots of jobs in the house. Do you ever help your Mum or Dad in the house? What sort of jobs do you do? Let me see you doing jobs in the house and I'll try and guess what you're doing.* *Now Mrs Peep loves being helped in the house and she hasn't got any help from her children today. If you offer to help Mrs Peep she will be very pleased.*

Get one of the class to rehearse meeting Mrs Peep and offering to help her in the house. This rehearsal before the event helps the class prepare for each stage of the drama: it is important if they are new to this way of working but becomes less important the more experience they gain.

Good morning, are you the Superhelpers? *Yes, I would be very grateful for your help this morning.*	11 Meeting Mrs Peep TiR
Organises asking them, from within the role, what jobs they can do.	Occupational mime
After a short while stop and thank them. *Let's sit down and have a cup of tea!*	
Moving out of role briefly, suggest that this could be a good time to find out what has happened to Bo Peep – get the children to remind you of the questions they need to ask.	OoR
Answer the children's questions and feed in the following information: Bo Peep had to get six sheep from the top field. She was a bit worried about what Farmer George had asked her to do. *I told her before she left not to worry, you can only do your best.* STOP THE DRAMA	TiR Mrs Peep information for role
We still need to find out what has happened to Bo Peep. What do you make of this message that came over the phone?	12 OoR

> From the National Park Hilltop Ranger:
> I believe that you are looking for Bo Peep. One of the shepherds I met reported that she went past his farm carrying a lamb. She told him she was taking it to the vet.
>   That reminded me that, earlier on, through my binoculars I myself saw a girl trying to get some sheep through a gate. Then I saw her picking up a lamb that was hurt.

Message input

STOP THE DRAMA

13 OoR

Summarise what they now know. Prepare to meet Farmer George again. What they have found out is taken back to Farmer George.

14 TIR Farmer George

Farmer George is very angry with Bo Peep. *She's let me down. I might lose the competition.*

15 OoR reflecting

Reflect on how they feel about what Farmer George has said. *Is he being selfish?*

16 TiR as Bo Peep. The other side of the story

Meet Bo Peep (TiR): she is very worried. *I went to get the sheep but found a lamb that had lost its mother. I tried to care for it and took it home but when I got back to the field the sheep had gone. I am worried about what Farmer George will say but he never showed me what I had to do. I haven't been trained properly and I tried my best. I couldn't leave the lamb.*

What am I going to do now? Farmer George will be very angry with me. I can't face him or my Mum. She'll be so disappointed that I let someone down. I think I'll run away and hide.

Make as though to run away and freeze. Then come OoR.

OoR reflecting

Reflect on how they feel about what has happened. *Was Bo Peep right to leave the sheep and take the lamb home? What should she do now? What will Farmer George say? Is she right to run away? What are they going to do?*

17 Children explaining to Farmer George

The children have to tell Farmer George what has happened and how they feel about it. He starts by being very angry and it is their job to calm him down.

His response is gradually to recognise that he has made a mistake.

18 Children devising a solution

He asks them to help him bring the sheep down from the mountain – he gives them a test of stealth (Grandmother's Footsteps). The children show they can help.

19 The resolution – the children winning

Conclusion – the children show pictures (tableaux) of themselves getting the sheep down from the mountain and showing Bo Peep what to do. They show the pictures that appear in the paper next week of the winners of the sheepdog trial and Bo Peep with the lamb she has helped.

Little Bo Peep – PLANNING SUMMARY

LEARNING OBJECTIVES

- to consider ideas of selfishness and competitiveness
- for children to gather and feedback information

NATIONAL CURRICULUM

programmes of study/attainment targets

Geography

- to become aware that the world exists beyond their own locality
- use geographical terms such as *hill, river, road*
- make maps and plans of real and imaginary places

As part of a study of a contrasting locality

- how localities may be similar and how they may be different

KEY STAGES IN THE DRAMA

1. Introducing nursery rhymes and changing them to story.
2. Contracting the drama and setting the context – where, who and what is happening. Remind them of the Superhelpers.
3. Collective drawing of the sheepdog trial.
4. Moving into role: *I am going to pretend to be someone in the story.*
5. OoR checking understanding. Put down a dog's bowl and come OoR.
6. TiR *Well, you look like very helpful people. This is my sheepdog, Fly.*
   OoR negotiating into the 'as if' world. *How can you show you are stroking this pretend dog?*
7. TiR: *I have to get a pen made for putting the sheep in at the end.*
   OoR discuss how Superhelpers can help and what they would have to do for him.
8. Occupational mime: building the sheep pen, defining the space.
9. Narration, then enter Farmer George (TiR1), describing the problem: where is Bo Peep?
10. OoR *How did Farmer George seem? What sort of mood was he in? What was the problem?*
    Preparing to meet Bo Peep's Mum.
11. Enter Bo Peep's Mum (TiR2) – she needs help in the house and then she will answer questions about Bo Peep.

12. OoR discuss what she said. Phone message brings new information to interpret.
13. OoR discuss what they know and prepare to tell Farmer George.
14. TiR1: Farmer George meets the Superhelpers and hears what they have found out.
15. OoR discuss Farmer George's reaction and prepare to meet Bo Peep.
16. Enter Bo Peep (TiR3): tells them of the injured lamb and going home. Prepare to meet Farmer George.
17. Children explain to Farmer George, who asks for their help to get the sheep and gives them a test of stealth (Grandmother's Footsteps).
18. Children devise a solution.
19. Still pictures of bringing the sheep down and the prize winning at the sheepdog trial.

Roles for Children	Superhelpers (or neighbours to the farmer, who have their own farm)		
Roles for Teacher	Farmer George	Mrs Peep	Bo Peep
The props/ role signifiers	Stick, shepherd's crook?	sweeping brush	hat

Other props: chairs for sheep pen, paper pens, cup for prize

Assessment, Recording and Reporting	
Attainment (reference to level descriptions) knowledge, understanding and skills	**PUPILS' RESPONSE – Evidence**
Progression(reference to level descriptions) gains in knowledge, understanding and skills	

Cinderella

Structure outline

Tell the children that we will be doing a story and in the story they will be Superhelpers (see Ideas 5)

1 OoR

The story starts in the Superhelpers' office. Some of the Superhelpers have been opening letters and some of them have been answering the phone. Remind them to answer, *Good morning. Superhelpers. Can I help you?* Rehearse the jobs the Superhelpers do in the office, ask the children what sort of requests for help they are getting.

It was an another busy day in the Superhelpers' office. All the Superhelpers were busily answering the phone and opening letters.

OoR narration

Look, everybody, I've got a letter here you should all listen to.

2 TiR Chief of Superhelpers

> 98 Rosewood Avenue
> Clifftop
> Liveshire
> Tuesday 10 September
>
> Dear Superhelpers,
> I have been told you know a lot about children's problems and you might be able to help me. I am very worried about our Cindy. She seems very sad a lot of the time. I would like to come and talk to you.
>   Yours Sincerely
>
>   Mr Parkinson.
>   (Cindy's Dad)
>
> PS Can I come soon?

STOP THE DRAMA

3 OoR

Negotiate meeting the father. Give them a chance to get ideas to talk to him. *What do we need to find out? What shall we ask him?*

4 TiR Cindy's father

Key pieces of information: Cindy's father has a new wife and daughter called Morella. Cindy and Morella do not get on very well. He does not know why.

My wife does not know there is a problem. When I mentioned it she says I am making a fuss. I have not told her I have come to see you.

I would like you to come and see for yourselves. I am having a party on Saturday night and I wondered if you came to help prepare the party, you could meet Cindy and Morella and see if you can see why they do not get on.
STOP THE DRAMA

5 OoR

Discuss what they have found out. *Why might the two sisters be not getting on? What jobs could you do so you could see what is happening and help the Dad?*

Mime work

Set up how they would help with the party. Practise some of the jobs.

Narration

The drama begins as the Superhelpers are getting the party ready. They don't know what Cindy looks like so they have to listen very carefully to what the sisters say to work out which one is which. They cannot tell her they are Superhelpers until they have found out what is going on.

6 TiR Cindy

Pick up a small bucket and cloth and while the children are doing their jobs talk to yourself as you clean the floor. *She never has to do anything. I have to clean the floor while she gets ready for the party. I have to do all the work while she does nothing. Well, I'm not going to the stupid party. She'll only get me into trouble anyway. I hate her. She's always singing songs so if I hear her I'm going even if I haven't finished this floor. And I don't care if she tells her Mum. She's not my mum anyway.*
STOP THE DRAMA

7 OoR

Reflect upon what Cindy has said. *What do you know now that you didn't know before? Are you ready to start the story again? I am going to be Cindy again. OK?*

Go back into role. If they talk to you just give very short answers. Even ask who they are to check that they get the idea of not saying Superhelpers. Go OoR and re-negotiate the not telling if someone does tell. Don't worry if they don't speak to you.

8 TiR Cindy

Continue with the cleaning of the floor and then you hear someone coming. *That's her. I can hear her coming! I'm going to my room.*

Without stopping the drama, exchange the bucket and cloth for a very fine hat to signify Morella. Move away from the Superhelpers. She sweeps in looking for Cindy. *Where is she? She's in big trouble with our Mum. She hasn't finished the floor. Right, I am going to tell on her.*

9 Change role TiR Morella

If they speak to you, explain who you are and what Cindy is supposed to have done and that it is not good enough.
STOP THE DRAMA

What do you need to say to Father and what could be the possible solution?

10 OoR

The drama from here on is about how these three communicate with each other and the children as Superhelpers will have to talk to each one.

Each role will present a particular attitude and the children need to find ways to help them understand what is happening and get them talking to each other.

Possible attitudes to be presented:

11 Hot-seating

Cindy: *I have to do all the work, she (Morella) doesn't do anything. My new Mum doesn't like me. I like reading, drawing and playing football, Morella just wants to watch television and play with her dolls. My new Mum is always nice to me when my Dad is there but not when he is not.*

Morella: *I didn't want my Mum to get married again. I don't like Cindy, she never wants to do the things I want to do.*

One option is to introduce the idea that Cindy has damaged one of Morella's dolls or toys. This adds another dimension for the children to deal with – if you are being treated unfairly or if you are not happy, is it OK to damage your stepsister's property?

Mum: *Morella shouldn't do the washing up because she has delicate skin. Cindy spends too much time on her own in her bedroom. She should be playing with dolls like our Morella. I have never seen Morella being horrible to Cindy. Morella is quite right to tell me if Cindy is not doing her jobs.*

Dad: *I thought they would play together. Cindy doesn't seem to be very happy. I've never seen Morella's Mum being horrible to Cindy. I always try to be nice to Morella because I want her to like me.*

12 Final forum theatre

The forum theatre (see Ideas 10) will involve the children taking Cindy's role and presenting how she feels and what she wants to one of the other three, or all of them one after the other in three forums. You play the other role.

It could be the children taking Dad's role and presenting the problem as he sees it to Mum or Morella.

Cinderella – PLANNING SUMMARY

LEARNING OBJECTIVES

- to introduce reception children to drama
- to create an opportunity for them to teach an adult
- to look at parent/child relationships
- to look at sibling relationships

NATIONAL CURRICULUM

programmes of study/attainment targets
English

- exploring, developing and clarifying ideas; predicting outcomes and discussing possibilities
- making simple clear explanations of choices, giving reasons for opinions and actions

KEY STAGES IN THE DRAMA

1. Set up Superhelpers' office – narrate 'another busy day' during occupational mime leading to the arrival of a letter.

2. Chief Superhelper with letter.
3. OoR negotiate speaking to the father.
4. TiR as father of Cindy.
5. OoR discuss what you have found out *or* Negotiate the setting up of the party with the class. Remind them to watch and listen carefully to see what Cindy and Morella are like.
6. TiR as Cindy.
7. OoR discuss what found out.
8. TiR as Cindy.
9. TiR as Morella.
10. Reflect on what we know now and decide whom we need to talk to.
11. possibles to hot-seat: Morella, Mum, Cindy, Dad
12. forum theatre: Cindy (children) and Morella (TiR); Cindy (children) and Mum (TiR); Dad (children) and Mum (TiR)

Roles for Children	Superhelpers (or servants to the family)				
Roles for Teacher	Chief Superhelper	Cindy's father	Cindy	her sister Morella	Cindy's Mum
The props/ role signifiers	Clipboard with letter	Walking stick	bucket and cloth	fine hat	carries a mirror
Other props:					

Assessment, Recording and Reporting	
Attainment (reference to level descriptions) knowledge, understanding and skills	**PUPILS' RESPONSE –** Evidence
Progression (reference to level descriptions) gains in knowledge, understanding and skills	

Sleeping Beauty

Session one

1 OoR contract	First negotiate the drama rules as usual: what is expected and how we work.
2 Setting the children's roles	Build the 'Mantle of the Expert' role for the children (see Ideas 5) of running a company organising parties for people.

Begin with a general discussion *What makes a good party?* List the ideas that the children come up with on a large sheet of paper. These will become their jobs.

Make sure that a range of jobs has been named. Add some yourself as you go along if not.

Set up the party-planning company. Choose a name for it. Decide on the working areas.

Or if you are setting up Superhelpers:
Set up the office in the usual way (see Ideas 5). Introduce a letter from the King or Queen asking for help to run a birthday party for their daughter as their ideas always go wrong.

Then start as above with the discussion about what makes a good party. Do the occupational mime (point 4) and skip to point 7.

3 TiR setting the context	As TiR1, the Manager of the Company, introduce the work that we have to complete in the next week. *These are the contracts that we have at the moment. We have parties for a five-year-old boy, Thomas, the ten-year-old twin girls, Stacey and Kelly, a seven-year-old girl, Samia, and a six-year-old boy, Sean.*

You can attach special interests or music likes and dislikes which can provide constraints for the work.

Produce signed contracts that *we are working to*. Figure 16 is an example:

We undertake to supply goods and services namely music, food, games, decorations and other agreed services for a party for

name ....

age ....

likes and dislikes........................

....

signed,

for Party Time

Figure 16 'Party Time' contract

Add at the end of your address to the workers: *These are the last orders for parties that we have at the moment so we must be on the lookout for future contracts that we might bid for. I'll leave you to get on with these parties now.*

> Setting an expectation

Groups work on preparing the ideas they have come up with: food, goody bags, games (bouncy castle), decor, poster, balloons, hats.

> **4** Occupational mime

TiR as manager, *If you need me I'll be in the office.*

As though it is being broadcast over the radio, announce, *We interrupt this programme to make a special announcement. Her Royal Majesty, the Queen Elena, is pleased to announce the*

> **5** Narrative as stimulus

Seventh Birthday Party for HRH the Princess Judith, on the Saturday at the end of the month. All the children of the town will be invited to a Grand Party at the Palace on that day.

6 TiR

As manager wander back into the factory area muttering about the need for more work and see if any of them pick up the possibility of the royal party. If not raise it with them.

Call the factory together. *Someone heard that there is to be a Grand Birthday Party at the Palace. What shall we do about this?*

Children's decisions

Building on their input, aim to put together representatives of each department to bid for the contract. Prepare them to go to the Queen. *What do the reps have to say?*

Session two

7 Setting the context

Visit the Queen. Set up the Palace hall. Ask the children what they think it would look like and put chairs or other markers down to show where things are.

Literacy connection

Use large pieces of paper to write the names of furniture or contents of the room, windows, banners etc. You could use these later in literacy work. Place the throne.

Defining children's role

The manager discusses approaching the Queen: *How would the representatives have to behave in the presence of the Queen? Particularly if we want to create a good impression and persuade her to give our company the contract.*

8 Forum theatre OoR

The representatives are placed in the appropriate place in the room with the other children gathered round them for forum theatre (see Ideas 10).

Enter the Queen (TiR2). Go OoR immediately after her first speech to check what their perception of the Queen is.

The negotiation takes place. Let the children win the contract if they show the right sorts of commitment. Go OoR to help them if they do not handle her right.

9 Occupational mime

Back at the factory. Set to preparing for the party. Each group to have specific responsibility this time as it is a big party and all groups are working on it. All can work on cake design – paper available.

During the work the Manager inspects and checks. Possibility of the Queen also to visit to inspect.

If there is not time, narrate the preparations for the big party as having happened and then move to:

| Narration |

Setting up the party in the hall at the Palace. The workers decorate, lay out food, prepare games, try out music etc. Manager says, *Remember you must keep an eye on security. No one must see the preparations till the day. So make sure no one unauthorised comes in here.* Put up big sign, 'No Entry'?

| 10 mime: setting an expectation |

TiR3, the Bad Fairy appears muttering, *Look at all this, just for her. Why should she have a big party like this? They never do this for me. I'll make sure it fails. They'll have a great surprise. Now where is that one that I used last time I wanted . . . mutter.* She thumbs through the folder she is carrying, labelled 'Spell Book'.

| 11 TiR as stimulus |

| Role signifier |

The children should challenge you because of the 'No Entry'. If so be very secretive about who you are and why you are there. Ask them questions about what they are doing. 'Exit', i.e. turn away and make to exit at a suitable moment to avoid difficult questions and/or to make it more intriguing. Then come OoR.

| Children's decision |

If they do not challenge you, look round and then exit.

OoR *Who was that? . . . What was she talking about? Should we find out more? How do we tackle her? She seems very secretive. What is she planning to do, do you think?*

| 12 OoR reflection |

Session three
Recap where we have got to. *What do we do about the intruder?*

| 13 OoR |

Do they seek to talk to her? If so she refuses to talk to *people who are organising a party for HER!*

Do they go to the Queen? If so she is annoyed and tells them not to poke their noses into what doesn't concern them, saying, *Just get the party ready and get on with your jobs, otherwise I'll get someone else to do the party.*

In any case they then 'find' a book titled 'Lucy's Diary' left lying near the throne, not at first realising she is the Bad Fairy. Dilemma – should they look inside?

| 14 Stimulus |

When they do look, they read her feelings at being left out of things all the time, and of the plan to put a spell on the Princess.

Lucy's diary entries

Tuesday
What a terrible day!! it has been awful. I can't stand all the fuss about Judith's party – it's making it much worse. It wouldn't be as bad if I had been invited. Leaving me out makes me so upset. It's not FAIR!!

Wednesday
Party! Party! Party! That's all you hear about. Birthday food. Birthday cards. Birthday presents. I'm going to give her a present she will never forget. Sometimes I wish she was *dead*. YES dead. Maybe DEATH will be my present for Judith.

Thursday
Why me? What have I ever done? Everyone's so excited for the party of the year. It will be the party of the year when I've finished – and then they'll be the ones that are upset. They'll see!! It's not Judith that I hate. She can't help who her parents are – but this is the only way I know of to make them suffer like I am doing.

---

15 Reflection and decision

Children to discuss in or out of role. For example if in role the Manager might say, *I don't understand what is going on here. Can you explain it to me? Why could Lucy hate them so much? What have they done to her? What are we going to do?*

S/he must convey concern over what might happen to the party: *Could you tackle Lucy again and ask her about the diary?*

If in this discussion the children suggest a usable reason for the jealousy, use it rather than the one suggested below. Also see alternative suggestion below for older, more experienced groups.

Optional: If the Queen has not been told yet, have the Queen come to check on the party. Do they tell the Queen and mention the diary to let her know how Lucy feels?

| **16** TiR |

Possible directions and outcomes: see Figure 17.

| **17** Children seek a solution |

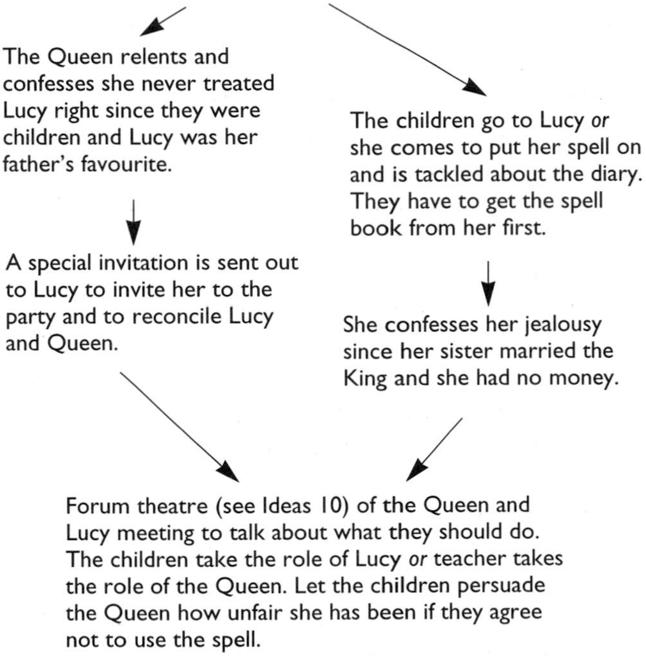

The Queen relents and confesses she never treated Lucy right since they were children and Lucy was her father's favourite.

The children go to Lucy *or* she comes to put her spell on and is tackled about the diary. They have to get the spell book from her first.

A special invitation is sent out to Lucy to invite her to the party and to reconcile Lucy and Queen.

She confesses her jealousy since her sister married the King and she had no money.

Forum theatre (see Ideas 10) of the Queen and Lucy meeting to talk about what they should do. The children take the role of Lucy *or* teacher takes the role of the Queen. Let the children persuade the Queen how unfair she has been if they agree not to use the spell.

Figure 17 Possible directions for the class to choose

The party to celebrate Judith's birthday goes ahead and has Lucy as the special guest.

| **18** The pay-off or reward for the children |

Note: here is a possible angle if used with a strong experienced group used to the darker side of fairy tales. If children do not supply a reason for Lucy's behaviour, say that ten years ago Lucy had a child when her sister the Queen was not able to have a child of own and the Queen stole it, saying it had died of an illness (in fact she hid it away with another family). The child is restored to Lucy at the party in point 18.

Sleeping Beauty – PLANNING SUMMARY	
LEARNING OBJECTIVES • to consider the ideas of feeling left out, jealousy • for the children to deal with injustice. **Focus** Children to identify the Bad Fairy's motives and feelings and change her mind to save Sleeping Beauty's life.	**NATIONAL CURRICULUM programmes of study/attainment targets** • non-chronological writing, making lists, writing invitations • planning and creating in the design curriculum • use of technical vocabulary of different sorts

KEY STAGES IN THE DRAMA

SESSION ONE

1. Negotiate the drama rules.
2. Build the 'Mantle of the Expert' role for the children.
3. Set up the party-planning company. Produce signed contracts.
4. Groups work on preparing.
5. Announce the *Seventh Birthday Party for the Princess, Judith*.
6. Enter as Manager muttering about the need for more work.

SESSION TWO

7. Visit the Queen (TiR2). 'Defining the Space.' Set up the hall.
8. Enter the Queen and the negotiation takes place.
9. Set to preparing for the party.
   Or Narrate the preparations for the big party.
10. Setting up the party in the hall at the Palace.
11. TiR3, the Bad Fairy, appears. If they do not challenge you, exit.
12. OoR. *Who was that?*

SESSION THREE

13. *What do we do about the intruder?*
14. 'Find' Lucy's diary left lying near the throne.
15. Children to discuss in or out of role.
16. (Optional) The Queen checks on the party.
17. Forum theatre: Lucy and the Queen meet.
18. Pay-off: the party to celebrate Judith's birthday.

Roles for Children	specialists at organising children's parties running a company (name chosen by them or given, e.g.) Party Time			
Roles for Teacher	Company Manager	The Bad Fairy/Lucy	The Queen	Judith if needed
The props/ role signifiers	clipboard	spell book	mace or crown	teddy bear

Other props: Lucy's diary: see point 14

Assessment, Recording and Reporting	
Attainment (reference to level descriptions) knowledge, understanding and skills	**PUPILS' RESPONSE –** Evidence
Progression (reference to level descriptions) gains in knowledge, understanding and skills	

Jill and the Beanstalk

Setting up expectation

Structure outline

Before starting the drama the children should have 'received' two letters, Letter Two enclosed with Letter One. The purpose of these is to raise the expectation of the class to the drama. Letters can provide a mysterious and stimulating introduction to drama. They can also provide material for literary work. Here, as one contains spelling mistakes, it is useful for spelling work.

Letter one

---

                                    1 Maple Gardens
                                         Littletown

Dear Superhelpers,
I have a strange problem. I found a large letter in my garden addressed 'HELP'. I have sent a copy to you. It is difficult to describe what the letter wants as I can't read it properly, but it mentions a big weed and there is certainly one in the garden next door to me. My garden is suffering from being in the shadow of the big weed and the owner won't do anything about it.
   Can you come down here to help me?
   Yours sincerely,

                                         Jane Clifton

Letter two
This letter should be very big and folded up to fit in a big
envelope with 'Helpp' on the front.

Der helpful peepul,
I got a big bad thing in my plants. It grows up into mi
gardern in the sky from down ther wer you are. it
hits my flouers and my veg tables and maks them fal
down. I am sad about the orful big weed and want it
to go awa. It groes from a gardun down ther. Pleez
can you helpe. Sorry my spelin is so bad.

  If you can help writ me a letur and find the
gardn were it iz. I wul pay yoo wiv a goldern eg if
you kills it.

  Thanks yoos. I can nut tels yoo my nam. I is
Frendy.

The first of these letters should have been read to the
children possibly up to a week before the drama and pinned
on a special 'letters' board. Say you cannot read the other
one and pin it up asking the children to decipher it.

Session one
Negotiate the rules and move into the drama. See the
'Introduction to the example dramas' for reference to
'contracting'.

> 1 OoR contract

Set up Superhelpers (see Ideas 5). This can be established
when the letters are first shown to the children, from a day
to a week before the first session.

> 2 Setting the
> children's roles

Enter TiR1, the Head of Superhelpers, carrying gardening
books. *What did you think of the two letters we had?* Re-read,
the children deciphering the big one for you. Discuss.

> 3 TiR setting the
> context

*We have a job to do here. What should we do about the weed?
We'd best go round and ask the neighbour about the problems.
Any questions you want to ask the neighbour about the big letter?*

Mark out the space which is to be the garden of Jane, the
neighbour.

> 4 Defining the
> space

OoR mark out the fences and gate using chairs and any other useful markers (e.g. PE cones, benches).

Head of the Superhelpers leads children into the garden looking for the neighbour. Knocks on the door – no answer.

'Looks up' to the neighbour's garden and describes the huge weed growing there. Walks round to the other garden and measures the weed (tape measure held by a number of children, or place the children round it).

5 Narration to set the scene

Goodness me, what a size! This is definitely a problem. It will be taking all the moisture from all these other plants. See, the potatoes are dying.

6 OoR reflection to establish belief

If necessary here go OoR to discuss what the Head of Superhelpers is seeing. Let them describe what they can 'see' of the effects of the big weed.

7 TiR sets activities for the children occupational mime

We must begin to get rid of it at once. What ways can we safely destroy it? What problems do we face? The children may suggest a range of possibilities: chopping it down, weed killer. Accept them but do point out that we have to do it without damaging anything around. Then set up tasks for the children in groups.

Dig round the weed and find its roots to put the poison in, to get rid of the weed. Measure it so we have a record. Draw it. Move plants and garden furniture that might be damaged.

As soon as they are occupied, tell them you are going to look for the neighbour, Jane.

8 TiR2 challenge for the children

Jack's mother, Mrs Brown, intervenes. Change role now very clearly. If the group needs a warning, tell them. Otherwise try just entering with a new role signifier, the broom.

Some notes on how the role of Jack's Mother, Mrs Brown, can be tackled

She is upset and does not want anyone interfering. She is alternately angry and sad; is also not very forthcoming about the 'weed' which she seems to hate and will not talk about. *What do you think you are doing in my garden and destroying my plant? How dare you. What do you want?* If they decide to tell her (you could discuss it OoR), she is very angry and will not let them do it – threatens to *have the law on them*, and has a big dog she will set on them if they try. She wants all of them out of her garden.

Stop and go OoR immediately after the first speech to check who they think you are now. Ask how they are going to handle her.

Tir2

She refuses to listen and makes them leave her garden. *In any case I do not want that 'weed' as you call it killed because I'll never see my son again if you do.*

OoR

Superhelpers retire to the other garden to consider what to do – must get her on their side. How to do that.

Mrs Brown goes into her house. *You've quite upset me, I must rest.*

Session two
What were you doing at the end of last session in our story?

But make the main recap of session one by going into role. Return as Head of Superhelpers: *I couldn't find Jane Clifton, but what happened here? I heard shouting,* and ask for their account of what has happened.

9 TiR1 checks understanding and recaps events

Are you ready for the next part of the drama?
As the Superhelpers sat and thought about what they should do now they heard someone trying to attract their attention from the other side of the fence.

Narrate OoR

Go to the other side of the fence to take on a new role: *Psst! Can I speak to you? I need your help, but I can't talk here where my mother might see me. I'll meet you round by the pond at the end of the road.*

10 TiR3 as stimulus for focus of drama

Who could that have been? It was definitely a girl. What will you want to ask her? Where is this pond?

OoR

They move to the 'pond' to talk to her. Jill tells her story.

Notes on the role of Jill
She is afraid and does not want her mother to know she is speaking to them. *Are you friendly, can you help us and not*

hurt anyone? Do you promise not to kill the weed? Can I trust you? Is she about? If you see her coming, tell me. She must not find me with you. Some of you must go and keep her busy.

She tells of Jack going up the weed, He has been missing up there for three days now and mother is very worried. If they kill the weed Jack might never come back. *I do wish he had not been doing this but he is my brother and I don't want him dead.*

She is reluctant to tell them what Jack has been doing. If the children say they know – since they know the story – then accept it.

OoR if necessary: They had a report of someone stealing from a Giant.

Jill wants to stop Jack doing what might lead to his death. *After all, Giants are very bad, aren't they?* (Children might bring up the 'friendly' letter at this point and Jill must be receptive.)

She might tell them of how she has been able to pay the rent. Jack came back after his first trip bringing a goose that lays golden eggs. If not they will discover that when they reach the castle. To help her they will have to go up the weed and see what has happened to Jack.

11 TiR puts children as teachers

Up the beanstalk. TiR3 as Jill looks up. *We're going to have to be very quiet when we get up there. We don't want to attract the Giant's attention. I expect, being Superhelpers, you are very good at moving about without making a sound? Mum says I'm not very good at it. I make too much noise. What do you think?*

Move about very noisily so that the children can criticise you. *Can you teach me how to move about very quietly?*

Have the children demonstrate and teach her. *Make sure you keep an eye on me when we get there, that I don't make too much noise. Will you do that?*

12 Movement and mime activity

OoR: Negotiation representing the journey: *We must show how we climb up the beanstalk and in drama we can all climb together, pretending we are on the beanstalk. Spread out and show me how you would be climbing, reaching for each branch, making sure your feet have a firm hold each time . . .* Use music with a steady rhythm to help with this, for example a section from 'Tubular Bells' by Mike Oldfield where there is a steady rising rhythm as accompaniment to the climbing. Practise the movement and get children to try to mime the effort, the size of the 'branches' etc. . . . . TiR3 as Jill leads the class in miming the climbing of the beanstalk.

Or the climb can be narrated by you with help from some volunteer children adding word pictures about what they saw on the way up, what the difficult stages were.

Optional: In groups show still pictures (tableaux) of difficult moments on the climb *where things could have gone wrong: how people helped each other so that no one did fall or get stuck.*

13 Possible extra work

Jill has to be kept quiet. TiR3 as Jill, noisily, *Hey, we're here* and moves noisily forward.

14 Testing the children out

If the children do not stop her then go OoR and discuss the problem she is causing. *You will have to put your skills at being quiet into practice and show how Jill should move and talk quietly, how everyone should hide and look for Jack.*

Carry out these trials and teach Jill.

Jill: *I can hear someone coming,* and she runs off.

Stop the drama and go OoR. Negotiate that you are going to change roles again and face them with their last and most important task.

In clear view put on a pinafore and pick up a duster. Giant's servant challenges them: *I know there is someone there. You made so much noise when you arrived. Come out and talk to me. Gosh, there are lots more of you than I thought. I heard one person. Are you like that Jack who keeps coming up here to steal things?*

15 TiR4 Giant's servant

Either s/he likes them and therefore warns them: *The Giant is nice but he does not like visitors. You must go back down the beanstalk.* If the children explain properly that they are looking for Jack and they will take him away and make sure he does not bother the Giant again, s/he tells them where Jack is and tells them to get him out quickly. *But you'll have to creep in near the Giant's chair and get the key from the hook there because he is locked up. I hope one of you is brave enough to do that.*

Or, if they do not handle her politely and diplomatically, stating the case for being there, she will be angry with them and will not listen, telling them, *Make sure you are gone by the time I get back or the Giant will lock you all up in the dungeon like he has Jack. And you'll never be brave enough to get the key because it is near where the Giant is asleep in his chair.* In this case let the children see whether they can see where you have hung the key. Then continue as above.

16 Game 'Keeper of the Keys'	Then play the game of children in twos creeping to where you have hung the keys as quietly as possible. You be the keeper but do it from outside the game not as someone guarding the keys. Call some of them back and give others a chance to try. Organise it to let one of the most shy or least able children win to boost their esteem.
17 Defining the space	They have to find Jack who is locked up. OoR set it up with the children laying out where the locked dungeon is, the passageway leading to it, the Giant's room and the route. Decide how the children find Jack, if the second possibility is chosen and they do not have the servant to tell them where he is.
18 TiR5 Freeing Jack	Become Jack crouched down in the corner of the agreed dungeon space and let the children make their way to you in the agreed manner. If they do not, i.e. they make noise or do not follow the agreed route, go OoR again and re-negotiate, *or* change role to the servant and confront them about the noise.

As Jack, be noisy and arrogant urging them to release you. They should challenge this and teach you about being quiet etc.

19 Jack and the children's dilemma	When they get you out, show them the golden egg and say, *I must go to get some more before we go down the beanstalk. There is something else there I want to get from the Giant. He has this really nice golden harp and I want to get it to give to my Mum.*

If the children do not automatically confront this, saying they have agreed to take him away and not steal, go OoR so that the children have to decide what to do. Whom do they side with at this point? Do they persuade Jack not to do it or go along with it? *After all he is a nasty Giant.*

Either they will strongly talk about this to Jack and he should gradually yield, even to the point of writing a note of apology. Jill will return here and thank the children for saving Jack. She has been away looking for him.

| 20 The persuading |

Or they let Jack go to steal the harp and he gets caught. Decide with the children how he gets caught by Jill, who meets him as she is coming back to find them all. Have a forum theatre (see Ideas 10) where the children as Jill have to argue the case against TiR Jack. Outcome should be the same.

Say goodbye to the servant – if they are friends with her at this point. She asks for the big weed to be killed.

Mime climbing down the beanstalk and then chopping it down.

| 21 Mime activity |

The story is told to Mrs Brown and they have a party.

| 22 Celebration |

Jill and the Beanstalk – PLANNING SUMMARY

LEARNING OBJECTIVES

- to use a traditional story and challenge traditional view of Giant and of Jack/Jill
- to raise the issue of things belonging to people
- to consider gender issues such as the roles of boys and girls

Focus

Children to meet a situation where they have to challenge someone who steals because she thinks giants are bad and stealing from someone with a bad reputation is acceptable.

NATIONAL CURRICULUM
programmes of study/attainment targets

This drama can relate to:

- using a traditional story to challenge the conventional view of the Giant and Jack and through the role of Jill
- moral and social education, particularly the issues of stealing and property, being neighbours

KEY STAGES IN THE DRAMA

Before the drama the two letters

SESSION ONE

1. Negotiate the 'doing of the story' and the rules of drama.
2. Set up Superhelpers.
3. TiR1: *What did you think of the two letters? What should we do about the weed?*
4. Mark out the space which is to be Jane's garden. Lead them into the garden.
5. Describe the huge weed.
7. Occupational mime to get rid of it. Tasks for the children in groups.
8. TiR2 Jack's mother, Mrs Brown, intervenes: *What do you think you are doing in my garden and destroying my plant?*

SESSION TWO

9. The main recap: *I couldn't find Jane Clifton, but what happened here?*
10. Narrate OoR: *They heard someone trying to attract their attention:* As TiR3: *Psst! Can I speak to you?* Jill tells her story.
11. *Can you teach me how to move about very quietly?*
12. OoR: Negotiate representing the journey – we can all climb together.
13. Optional: In groups show still pictures of difficult moments on the climb.
14. Jill has to be kept quiet.
15. Jill runs off. TiR4 Giant's servant: *I know there is someone there. Either she likes them and therefore warns them or She will be angry with them and will not listen.*
16. Game like 'Keeper of the Keys'.
17. They have to find Jack who is locked up.
18. Freeing Jack.
19. Jack wants to steal.
20. *Either* they oppose Jack, *or* They let Jack go back to the harp, followed by forum theatre where the children as Jill argue the case against Jack.
21. The Finale . . . mime climbing and chopping down the beanstalk.
22. Celebration.

Roles for Children	Superhelpers (or people who run a garden centre and know about how things grow)				
Roles for Teacher	Head of Superhelpers	Jill	Jack's mother	Giant's servant	Jack
The props/ role signifiers	clipboard	empty seed packet 'Giant Beans'	broom	pinafore and duster	golden egg

Other props: a big old key for the Giant's dungeon

Assessment, Recording and Reporting	
Attainment (reference to level descriptions) knowledge, understanding and skills	PUPILS' RESPONSE – Evidence
Progression (reference to level descriptions) gains in knowledge, understanding and skills	

Part III

Seven more dramas

Baby Bear Did It

Structure outline

Explain that some of our drama will take place in the Three Bears' kitchen, where they eat their breakfast.

| 1 OoR |

Set up the kitchen. Discuss how the children want it: *What did the kitchen look like before Goldilocks came to visit? How many Bears sit at the table? What will be on the table? How many chairs will there be? How many bowls will there be?*

I am going to be Baby Bear sitting at the table. Daddy and Mummy Bear have just gone for a walk. I want you to watch him and listen to him and then we will talk about it. Are you ready to start? I will be Baby Bear when I sit down.

2 Setting up Baby Bear TiR

Baby Bear sits with his head in his hands. *I don't want this porridge. I WANT to go on the WALK to the lake. They can't make me eat it! I'm going to throw my Dad's away.*

He pulls his Dad's chair back and takes the porridge to the kitchen sink. *I better not – he'll shout.*

He pulls his Mum's chair back and takes the porridge to the kitchen sink. *I better not – she'll shout.*

He takes his porridge to the kitchen sink and pours it away. *There! They won't know. They'll think I've eaten it!*

He knocks his chair over. *I don't care. I'll catch them up and tell them I've finished my porridge.*

He runs out.
STOP THE DRAMA

3 Reflection OoR

What did you see? What did Baby Bear say?

Prepare to meet Goldilocks. *The next day. Goldilocks is sitting on a log in the forest near the Three Bears' cottage. I want you to look at Goldilocks and listen to what she says and then we will talk about it. You'll know when I am pretending to be Goldilocks because I will wear this hat.*

4 Goldilocks TiR

I didn't do it. It's not fair. I'm not going to help people again.
STOP THE DRAMA

OoR preparing for questioning

What do you want to ask her?

There are key points you will make and the children will have to extract: *I have been blamed for something I didn't do. I was walking past Baby Bear's house. I saw him run out of the house and leave the door open. His face was very red, he looked very cross. I went to the house and there was a terrible mess in the kitchen. All the chairs were the wrong way round and one had been pushed over. Porridge had been poured down the sink. I went upstairs to see if Mrs or Mr Bear were there and I tripped on one of Baby Bear's toys and next thing I knew there were the Three Bears standing around me. Baby Bear was crying and saying, 'She did it, Daddy, she did it!' And now I'm in trouble!*

Questioning Goldilocks TiR

If you see Baby Bear, will you keep him there until I find him because I want him to tell the truth so that I am not in trouble.

5 Meeting Baby Bear TiR

Move straight into the role of Baby Bear by removing Goldilocks's hat and picking up a fishing rod and sandwich box. Baby Bear is not initially aware of the children and sits by a bin going through his sandwiches.

Oh no! She's given me tuna. I hate tuna! I wanted jam. He throws the sandwiches in the bin.

Oh no! She's only given me one chocolate bar. I wanted three. Oh no! I hate brown bread and apples. He throws them in the bin.

6 Dialogue with Baby Bear TiR/OoR

He notices the children. *Who are you?*

The children will tell him what they know. It is important that if they say anything Baby Bear might be uncomfortable with, you will start to move away to fish somewhere else. Go OoR if necessary to discuss with them why he is moving away from them at certain times. This means that the children will have to work hard at keeping you there.

There are possible learning areas to explore, and these can be oriented according to what the children perceive as the problem.

How to play Baby Bear: Baby Bear loses his temper very easily. Baby Bear doesn't like the food he is given. Baby Bear does not tell the truth. All these can be related to the fact that Baby Bear does not have any friends.

The task for the children is to befriend Baby Bear and get him to say what really happened. They must try to convince him not to throw food away and to tell his Mum and Dad what really happened.

> **7** Use of forum theatre to resolve the issues TiR/OoR

They can play fishing with him to gain his trust. Eventually he tells them what happened and how sorry he is. The children negotiate with him about telling the truth.

The children must decide whom he needs to speak to and help him to rehearse what he needs to say. Again, forum theatre (see Ideas 10) can be an excellent way to structure these meetings. They can also inform him on healthy eating and a balanced diet.

The children help Baby Bear say sorry to Goldilocks, and her hat on a chair symbolises her. Initially he may do it poorly but with the help of the class he will improve ability to communicate. What is important is the moving in and out of role to discuss the response of the characters and how to deal with them.

The drama finishes with a photo album of still images of the children playing with Baby Bear.

> **8** Tableaux

Baby Bear Did It – PLANNING SUMMARY

LEARNING OBJECTIVES	NATIONAL CURRICULUM
• to introduce reception children to drama • to create opportunity for them to put right an injustice • to look at child/child relationships and 'taking the blame'	**programmes of study/attainment targets**

KEY STAGES IN THE DRAMA

1. Set up Three Bears kitchen.
2. They witness Baby Bear leaving his food and pushing over the chair.
3. Discussion about what they have seen.
4. Class meet Goldilocks – they find out she is being blamed for what has happened.
5. Move straight into role as Baby Bear going fishing and throwing his food away.
6. Getting Baby Bear to talk about what he has done and deciding whom he should speak to and what he should say.
7. Teaching Baby Bear how to behave – using forum theatre – speaking to Goldilocks, Daddy Bear and Mummy Bear.
8. Other developments: using tableaux, pictures of Baby Bear playing with the children, eating his porridge, writing to Goldilocks's Mum

Roles for Children	not specific	
Roles for Teacher	Goldilocks	Baby Bear
The props/role signifiers	hat	fishing rod

Other props: Table, three bowls, spoons etc., three chairs – one smaller chair.

Assessment, Recording and Reporting	
Attainment (reference to level descriptions) **knowledge, understanding and skills**	**PUPILS' RESPONSE –** Evidence
Progression (reference to level descriptions) **gains in knowledge, understanding and skills**	

The King of Spring

Structure outline

Tell the children that the drama will begin after we have had a walk around the outside of the school.

1 OoR contract

Negotiate that everyone will be in the drama including yourself, and you will be a king for part of the drama and a wizard in another part.

Take the class on a walk around the outside of the school, or to a nearby park. The purpose of the walk is to observe the effect of the seasons on plant and animal life. (For the purpose of this drama let us assume it is winter. It does not have to be, however, since the content learning of the session will be the current season.)

2 OoR The stimulus

During the walk stop every now and then and get the children to notice what happens to plants and trees during winter.

3 OoR key questions during the walk

At some time make a point of noticing a bird. This will be used later in the drama and will also highlight the point about migration for the winter. However, do not tell the children that the bird will be used in the drama.

4 Building in a point of reference

Begin the drama by telling this story. *There was once a King. A good King. He was King of the Land of Spring. In the Land of Spring it was always Spring. Daffodils and crocuses were always in bloom. The fields were full of lambs and baby rabbits. In our drama we are going to meet the King of Spring. I want you to just look at him and listen to him to begin with and then we will stop the drama and talk about it.*

5 OoR back in the classroom

Moving into role

You'll know when I'm pretending to be the King because I will wear this crown and you'll know when I am your teacher again because I'll take my crown off.

6 TiR

Move to a chair with a crown and a large spell book with one page obviously torn out. Open it, looking very worried. *What am I going to do? He is coming back today. I won't be able to answer his question. I'm so worried. Look what he has done to my book! And this note that he left.*

7 OoR

Place the crown and spell book back on the chair and ask the children about the King. *How did he look? Could you tell whether he was happy or sad by the way he looked and what he said? What did he say? What questions do we need to ask him so that we can find out more?* The class decide upon questions to ask the King.

8 Key information
TiR hot-seating

The teacher role will share some key information but it is important not to give the information too quickly or easily. The children have to work to find out more.

This process will involve coming in and out of role to summarise and reflect upon the hot-seating of the King. The wizard's note will be shown to the children

> It's time for me to take a hand
> And make this into Winterland
> The Winter Wizard

Place the crown and spell book back on the chair and ask the children about the King.

9 OoR

After the hot-seating of the King summarise *what we know, what we think we know* and *what we can guess* has happened.

10 Narration

The King was sitting up in bed. He couldn't sleep. He was worried. He didn't know what to do. If the Winter Wizard returned and changed the land into Winterland he would not be able to be King any more. He didn't know anything about winter. He wouldn't be able to help his people. He was just about to cry when a little bird landed upon the window ledge. The little bird told the King that she had been flying over (name of school) and she had seen some children who knew lots about winter. The King wished he could meet them.

Ask the children how they could help the King.

11 OoR

Set up the space to represent the throne room. Two chairs for the entrance, perhaps two guards who stop people rushing in and tell the King who has come to visit him. Talk about how they should approach a King and rehearse this, deciding who will knock on the door, tell the guards etc.

The rehearsal is important in two ways: to make the children feel secure in what is happening and to develop an appropriate atmosphere for the drama to work.

The children solemnly make their entrance and the King says: *I am very grateful for your help. A little bird saw you all outside and realised that you knew lots about winter. Could you teach me ten things about winter?*

12 TiR

What might we put in the list of facts about winter? Are there any special words? Do we need to check the spelling? Who will tell the King about each fact? The class can be divided up into groups of two or three to remember the different things they are going to tell the King. Prepare the class to meet the King.

13 OoR

As the King, write down the children's ideas. When you get to idea ten, stop as if you can hear someone coming. Go to the classroom door and come back to the class. *There isn't much time. I will leave this list on my throne and the Wizard will see that I know lots about winter and his plan will not work. I must make you into an invisible wall. You will not be seen.*

14 TiR the King

Organise the class to sit in a semicircle around the outside of the space. Make a contract with them that they must be very careful that the Wizard does not suspect that they are there. *Are you ready for the most important part of our story?*

15 OoR

Enter into the throne room wearing the Wizard's hat. *Good, he's not here. He must be packing to leave and then I am in charge! I'll sit on his throne just to prove it. Must make sure there is no one around.*

16 TiR the Winter Wizard

Look round and particularly to make the children stand very still. Go to the throne and find the list of facts about winter and begin to read them. *What does this mean?* Read out some of the contents devised by the children. *This means that he knows about winter. That will ruin my plans. I have to think carefully about this.*

There are options in the way that you respond to this.

Option 1: Leave in a huff and vow never to return. Return as the King to explain what has happened.

Option 2: Fold up the paper and say you are going to throw it away. Stop the drama and talk about how the children can help the King if he hasn't got the piece of paper. The invisible wall can chant the different facts.

Each little group of children can whisper the facts about winter so that the Wizard will see that destroying the list will not work.

Rehearse this second idea and the scene with the Wizard trying to take the paper away. Re-run this time with the children chanting or whispering the facts until the Wizard leaves frightened, saying he is never going to return.

Whatever strategy is used, the children will win and then explain to the King what has happened.

The King of Spring – PLANNING SUMMARY

LEARNING OBJECTIVES	NATIONAL CURRICULUM programmes of study/attainment targets
• to consider the differences between the seasons • to examine the effect of these differences upon the environment • for the children to teach an adult • to use writing as a means to hold on to ideas • to use first-hand experience as the basis for a drama	**Geography** • The effects of weather on people and their surroundings, e.g. the effect of seasonal variations in temperature on the clothes people wear **Science** • To relate simple scientific ideas to the evidence before them • To make simple comparisons • To try to explain what they found out, drawing on their knowledge and understanding

KEY STAGES IN THE DRAMA

1. Set up the drama by explaining that it will begin with a walk around the school to look at the effects of the seasons.
2. The walk: note how the environment is effected by the seasons.
3. Note one bird.
4. OoR: tell story; discuss what the land of spring would look like.
5. Children look at TiR as the King of Spring.
6. OoR discuss how he looks and feels.
7. Hot-seat the King for more information.
8. OoR recap what we know or think we know and need to know.
9. Narration: the King's worries.
10. OoR set up the throne room and rehearse visiting the King.
11. Meeting the King.
12. OoR: listing the facts about winter.
13. TiR: the King notes down the facts.
14. Preparing for the visit of the Wizard – contracting the invisible wall.
15. TiR as the Wizard discovering the King's new-found knowledge.
16. Alternative endings: the Wizard leaves or he keeps the paper and the children have to help the King.

Roles for Teacher	King of Spring	Wizard
The props/role signifiers	crown and spell book	wizard's hat

Other props: chair for a throne, paper and pens for list of facts

Assessment, Reporting and Recording	
Attainment (reference to level descriptions) knowledge, understanding and skills	**PUPILS' RESPONSE – Evidence**
Progression (reference to level descriptions) gains in knowledge, understanding and skills	

Humpty Dumpty

Pre-drama activity

1 OoR collective storytelling

Sit in a circle. Negotiate the drama rules, what is expected and how we work. *What kind of stories do we tell children in the nursery or first class? How do we make them interesting?*

Demonstrate changing nursery rhymes into narrative and using traditional stories. In a collective form tell the story of a nursery rhyme in narrative form: *There was once a girl called Mary and she was given for her birthday a very special present, a little lamb. She cared for the lamb and everywhere she went the lamb followed her . . . even into school!*

Or 'Jack and Jill'. *Or* 'Little Miss Muffet'.

Then do the same and get the children to do it for 'Humpty Dumpty'.

Structure outline

2 OoR building the context collective drawing

In small groups, or with class teacher as scribe, the children draw the rooms of the castle, putting furniture and special objects in them.

3 Setting up the children's roles – mime

Humpty lived in a very nice castle, with lots of servants. What sort of jobs did they do in the castle? The space is arranged as one of the castle rooms. Chairs are used to indicate doors, walls and tables. They are placed to show the geography of the room. *Is it a throne room or a great dining room?*

As a whole class the children with the teacher demonstrate what some of the jobs would look like. Children choose their own jobs, on their own or in pairs or threes.

The teacher uses narration to set the scene: *It was a bright sunny morning and the servants were busy doing all the jobs that needed to be done in the castle. Shelley was cleaning the silver candlesticks, Robert was dusting the big table and Marvin sweeping the floor. As they were working, Jonathan, the Chief Servant, came in with some very important news.*

TiR tells the children: *The King is going to hold a party for the whole of Nursery Rhyme Land. All the famous people will be there: Jack and Jill, Little Bo Peep, Miss Muffet and of course Humpty Dumpty. He is such good fun at a party because he tells such funny stories and knows so many good games.*

> **4** TiR as Chief Servant, children as servants

It may be that a child says that he cannot come because he has fallen off the wall. It is important that this is accepted with worried concern by TiR. *When I have got things organised here, I will go and find out what has happened. There isn't much time so we need to make some important decisions.*
STOP THE DRAMA

What do we need to do to get ready for the party?

> **5** OoR

Children decide upon jobs that need to be done to get ready for the party – in groups or as a class. Possibilities might include: invitations – nursery rhyme characters; menu; music; games; presents list.

When these activities are almost complete the Chief Servant interrupts with news of Humpty's accident. *There are three people who have seen what has happened – three of the King's men. They were passing in a long column. One was at the front, one was at the end and one was in the middle.*
STOP THE DRAMA

> **6** TiR as Chief Servant

Children are asked to think of questions for each of the King's men to find out what happened. *What did he see? Where was he in the line? What time did you go past?* Each soldier comes to report what he saw.

> **7** OoR

He was lying on the ground. We tried to put him together. We had to take him to hospital. He's going to be all right but he has broken his arm and his ankle. Went past at 10.10 am.

> **8** TiR soldier at the back of the column

9 OoR	*Let's write down what we know so far.* Do that on a large sheet of paper.
10 TiR soldier at the front of the column	*He was looking up at the wall. He was shouting something. It might have been Tom or Kitty or something. Then it started to rain. Went past at 10 am.*
11 OoR	*Write down what we now know and what we might guess.*
12 TiR soldier in the middle of the column	*He was climbing up at the wall. He looked nervous. He was trying to reach for something. It was raining. Went past at 10.05 am.*
13 OoR	*Write down what we now know and do we need to ask anything else of the soldiers?* This is a good time to take a break if you want to do the drama in two sessions
14 TiR Chief Servant	The children tell the Chief Servant what they have found out. He tells them the King is coming to see how the preparations for the party are going. He is not in a very good mood because of what has happened to Humpty. STOP THE DRAMA
15 OoR	*How shall you handle the King?* Contract that they are a little bit afraid of him. *He is very powerful and you must be a bit careful if he is in a bad mood. Make sure you are all doing what you should on the preparations when he arrives.*
16 TiR the King	Servants back to occupational mime on preparations. The King asks them about the preparations. He is very unhappy. *Humpty Dumpty was going to tell some funny stories and sing a song. He has spoiled everything now he has not turned up. I have banned him from the party and you must tell him that.* STOP THE DRAMA
17 OoR	*Is the King right not to allow Humpty to the party? How will the servants break the news to Humpty?* The class prepare to meet Humpty? *Where will this happen? How should the servants behave to Humpty?*

Children then speak to Humpty. He has a bandage round his arm and a walking stick. He tells them about trying to save the King's favourite cat – Tom. *The wall was wet and I fell. I knew the King would want the cat at the party and would miss him terribly if he did not turn up.*
STOP THE DRAMA

| 18 TiR Humpty |

Humpty must tell the King what really happened. *You must take the role of Humpty and explain what happened.*

| 19 OoR |

A forum theatre is set up with two chairs, one to represent Humpty the other the King (TiR).

The King is very angry. *He spoilt my party. I don't want him here.*

| 20 Forum theatre |

Humpty tells the King what really happened.

The King listens and gradually his mood changes (depending on how well the children argue Humpty's case). He thanks Humpty for trying to save the cat. *However, it is still impossible for you to come to the party because you can't dance or won't be able to cut your food or use a knife and fork. You look horrible with cuts and bruises and that horrible bandage. It will upset people.*
STOP THE DRAMA

Should the King ban somebody just because they are hurt and look different? What do they need to do to show the King that Humpty should come to the party? What plans can they make to help Humpty eat his food, dance and take part in the party?

| 21 OoR |

The class draw up plans for the inclusion of Humpty and present these to the King.

Tableau work: (1) The party photo album. Groups make different pictures to show how they can help Humpty to enjoy the party. (2) Humpty gets help to get the cat down – pictures showing how this happened and later at the party.

| 22 Possible follow-ups |

Humpty Dumpty – PLANNING SUMMARY

LEARNING OBJECTIVES	NATIONAL CURRICULUM
• to give children the opportunity to build a story on to a story they already know • to create opportunities for finding out information through asking appropriate questions • to challenge children to look critically at the idea of exclusion because of physical disability	**programmes of study/attainment targets** **History** • to sequence events . . . in order to develop a sense of chronology **English** • opportunity to listen carefully and to show their understanding of what they see and hear by making relevant comments • remember specific points that interested them and to listen to others' reactions

KEY STAGES IN THE DRAMA

1. Collective story telling teachers: 'Jack and Jill' with children 'Humpty Dumpty'.
2. Collective drawing.
3. Setting up the community roles: *what jobs did they do?* occupational mime.
4. TiR Chief Servant announces party.
5. Return to occupational mime: big party – invitations and plan for party.
6. TiR: Chief Servant – news of accident – seen by King's men.
7. OoR: questions for the King's men – went to hospital.
8. TiR: King's man 1 – children question.
9. OoR reflect on what they have found out – write it!
10. TiR – King's man 2.
11. OoR: reflect on what they have found out – write it!
12. TiR: King's man 3.
13. OoR: reflect on what they have found out – write it!
14. Servants report to Chief Servant what they have found out; he tells the servants the King is coming to see the preparations for the party.
15. OoR how to handle the King.
16. TiR as the King: tells the children Humpty is not allowed to go to the party.
17. OoR reflect on King's reaction.

18. TiR as Humpty: what kind of party – if not how do they explain it to him?
19. OoR reflect and set them up to take Humpty role to the King.
20. Forum theatre: children as Humpty explain what happened.
21. Class draw up plans for the party and present them to the King.
22. Possible follow-ups: the party photo album and tableaux entitled 'Humpty gets help to get the cat down'.

Roles for Children	Servants to the King			
Roles for Teacher	Chief Servant	3 King's men	The King	Humpty
The props/ role signifiers	Staff of office	bands, crown, waistcoat	crown	bandage and walking stick

Other props: paper, pens, Polaroid camera

Assessment, Recording and Reporting	
Attainment (reference to level descriptions) knowledge, understanding and skills	**PUPILS' RESPONSE –** Evidence
Progression (reference to level descriptions) gains in knowledge, understanding and skills	

The Giant's Coat

Structure outline

1 A hook to interest them	Hold up a coat with all the seams torn and try it on. *This is my favourite coat.* If the children laugh, ask what the problem is. If they do not, 'find' the tears yourself. *Oh dear, what am I going to do with this? Who would be able to help with mending something like this? What skills would you need? What would they do exactly?*
2 Negotiating the doing of drama	*I want to do a story about a group of people who work very hard making clothes for people. I wonder if you'd help me with it. We could do it together. You will be the clothes makers in the story. What would you be doing if I walked into your workshop now? Who will you work with?*
3 Defining the space or occupational mime optional task	*This is the workshop. Is that all right? What will you be making? What do you have to do to do that? Where will your part of the workshop be? Show me how you work at making something you have designed.*
	What designs do you have for suits and clothes and shoes? Could you draw those for your customers? Show how you pretend to draw out the designs for a particular client. What size is your paper? What are you using to draw it?
	If you have time give them some paper in groups to draw their latest design for a client. Or do this later as a separate activity.
4 Sound tracking to help build belief	*What machines do you have to help make the clothes? What sorts of noise would visitors to your factory hear?* Conduct this like a piece of music, louder and quieter.

(This could be the basis of a music lesson to produce a piece of music with the class which can then be used as part of the drama.)

Once they have the idea the children can mime actions and create the sound at the same time.

Are you ready for the story to start? It starts with a visitor who came to the factory every day. Who do you think that might be?

The clothes makers were working in their shop one day when the postman came.

5 Narration

Stagger in carrying a postbag and out of it pokes a large letter. *I wonder what you've got today. I've never delivered anything like this before. What do you think it is? Is it all right if I stay while you open it? I'm really interested.*

6 TiR brings the letter (usable for literacy work)

Get the children to open the letter (see 'other props' in the summary for ideas about the letter).

> Clothes makers,
> My coat is badly torn and you must make me a new one. I found your address in an old newspaper. Send me a design at once. If you make me a really good coat I will pay you well. I cannot come to meet you because I do not like people. You can write to me by getting the post deliverer to leave a letter on the big stone on the mountain. Do not keep me waiting.
> Impatiently,
>
> Blunderstone

Negotiate the next stage either in role as the postie or by going OoR. *What is that all about? What are you going to do? What does he sound like from the letter? Are you going to write to him? What will you say? What do you need to know to make the coat? How can you do that without meeting him?*

7 Writing in role

You need to answer the letter. What will you say? I will deliver it to the mountain for you and we will see what happens.

Write the reply and that ends the session.

Here is an example reply from the children, but see below (Figure 18) for the possible choices they can make.

> Dear Giant Blunderstone,
> How are you?
> We will design a jacket for you, but you are very rude and we will only do it if you are more polite. We will want some of your gold. How wide are you? How big are you? Measure in metres, please. Please choose one of the jackets and tell us.
>   What is your other name?
>   from,
>
>   The clothes makers

Leaving it till the next session gives you a chance to have replies ready.

Option

Instead of writing replies to and fro it is possible to tape the letters. This can be very good for assessing speaking and listening. Get someone else to tape the Giant's voice for you and, if you have the facility, distort the voice a bit on the tape.

Session two

Honouring the class's decisions

Possible ways of developing: choices for the class (see Figure 18.)

The Giant is not met (see below). The TiR as the post person is the go-between.

The Giant's reply:

> Clothes makers,
> I am sorry if you think I was rude. I cannot talk to people. You will have to put up with my bluntness.
>   I like your work.
>   Here is the size of my foot. I do not understand 'metres'. You will have to work out what I am like from that. I will pay you 500 gold coins. I cannot meet you. I hate people.
>   Blunderstone

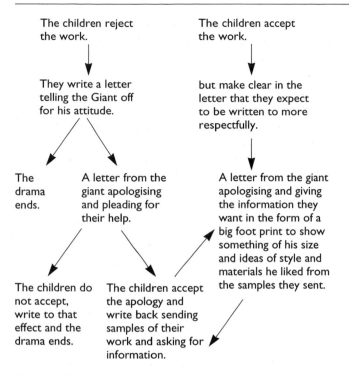

The children reject the work.

↓

They write a letter telling the Giant off for his attitude.

The children accept the work.

↓

but make clear in the letter that they expect to be written to more respectfully.

↓

A letter from the giant apologising and giving the information they want in the form of a big foot print to show something of his size and ideas of style and materials he liked from the samples they sent.

The drama ends.

A letter from the giant apologising and pleading for their help.

The children do not accept, write to that effect and the drama ends.

The children accept the apology and write back sending samples of their work and asking for information.

Figure 18 The clothes makers choose to accept the work – or not

The clothes makers have to begin to estimate his size and work out relative sizes, using the footprint as a guide. A group task can be set. There are several stages. The children measure their own size in their own footprints and so get a rough guide as to his size. They can move on to measuring the foot print, at 0.5 m or 1 m, and then measuring the number of footprints that make up an arm or a chest size as already worked out in. Then they measure out the jacket in the material(s).

9 Maths

Making the jacket. If you want a simple ending this stage can be simply described, written about or just drawn.

10 Technology and design

If you want to make it the focus of curriculum work, the jacket can actually be made in a variety of ways: out of sugar paper; out of a range of materials so the children get different textures, etc.; so that they have to look at how to join different materials together (this list can be added to depending on what you want to do).

11 Other developments

The drama can be finished with the making of the coat and sending to the Giant, who thanks and pays them.

It is possible to take the drama further and into the SMSC curriculum. There can be further communications with the Giant: *Why won't he meet us? Why doesn't he like people? Is it possible to make friends with him? Shall we write to him again?*

Notes on creating The Giant as a role

There can be a problem if you want the Giant to appear and not just work through a go-between. It destroys the imaginative pictures and ideas of size that the children have in their heads. On the odd occasion I have introduced him as TiR it has not really worked. It is a let-down.

I have always let the children befriend him by letter or tape or send pictures, but made him very shy, or very hurt by having trusted humans and been let down so he will never trust them again except the group and then not to meet them.

One student of ours had to keep the Giant in being by letter for nearly a whole term with her class of reception children and justified it by having the Giant set more and more tasks in more and more curriculum areas in his letters. They never became bored with him and would not let him go. He was an excellent motivator.

The Giant's Coat – PLANNING SUMMARY

LEARNING OBJECTIVES	NATIONAL CURRICULUM programmes of study
• to utilise 'Mantle of the Expert' with regard to maths and technology • to reinforce idea of measuring to infants. Originally planned for reception and Year One mixed-age class	**Using and applying mathematics** • providing a practical task, in a fictional (but feeling like real) problem • considering the properties of shapes and comparatives, e.g. 'bigger than' **Shape, space and measure** • practical experience using a variety of materials

- working with shape and patterns that can be seen or visualised
- using common non-standard and standard units of length
- choosing and using simple measuring instruments

Design and technology
- designing and making a product
- work with a range of materials and components
- most of NC 3 Designing Skills and 4 Making Skills

KEY STAGES IN THE DRAMA

1. The coat with all the seams torn. *Who would be able to help with mending?*
2. *A story about a group of people who work very hard making clothes for people.*
3. *This is the workshop. Show how you work at making something you have designed.*
4. *What machines do you have to help make the clothes?* A piece of music.
5. Narration: *The clothes makers were working.*
6. Stagger in carrying a postbag: *Is it all right if I stay while you open it?* The letter: *What are you going to do? What does he sound like from the letter?*
7. Write the reply: The children accept the work *or* they reject it. TiR: *I will deliver it to the mountain for you.*

SESSION TWO

8. The Giant's reply.
9. The clothes makers have to begin to estimate his size: a group task can be set.
10. Making the jacket.
     The drama can be finished with the making of the coat and sending to the giant.
11. Other developments. There can be further communications with the Giant. Why won't he meet them? Why doesn't he like people? Is it possible to make friends?

Roles for Children	The clothes makers, who are very skilled at designing and making all sorts of clothes
Roles for Teacher	The post deliverer
The props/role signifiers	sack of post

Other props
- For the introduction a coat with the seams torn and needle and thread.
- A letter from the Giant. This could be one large sheet or written really huge on a role of paper. I once did this and had children help me unroll the letter, tearing off at the end of each sentence and laying that sentence out on the hall floor. The letter in the end was gigantic and readable by all the children at once. They put it up on their classroom wall.
- A large footprint cut out of paper that is 0.5 m or 1 m long and a suitable width, depending on the size you want to use (e.g. 30 cm). The coat can then be constructed in scale to the footprint.

Assessment, Recording and Reporting	
Attainment (reference to level descriptions) knowledge, understanding and skills	**PUPILS' RESPONSE –** Evidence
Progression (reference to level descriptions) gains in knowledge, understanding and skills	

The Pied Piper

Structure outline

Tell the class they are going to look at a picture of a famous painting by Pieter Brueghel. *What do think the children are doing? How are they dressed? What does that tell us about when this picture was painted? Do children still do the same kinds of things?*

Using this discussion, set the time and place of the drama, long ago, in a simpler age when families worked together to survive. The picture is a means to make that time shift and look at the implications for family life.

Question the children further: *What do you think life might have been like for these children, in particular, where would they get food from and what food could they make themselves? Tell me something about how they might have made bread in those days?*

Spend some time clarifying the processes that go into the making of bread, including short miming activities such as mixing and pouring. Discuss what 'kneading the dough' means and how it is done. *I want you to work in groups of about five. Be a family living at this time and decide who you are going to be in the family – the mother or father, or one of the children. If you are going to be a child I don't want you to be any younger than you actually are. So no babies please. Is that agreed? And you are all people, no animals.*

Move the children into role as families in a community.

The bread-making offers an occupational mime that will bind the class together in a single community and will introduce a relationship of parents and children. This will be

> **1** OoR setting a historical context

> **2** Moving the children into role

important later in the drama. *I want you to show me a still picture or tableau of a family making bread in these days.*

Key questions: *What do we need – what implements? What ingredients? What do you have to do? Making dough – kneading dough – carrying bags of flour – heating the oven – old-fashioned oven. How do you involve the children in making bread? You can also think about how you are going to keep the small children busy while you are making your bread. You might give them a piece of dough to play with and make a shape out of.*

| **3 Tableaux** | Groups move into their own spaces to make their still picture. Highlight one or two groups at a time getting the children to comment on what they think the others are showing of the bread-making process etc.
STOP THE DRAMA |

| **4 OoR** | Tell them they are going to meet somebody who is very important in the town. Look at and listen to what this person has to say and then we will talk about it. |

| **5 TiR the Mayor** | Put on the Mayor's chain of office and give a short election 'thank you' speech. *Can I tell you how pleased I am to be elected once again as Mayor of this wonderful town.* Promise better housing, better education etc.
STOP THE DRAMA |

| **6 OoR** | Discuss what the Mayor said with the class. *Who do think that was? What was he telling the townspeople? Why was he thanking the people, what had they done? What promises did he make to them?* |

After some discussion move the drama on six months.

| **7 Narration moving the drama on** | *The town has changed a great deal since the Mayor spoke to the people. I will now read to you part of the story.*

Read the section of the story or the Browning poem describing the effects of the invasion of rats (for list of editions see summary). |

| **8 Whole-class tableau OoR** | Ask the children to return to the family groups they made earlier and divide the class so that the groups stay together but the class is split. *The two sides of the classroom represent* |

two sides of the street in the town of Hamelin. Make your picture of the family in the kitchen making bread once again.

Place a picture of a rat in each tableau of the bread-making and ask the children to change their still picture to show what happens after the rats have come. The picture now shows how the family respond to the rat in their kitchen. This is planned before each side of the class looks at the pictures and you comment on them.

9 Tableau 2 to show change

STOP THE DRAMA

You are now all going to be the adults in the town. You go as a group to see the Mayor. While you are very angry about the situation, the Mayor is very powerful and nothing will get done if you upset him by just shouting at him.

10 OoR contract how they must handle the Mayor

It is important to spend time setting up the Mayor's parlour. Have a desk in between you and the townspeople. This will help create a barrier and distance between the Mayor and the townspeople.

Rehearse how the townspeople will go into the room, who will knock, how they will go in, their demeanour and most importantly their questions or statements and who is going to talk. This gives you an opportunity to be prepared for their questions as well as clarifying who is going to do what in the improvisation. *When I put this chain on I will be the Mayor and you will be the townspeople who have come to complain about the rats. What will you say to the Mayor when you meet him? Will you be polite? How will you show how you feel? Remember he is very powerful and he has agreed to see you so he is not trying to avoid you.*

It is very important to be clear about what sort of attitude you are going to adopt as Mayor. Instead of the arrogant, dismissive and possibly aggressive Mayor, which is what the children may expect, you will be contrite and humble. This will surprise the children and will undermine their attempts to blame the situation on you.

The Mayor listens to their complaints and is very sympathetic: *Don't worry, I've already sorted it. I've heard of someone who can help us. I'll read you this newspaper report I've found.* Staying in role you show them a newspaper article reporting the Pied Piper's great feats.

11 TiR the Mayor

THE WEEKLY NEWS

Mystery Man Rids Town of Swarm of Bees

THE PIPER SAYS IT'S ALL IN A DAY'S WORK!

A mystery man was reported to have singlehandedly removed a swarm of deadly bees from the city of Delhi in India. The bees which had stung seven people to death, including a small child, were causing havoc. The man who arrived quite by chance offered his help and within one day the bees had gone!

Nobody is quite sure how he did it but, to quote a spokesperson for the palace, 'The royal family are delighted and have made a large gift of some jewels and gold coins. He didn't leave his name but he was told he would always be welcome.'

When asked where the man was staying, the spokesperson, quoting the man, said he had moved on 'because there was so much still to be done'.

I've already contacted him and he is on his way here now to help us get rid of the rats.
STOP THE DRAMA

12 OoR

Ask the children about how the Mayor dealt with them. Do they have any worries about the Piper and what actually happened in the story?

Move the story on to the meeting with the Piper. Set up two chairs. The children will hear just one side of the conversation. On the blackboard or a flipchart, have the Mayor's words written out but the children do not see this until you have played the scene.

13 TiR as Mayor Overheard conversation

Play out the following scene as the Mayor, leaving pauses for the imagined responses of the Pied Piper: *Thank you very much for coming so quickly! . . . Of course, of course. I will be*

as quick as I can. The problem is rats, thousands of them, and the people of Hamelin are getting very upset. You see . . . Well, as soon as possible. Today in fact . . . Well, that's brilliant. Wonderful . . . Ah! We are not a rich town. We haven't got a lot of money. These are poor people . . . No, please don't go! All right, 500 Crowns. You drive a hard bargain, Mr Piper.
STOP THE DRAMA

Discuss what the children think the piper was saying to the Mayor. *What would you have said in his place? What is he after?*

OoR

When you have agreed upon what the Piper said, re-run the scene with children taking the part of the Piper.
STOP THE DRAMA

14 Replay the scene

Reflect on the drama with the class. *What has the Mayor promised? What happened next in the story?*

15 OoR

Narrate the story up to the point at where the Piper returns to the Mayor to collect his money.

The children decide what the Piper would say to the Mayor when he goes to collect his money.

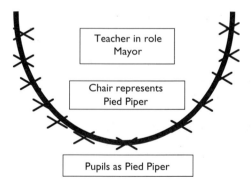

16 The Piper returns for his money forum theatre (Figure 19)

Figure 19 Forum theatre

Ask for a child to take the role of the Piper to begin the meeting with the Mayor.

I wanted to thank you for doing a very professional job. The whole town is so relieved. There is one small problem, however, and I really am very sorry about this. I won't be able to pay you all the money I promised. I only have 100 Crowns.

TiR the Mayor

The children can either swap in to the chair to respond to the Mayor or just speak from their chairs. The Mayor becomes more awkward and insistent: *I haven't got the money and will not be able to pay you.*

During this scene it is important to stop and discuss out of role the way in which the Mayor is behaving and also the alternatives the Piper has in dealing with him.
STOP THE DRAMA

What happened in the story? What did the Piper do to get revenge?

In the next phase of the drama the class remake the street they made earlier with the families in the kitchen.

17 The children leave

Narrate the part of the story where the Piper takes the children. Signal to the children in the tableau and they move away from the families leaving the parents.

18 Thought-tracking

Get them to sit in a circle in the middle of the street. Explain that you are going to thought-track the parents (see Ideas 10). Touch each one on the shoulder and they describe how they feel about the loss of their children.

Move to the children sitting in the circle and ask them, *What lovely things could they see and hear when the Piper was playing his music? What would tempt them to follow him?* Touch their shoulders and they voice their thoughts.
STOP THE DRAMA

19 OoR

Reflect on the drama with the class. *If you were the parents of the children who had been taken away by the Pied Piper, what would you say to the Mayor?*

20 Tackling the Mayor TiR

The class return to the forum theatre set up with the Mayor, this time as the parents of the children after they have been taken away.

The children question the Mayor. *I wasn't to know the Pied Piper would take the children. I was just trying to save money. I made a mistake. You elected me! I got rid of the rats didn't I? I did it for you. We couldn't afford what he wanted. I only lied to help the town. I thought I could get away with it. I didn't think he could do it, but I wanted to try anything.*
STOP THE DRAMA

Reflect on the Mayor's attitude with the class. *Could the townsfolk have avoided what happened?*

21 OoR

Discuss the actions of the Pied Piper. *What do you think of what he did? Was it right? Could he have done something else? If you were the parents of the children who had been taken away by the Pied Piper what would you say to the Pied Piper?*

The parents made their way sadly to where they last glimpsed their children. They arrived at the foot of the Mountain. There they found one child and eagerly approached him or her.

22 Narration. Set up the context

OoR: *Decide what questions you want to ask the child.*

23 Hot-seating the child who was left behind TiR

Notes for the TiR: You were left behind. You had no shoes and could not keep up with the others. The huge door in the Mountain had closed before you could get there.

Describe the glimpse you had of the wonderful land you saw in the Mountain.

Prepare the class for going to the Mountain. *Now they know where their children are, what would the townsfolk do? Who do they wish to speak to? How will they get the door of the mountain open?*

24 OoR

Probably they will ask to see the Pied Piper. The key to this role is the inability to see the injustice of taking the children to punish the Mayor. At this point no amount of money is what he wants. *I was made to look a fool by your town and nothing you can do will make amends. I do not care about the money now, I wanted you to learn that there are consequences to what you do.*

25 TiR possibilities

Or they may ask to see one of the children. The attitude here is, *Why should we leave? It's wonderful, no school, all the food we like, all the toys we have ever wanted.*

If they try to load the responsibility on to the Mayor, say how sorry you are, *but I cannot see what to do. I am so upset that I do not want to be Mayor any more. I tried my best. You will have to find your own solution. I give up being the Mayor. You will have to find a new Mayor.* Put down your mayoral chain and walk away.

In any case the class will have to work at convincing the child or Piper the consequences of their actions. The important issue is that, as the Piper, you will let them win but make them work for a solution.

26 OoR

Reflect on the drama with the class: how to convince the Piper that he has been too harsh. *Why do they want the children back? Can they show him what the children mean to them?* For example: the class could demonstrate through tableaux or write letters to the Pied Piper describing what life is like without the children.

27 Finale

In return the Pied Piper returns the children to their homes and the class make still images of 'The Return of the Children'. These are photographed and make a display with the letters to the Pied Piper.

The Pied Piper – PLANNING SUMMARY

LEARNING OBJECTIVES	NATIONAL CURRICULUM programmes of study/attainment targets
<ul><li>to consider the nature of justice as against revenge</li><li>to give the opportunity for children to examine methods of negotiation</li><li>to give the opportunity for children to use a traditional story as a basis for creating new narrative</li></ul>	**Art** <ul><li>Introduced to the work of artists, from a variety of cultures and the past</li><li>Describe works of art, in simple terms</li></ul>**History** <ul><li>The everyday life of men, women and children from the past</li><li>To identify ways in which the past is represented</li></ul>**Science** <ul><li>To describe the way some everyday materials change when heated</li></ul>

KEY STAGES IN THE DRAMA

1. Using Pieter Brueghel's painting *Children's Games*, set the context in time.

2. Move the children into the role of families in Hamelin.
3. Tableaux of the bread-making.
4. OoR introduction TiR as the Mayor.
5. TiR as the Mayor – giving the election 'thank you' address.
6. OoR reflect on the Mayor's words.
7. Narration moving the drama on in time.
8. Whole-class tableaux of family groups as two sides of the street *before* the rats.
9. Whole-class tableaux of family groups as two sides of the street *after* the rats.
10. OoR negotiate the handling of the Mayor.
11. TiR as the Mayor meet the people of Hamelin about the rats.
12. OoR reflect on the people's meeting with the Mayor.
13. Overheard conversation of Mayor and Piper.
14. Replay scene of the Mayor meeting the Piper – children create the Piper's dialogue.
15. OoR reflect on the drama so far and what to do.
16. Forum theatre: the Piper returns for his money; children take Piper's role.
17. Re-making the street: tableaux before and after the children are taken.
18. Thought-tracking the parents: life without the children.
19. Reflect on what has happened to the village and what to say to the Mayor.
20. Forum theatre: children as parents meet the Mayor.
21. OoR reflect on what he said.
22. Narration: setting new scene, to the Mountain.
23. Hot-seating the child who was left behind.
24. OoR prepare for meeting someone at the Mountain.
25. TiR meeting a child or the Piper outside the Mountain – persuading them to return.
26. OoR reflect on getting the children back.
27. The return of the children – still images of the resolution.

Roles for Children	The families who live in Hamelin		
Roles for Teacher	The Mayor	The Pied Piper	The child who was left behind
The props/ role signifiers	Chain of office	Pied Piper's flute or recorder	A broken sandal

Other props: *Children's Games* by Pieter Brueghel – poster or transparency
Pictures of a rat – A4 size.
A copy of the story of the Pied Piper of Hamelin.
Pied Piper Books: *The Pied Piper of Hamelin* by Robert Browning, illustrated by Alan Howard (Faber & Faber, 1967); *The Pied Piper of Hamelin* by Robert Browning, illustrated by Kate Greenaway (Frederick Warne, 1888); *The Pied Piper of Hamelin* by Sara and Stephen Corrin, illustrated by Erroll Le Cain (Puffin, 1988), including an account of the 'real' history; *The Pied Piper of Hamelin* by Robert Browning, illustrated by Andre Amstutz (Orchard Books, 1993); *The Pied Piper of Hamelin* by Patrice Baldwin in *The Drama Box* (Collins, 1994).

Assessment, Recording and Reporting	
Attainment (reference to level descriptions) **knowledge, understanding and skills**	**PUPILS' RESPONSE –** **Evidence**
Progression (reference to level descriptions) **gains in knowledge, understanding and skills**	

The Billy Goats Gruff

Structure outline

Read the story of 'The Billy Goats Gruff' up to the point where the Troll falls into the water.

1 OoR stimulus

Key question: *I wonder what became of that Troll?* Discussion. This is an open-ended question and gives you the opportunity to value the contributions of the children.

One corner of the classroom is set aside for Mrs Green's cottage – two chairs for the door and a chair with her wool and knitting needles. Two chairs represent the bridge where the Troll lived.

2 Setting the context

In the space between is a hill where the children of Newhill play on their way home from school. Move the children into a space and point out the Troll's bridge and also the small cottage where Mrs Green lives. The children will meet Mrs Green later. Set up the situation as follows.

On their way home after school the children play on the hillside above the Troll's bridge. You are going to be those children in the story. Think of a game you can play. Listen to their suggestions. Tell them they never play fighting games because they are not allowed!

3 Children in role as children of Newhill

Tell them to listen to the story and to freeze when they hear the sound of someone going over the bridge.

Narrate the story: *It was a beautiful summer's afternoon. The children of Newhill had finished school and were on their way home. They were playing games. Some were playing . . . others were playing . . . (use the suggestions they have come up with and are demonstrating).*

Suddenly there was a great splash from the bridge and the children all stopped and looked towards the bridge.

4 Moment of significance thought-tracking

What did the children think made the splash? Move around the group and touch each child on the shoulder. The children can offer suggestions as to what caused the noise; again it is open-ended and some children may not offer an answer. This is not important, it offers an opportunity for assessment of who is confident enough to speak in front of the rest of the class.
STOP THE DRAMA

Sit the children around your chair and tell them: *We are going to move the drama on to a few days later. You are going to play on the hill again and this time I am going to pretend to be somebody in the drama. Listen very carefully and see if you can guess who this person is and what they want.*

5 TiR the post delivery

Take the role of someone delivering mail. Choose somebody whom you want to bring into the drama, a child who would benefit from having a special role in the drama.

The children return to their games as in the earlier part of the drama and, as the children are playing, shout: *Special delivery for Margaret Jones* (use the name of the chosen child) *and the children of Newhill.*

Make quite a bit of this, asking around to find Margaret, getting her to sign a special form etc. All of this will add to the tension.

When she has opened it, the children can begin to decipher whom it is from. Then stop the drama to gather round and read the letter together.

6 OoR sharing the letter

Rose Cottage
Greenfield Lane
Newhill

20 May

Dear Children of Newhill School,
I need your help. I have heard you know a lot about Trolls. I have a Troll in my shed. He is very wet and he is

not very happy. He says he has had to leave his home under the bridge and he is very worried about the Troll eggs he was looking after. If he does not go back they will not hatch. He is afraid of the Big Billy Goat.

I have tried to help him before but he shouts at me and I am a bit frightened of him. Please can you help?

Best wishes

Mrs Green.

Review the letter, in particular the section that refers to knowing 'a lot about Trolls'. Tell the children that before you can help Mrs Green and the Troll they must make a special book that will show they are Troll experts. It will be called *Everything You Need to Know about Trolls*. Children discuss with you what skills they need to be a carer of Trolls.

> **7** Task writing the big book

Time must be set aside to make a 'big book' on the subject of caring and looking after Trolls. A book on caring and looking after pets can be used as an example. Possible areas for discussion might be: the skills needed to catch a Troll without frightening it or harming it; how to talk to a Troll; what frightens a Troll; how to move a Troll's eggs; how to keep a Troll's eggs warm.

End of session one

In between sessions the work on the book takes place so that by the beginning of the next session the children have developed and shared their expertise and are ready to share it with Mrs Green.

Session two

Recap last session and prepare them for the meeting with Mrs Green. This is done by discussing the letter and deciding what questions they would like to ask her. It is also worth talking about how to behave when you go to visit someone else's house. *We are going to visit Mrs Green's cottage and I am going to be Mrs Green. What do we need to remember when we visit someone in their house for the first time? What do we do when we are being polite?*

> **8** OoR preparation for hot-seating Mrs Green

The key points for playing the role are: Mrs Green knows about the Troll's eggs; she has been watching the Troll for

> **9** TiR Mrs Green

some time; she has tried to help him by putting a notice by the bridge saying:

> Do not cross this bridge
> Troll looking after eggs
> Please be very quiet

To her surprise the Troll pulled up the notice and put it under his bridge, she doesn't know why; she has heard the children are Troll experts and she needs their help.

The children explain and advise about what to do. They will need to speak to the Troll.

10 OoR preparation for meeting the Troll

Explain to the children that in the next part of the drama you are going to be the Troll in the shed: *I cannot look like a Troll but I can pretend to be one. You will not be able to see him, so you can imagine what he looks like.*

Discuss what he might look like. They prepare to meet him: *If you went to talk to the Troll, what sort of mood do you think he will be in? What will you say when you approach the shed door? I am going to use two chairs for the shed door. I want you to show me where you would talk to him? How far away do you need to be at the beginning? Is there anything you need to take with you?*

Having set up the space and discussed how the children will approach the first meeting, sit behind the chairs and run through the first conversation. The Troll will be very resistant at first, in fact the first conversation may only last a few seconds before you come out of role and discuss ways of approaching him. This shifting in and out of role is very important for the success of this dialogue.

11 TiR meeting the Troll

The key points for the role play are: the Troll doesn't initially want to talk to anyone; the Troll doesn't trust the children: *You're after my eggs like those Billy Goats*; the Troll has brought Mrs Green's notice with him and is trying to read it: *What's these letters? Is it 'come and see the Troll's eggs'? I know that's a curly 'C' and that's a 'T' for Troll. Is it 'Come across the Bridge – Look at the Troll's Eggs'? I think it is? I wish I could read these letters.*

The children must work at gaining his confidence, tempting him out and helping him read the notice. This will mean moving in and out of role to discuss, plan and reflect on the drama.

There are several possible ways in which the drama can go.

> **12 Possible ways forward**

In these possibilities there is a technology focus: the design of a new bridge to house the Troll away from the Billy Goats; a plan to move the eggs to the new home or bridge; a receptacle to hold the eggs while they are being moved. It should keep them warm and cushion them against any bumps while they are being transported.

In these there is a literacy focus: a letter to the Billy Goats explaining the problem and agreeing on them not crossing the bridge until the eggs are hatched; helping the Troll to make a new notice or designing notices to be put near the bridge.

The Billy Goats Gruff – PLANNING SUMMARY

LEARNING OBJECTIVES	NATIONAL CURRICULUM
• to use drama to learn how to deal with a difficult character • to use the drama to give writing a real purpose • to consider the technology related to moving delicate objects	**Programmes of study/attainment targets** **English** • Pupils' writing communicates meaning in both narrative and non-narrative form. • Letters are accurately formed and consistent in size. **Design and technology** • Designing and making a product. • Working with a range of materials and components. • Most of NC 3 Designing Skills and 4 Making Skills

KEY STAGES IN THE DRAMA

1. Read the story up to the splash of the Troll in the river.

2. Setting the context – a hill near the village of Newhill.
3. Children in role playing on the hill.
4. Moment of significance – the splash: thought-tracking the children.
5. A few days later – the arrival of a letter (TiR).
6. OoR sharing the letter.
7. Creation of a big book: caring and looking after Trolls.
8. Preparing to meet Mrs Green.
9. Meeting Mrs Green (TiR).
10. Preparing to meet the Troll.
11. Meeting the Troll (TiR).
12. Possible ways forward.

Roles for Children	The children of Newhill School	
Roles for Teacher	Mrs Green	The Troll
The props/role signifiers	knitting needles and wool	not seen – just heard

Other props: chairs; anything required from the children's ideas

Assessment, Recording and Reporting	
Attainment (reference to level descriptions) knowledge, understanding and skills	**PUPILS' RESPONSE –** Evidence
Progression (reference to level descriptions) gains in knowledge, understanding and skills	

Hansel and Gretel

Structure outline

Negotiate the rules and moving into the drama. See the 'Introduction to the example dramas' for explanation of 'contracting'.

I OoR contract

Set up forestry work. Have ready some examples of the sorts of equipment a forestry worker might use, the more interesting the better. *I am going to bring in some things that show what your job is going to be in the story we are doing today. You must look carefully at them, no touching, and tell me what the things are and what you think the job is. What work would be done with these?* Obviously safety is a factor here and you must bring in only what you think is right.

Now I am going to begin the story. Listen carefully and tell me what is happening after I stop and become (teacher's name) again.

2 TiR I moves class into role

Enter as the Chief Forest Ranger. *Today we have to get on with taking the photographs for our information boards for the new visitors' centre. So I need you to tell me what you are working on and where we can get photos to illustrate each of our activities in running this forest.*

Who was that and what was she talking about? What special thing is being made for visitors to the forest? So what is she asking you to do? Can you do that? What sort of things might you want to tell her about and show her for the photos?

OoR check they understand

Possible activities: clearing spaces for planting, planting, tending young trees, thinning, tree felling, branch lopping, clearing dead trees, burning, clearing trunks, transporting tree trunks, clearing paths, testing trees to find diseased trees, working with hand tools, machinery, hands; tools: sharpening, cleaning, repairing; machinery: repairing, maintaining, cleaning.

Go back into role to hear their ideas about what work is going to be photographed for the visitors' board.

3 TiR sets occupational mime

Send them to set out their work areas in groups. *I'll be visiting so that you can show me your work in a moment. You have to decide on what you want to show me. I'll be coming round each area to have a look.*

4 Teaching about tableau

Ask them to prepare tableaux (or still photos) of the work in progress for you to look at. *Then choose the best picture for the photograph and freeze what you are doing so that the Ranger can take the picture. So show me your work one group at a time.*

Cross curricular work

If you can, take instant photos to help make a map of the forest and activities for the visitors' centre in another lesson. (A Polaroid camera helps here and is very useful in drama work.)

Optional task to reinforce caring

What safety procedures do we have to ensure the safety of the workers and the public? Groups set up to show the operation of safety in the working areas. TiR1 carries out an inspection of tools and safety procedures.

TiR1 ends the inspection of work sites. *Right, I am satisfied with this and that you know what needs yet to be done. What jobs have you got to do for preparing for the tours of the forest by the public?* Discuss.

You know that no unauthorised persons are ever allowed into the forest where felling is taking place but, as the visitors' centre is not open yet, there should be no one but yourselves around. Keep your eyes open because people are keen to see what we are preparing.

5 Narration sets up key moment for drama

The workers are hard at work. The visitors' centre is not yet ready to be opened but parts of the forest are being prepared for visits by the public. Fencing and signs are being prepared.

Enter as Hansel (or Gretel), searching, obviously upset and frightened. If the children take notice of you, hide behind a tree. Do not answer them if they challenge you.

OoR: Who was that? How was he? What was he doing? What are you going to do about him? What is your responsibility? How do you find out more?

They try to approach him but he runs and hides and refuses to talk.

How are you going to catch him?

7 OoR

Possible end of first session – or when he is caught

Session two
What were you doing at the end of the last session in our story? How did you catch (OR were going to catch) the intruder?

8 OoR recap events

The foresters interview him. As Hansel do not talk. Show by the way you sit, the way you do not look at them, that you are frightened.

9 Hot-seating of key TiR2

At a suitable point very soon after starting come OoR: *What are you going to do? How do you think he is feeling? You can't let him stay here but how can you take him somewhere if you know nothing about him? How are you going to get him to talk?*

OoR reflect on Hansel's attitude

Action must be decided by the children: how to get his trust first? Play with him? Show him their work? Talk about other things? Get him some food?

Handling Hansel in the hot-seating: As the foresters show more consideration, begin to talk. How much information to give at this stage? At the very least, *I am lost in the forest* is revealed. Reveal home address: 6 *Hilltop, Forest Edge*.

Only if they are really good at making him feel better, he tells them what has really happened: *Mother left me picking some berries in the forest and told me she was going to look for some water and she would be back in a while. I must have wandered. I expect she could not find me.*

Whatever the case, he still basically loves his mother and does not understand what is going on, but can be a bit reluctant to go home in case he gets into trouble for being out so long. He thinks it is his fault he got lost and is confused as to why his mother left him alone.

There are several possibilities at this stage.

10 responsibility for the children

If the children get his address and decide to take him straight home, move straight to Step 11 below.

Phone his mother? He gives the telephone number if asked. This introduces Mother (TiR3). Negotiate setting up where mother is in his house and what she is doing when the phone rings. One of the children volunteers to make the call. If necessary discuss how to pretend and mime making the call. Negotiate the convention of not looking at mother as you talk because she is somewhere else

Possibly sit in chairs in front of the children but facing in opposite directions. As Mum pretend to be happy to hear that he is safe but also, *I'm afraid I can't come to fetch him. I don't have a car and it's too far to walk. Can you bring him back?* The forester gets the address, if they do not already have it.

11 Getting him home

Hansel's reaction to news of being taken home: *Can I not stay here for a while with you? You seem very friendly people and I like the forest now I know I am safe.*

The children should tackle this reluctance and might ask questions about it. See possible information to use as Hansel, listed at Step 9. Map of forest area is now used to locate the route to the house.

12 Whole-class story making

The journey to the house. Decide which children are going in the car or Landrover and devise a group story, made on the spot by the children and yourself, to describe who goes, the transport they use, the route they took and what they saw.

What happens when he arrives home? OoR discuss with whole group how the representatives should handle handing him over.

Set out the space so that the rest of the class are gathered round to watch, as though behind invisible walls, and make the convention that they can stop the action if they see things they want to talk about and at that point you will come OoR to let them advise the representatives, but they cannot talk directly to Mum.

Make it so that you change role to mother and that Hansel is there but represented by his role signifier. Get the children to give an answer from him if it is necessary. Otherwise they handle the situation as the foresters or representatives.

If they have phoned so Mum knows he is coming	If they have not phoned so Mum does not know he is coming	
She is 'happy' to see him but give glimpses of not being happy. *I don't know what your Dad will say. How could you have run away like that?*	She thinks he is dead of course. Betray shock but recover very quickly. *Hansel, it's you. I thought you were . . . I mean it's wonderful to see you. You're a very naughty boy worrying your mother like that.*	**13** TiR3 Mum challenging the children to spot signs of lying

Go OoR to discuss their impression of the mother. In both cases if the children are suspicious let them decide how to find out more.

If they are suspicious let them listen in on the house and hear one side of a conversation, mother talking to an imaginary Hansel, complaining about how little money she has to keep and feed him and how he must learn to look after himself in the world. She will have to let him go.	If they are not suspicious they return to work and then overhear mother talking to Hansel as she takes him into the forest again, to leave him.	**14** Overheard conversation

Either way they learn that he is not wanted and that it is because she has very little money.

15 Challenge for the class	How to teach her parental responsibility? They have to sort out Mother trying to get rid of him – money worries, she is on her own and cannot manage.

Possible directions and activities:
Thought-track Hansel, showing how he feels inside.

The class as the foresters hot-seat mother to help her solve her problems. In this they teach mother of the dangers to Hansel in the forest, setting up tableaux to show the problems he faces.

Forum theatre of how Hansel should tackle his mother and tell her how he feels. TiR3 as mother while the class take the role of Hansel and prepare beforehand what they should say. Volunteers take Hansel's seat and hold the teddy bear. Others can intervene, stop the dialogue and take over or suggest activities to help with the money problems.

Some examples of class choices from classes who have experienced the drama:
Mother realised the error of her ways but they decided she would have to be monitored to see that she didn't try to get rid of him again.

They did not trust her and decided to take on Hansel and look after him themselves.

They tried to leave money on the doorstep for mother to find, as they thought that was the only problem. TiR then took the money in and, as they watched talked about what she was going to spend the money on for herself. The children then confronted her and taught her how selfish she was being.

16 Debrief	Discussion of the drama. What was the drama about? How did they help Hansel? What had they learnt about their job? What had they learnt from helping Hansel and his Mum?

Hansel and Gretel – PLANNING SUMMARY	
LEARNING OBJECTIVES • to consider how a parent should treat a child • to learn the role of carers, environmental and personal Could be: • to consider child abuse (using a fairy story and drama to focus difficult material and help safely distance it) Originally designed for a Year One class working on Science: 'Green plants as organisms', such as trees. • to build on work in class on growing things	**NATIONAL CURRICULUM programmes of study/attainment targets** This drama can relate to **the SMSC curriculum**, particularly • to learn to help others, particularly those who are victims • to learn to act on a sense of what is right, what is wrong **Geographical Skills 3d** • making a map or plan of an imaginary place, using pictures and symbols

KEY STAGES IN THE DRAMA

1. Negotiate the rules and set up forestry work.
2. Enter as the Chief Forest Ranger. *Today we have to get on with taking the photographs.*
   OoR check they understand: *What sort of things might you want to tell her about and show her for the photos?*
3. Working in the forest: *I'll be visiting so that you can show me your work in a moment.* Show work under way: photos of the work towards tableau training. Optional-groups set up to show the operation of safety in the working areas. TiR1 carries out an inspection of tools and safety procedures.
4. TiR1 ends the inspection of work sites.
5. Narration: *The workers are hard at work.*
6. Enter as Hansel (or Gretel), OoR: *Who was that?*
7. They try to approach him but he runs and hides and refuses to talk. OoR *How are you going to catch him?*

Possible end of first session – or when he is caught.

SESSION TWO

8. *What were you doing at the end of last session in our story?*
9. The foresters interview him. As Hansel (Gretel) do not talk. Show that

continued . . .

you are frightened by the way you sit, the way you do not look at them. OoR *What are you going to do?* Action decided by the children: how to get his trust first?

Handling Hansel in the hot-seating. As the foresters are more considerate, begin to talk. Only if they are really good at making him feel better, he tells them what has really happened.

10. Possibilities at this stage: If the children get his address and decide to take him straight home move straight to Step 11. Phone his mother? He gives the telephone number if asked.
11. Getting him home: Hansel's reaction to news of being taken home. Map of forest area is now used to locate the route to the house.
12. The journey to the house. What happens when he arrives home? OoR discuss with whole group how the representatives should handle handing him over. Have they phoned so that Mum knows whether he is coming or not?
13. Mum challenging the children to spot signs of lying.
14. Overheard conversation: Mother tells Hansel how poor they are.
15. How to teach her parental responsibility?
    Possible directions and activities: Thought-track Hansel, showing how he feels inside; the class as the foresters hot-seat Mother; forum theatre of how Hansel should tackle his mother.
16. Debrief.

Roles for Children	Foresters who are planning a visitors' centre in their forest		
Roles for Teacher	Chief Forest Ranger	Hansel *or* Gretel. (We do not have both of them and there is no cottage or witch in this use of the story.)	Mother
The props/ role signifiers	badge	teddy bear	threadbare coat

Other props: Forester's equipment as opening stimulus. Map of the imaginary forest and surrounding area including some houses on the edge of the forest, on the top of a hill. This can be prepared in outline before the drama and added to with the children's ideas for the visitors' centre and routes during phase one of the drama, and including placing the photos taken of work in progress.

Assessment, Recording and Reporting	
Attainment (reference to level descriptions) knowledge, understanding and skills	PUPILS' RESPONSE – Evidence
Progression (reference to level descriptions) gains in knowledge, understanding and skills	

Developing a school policy for drama: the key elements

If you wish to develop the use of drama as a school, it will be necessary to produce a policy to work to, and many of the chapters in the book will provide direction and content for such a policy. Here is a checklist of areas it might include:

WHAT IS DRAMA?

An active, fictional approach to learning where teacher and pupils use role and other techniques of the art form to examine key elements of a story. The fictional exploration focuses learning, with reflection in and out of role as a vital ingredient of that learning process.

WHY USE DRAMA?

Aims

- drama for developing language (relating drama to English): speaking and listening in the NC for English; a 'real' reason to read and write (again contributing to the NC); for literacy work
- drama integrated into the schemes of work for the above, together with a cross-curricular approach to provide context for learning in many other subjects, including history, technology, maths etc.
- tackling the SMSC curriculum; teaching Citizenship
- drama as a subject: children's learning of how to do drama.

Implementation approaches

- a co-ordinator for drama – possibly part of the English remit? Review your current position. Prioritise needs. Assess implications of change. Draw up an action plan, implementation and reviewing strategies. Involvement of governors, parents and colleagues

- short, medium and long term curriculum planning
- the opportunities to share work and work together, particularly in using role
- use of story; availability of suitable materials
- use of TiR
- other techniques, such as forum theatre, tableaux, thought-tracking
- progression and development
- assessment, recording and reporting
- special needs and equal opportunities
- training needs
- books on drama.

Logistics

- planning use of spaces
- allocation of adult input (e.g. to input to nursery work for story and theme corner)
- how drama can be integrated with theme corner or role-play area work; the necessity of adult input
- other resources, e.g. useful props as role signifiers for TiR – walking stick, hats, coats; materials for setting up a situation, e.g. chairs and bowls for 'Baby Bear Did It'.

Relationship to other key drama elements of the school

- the school play
- assemblies and other performance work

Use of outside agencies

- regional arts association
- advisory support
- visiting performers
- visiting theatres
- children's responses to seeing drama.

Bibliography

There is a dearth of material for drama for early years children, and no books specifically for ages 3–7 about developing TiR work for them. That is one of the main reasons we decided to produce this book. However, we indicate what we know to be available. Apologies if we are ignorant of key material, but let us know.

Practical drama with theory

These books include material for older children, some of which can be adapted for younger.

Baldwin P. (1992) *Stimulating Drama: Cross-curricular Approaches to Drama in the Primary School* (London: National Drama). Practical set of lessons with two specifically for early years and others adaptable.

Baldwin P. and Hendy L. (1994) *The Drama Box and Book* (London: Collins). A collection of materials: stories, tapes and structures for primary drama, including six theme-based for early years.

Booth D. (1994) *Story Drama* (Markham, Ontario: Pembroke Publishing). A very interesting and stimulating account of the process of using stories through drama with some very useful example dramas.

Clarke J. (1994) *Hands on Drama* (Norwich: Norfolk Educational Press). Includes five useful ideas for early years' lessons and some good explanations of practice.

Dudley Advisory Service (n.d.) *Drama Tried and Tested: A Drama Approach to the Primary School National Curriculum* (Dudley LEA; available from London Drama). Four drama structures, adaptable for different ages.

Ewart F. G. (1998) *Let the Shadows Speak: Developing Children's Language through Shadow Puppetry* (Stoke on Trent: Trentham Books). Interesting on the use of role through puppets; parallel to TiR.

Fullwood R. (1994) *Drama: Ideas for Infant Teachers* (published by R. Fullwood; available through London Drama). Useful ideas for beginnings and some very interesting TiR set-ups.

Fullwood R. (1996) *Infant Drama through Topics* (published by R. Fullwood; available through London Drama). Sixteeen lessons on ten common infant topics. Good starting points.

Kempe A. (ed.) (1996) *Drama Education and Special Needs* (London: Stanley Thornes).

Very useful not only for special needs but also for early years. See especially Melanie Peters's chapter on drama and story.

Kitson N. and Spiby I. (1995) *Primary Drama Handbook* (London: Watts). A simple and effective account of theory with five good early years examples, including 'The Pirates' and 'The Farm'.

O'Neill, C., Lambert A., Linnell R. and Warr-Wood J. (1986) *Drama Guidelines* (London: London Drama/Heinemann). Including four early years lessons which are very adaptable. See particularly 'The Sad King'. Contains short but very useful definitions of key ideas, like TiR.

Peters M. (1994) *Drama for All* (London: David Fulton Publishers). Drama in the curriculum with pupils with special needs, including an appendix with much very adaptable material.

Readman G. and Lamont G. (1994) *Drama: A Handbook for Primary Teachers* (London: BBC Educational Publishing). A very practical and powerful account of work including early years material.

Winston J. and Tandy M. (1998) *Beginning Drama 4–11* (London: David Fulton Publishers). Some useful dramas and ways of approaching drama, with a useful section for early years, including adult intervention.

Books essentially on theory, never exclusively

Bolton G. (1984) *Drama as Education* (London: Longman). A key text on the development of educational drama.

Bolton G. (1992) *New Perspectives on Classroom Drama* (London: Simon & Schuster Educational). Very good on the theory with two examples of early years practice.

Clipson-Boyles S. (1998) *Drama in Primary English Teaching* (London: David Fulton Publishers). A useful résumé of theory relating to drama, oracy, English and National Curriculum. Useful on assessment and drama's link to reading and writing. Some practical examples.

Davies G. (1983) *Practical Primary Drama* (London: Heinemann). An early text, with emphasis on workable ideas, with clear awareness of the anxieties of beginners. See good ideas for beginnings from story.

Fleming M. (1994) *Starting Drama Teaching* (London: David Fulton Publishers). Explores some of the ideas behind drama and a good lead into drama.

Heathcote D. and Bolton G. (1995) *Drama for Learning: Dorothy Heathcote's Mantle of the Expert Approach to Education* (Portsmouth, NH: Heinemann). A key book on a key method for teachers using drama.

Morgan N. and Saxton J. (1989) *Teaching Drama: a Mind of Many Wonders* (London: Hutchinson). A useful account of the nature of drama; see the analysis of the types of teacher roles.

Peters M. (1995) *Making Drama Special* (London: David Fulton Publishers). Developing Drama for pupils with special needs.

Rooke C. *Drama: Policy and Practice in the Primary School* (Barnsley LEA; available from London Drama). Very useful summary of policy, approaches and giving examples.

Wagner B. J. (1979) *Dorothy Heathcote: Drama as a Learning Medium* (London: Hutchinson). Still a seminal book for understanding one of the most important educators of this century.

Woolland B. (1993) *The Teaching of Drama in the Primary School* (London: Longman). A very useful combination of theory and practice with examples and a good chapter on early years drama.

Books defining the range of drama techniques

Barlow S. and Skidmore S. (1994) *Drama Form: A Practical Guide to Drama Techniques* (London: Hodder & Stoughton). Some useful ideas illustrating uses of drama conventions.

Neelands J. (1990) *Structuring Drama Work* (Cambridge: Cambridge University Press). A very good account of the strategies and conventions used in drama.

Background material for reference in policy-making

Department of Education and Science and Welsh Office (1989) *Drama 5–16: Curriculum Matters 17* (London: HMSO). Old now, but the only document of its type produced about the role of drama in the curriculum.

Department of Education and Science and Welsh Office (1989) *English for Ages 5–16* (The Cox Committee Report, June version) (London: DES). See especially chapter 8 which still has a lot to say to us about the nature and importance of drama in education. A pity it has never been properly implemented.

Moyles, J. ed. (1994) *The Excellence of Play* (Milton Keynes: Open University Press). See especially N. Kitson, 'Please, Miss Alexander: will you be the robber? Fantasy play a case for adult intervention', which explores some key ideas about the use of role-play.

SCAA (1995) *Desirable Outcomes for Children's Learning on Entering Compulsory Education* (London: School Curriculum and Assessment Authority). Essential reading to help plan Early Years' Drama.

A useful source for obtaining books on drama is: London Drama, Central School of Speech & Drama, Eton Avenue, London NW3 3HY.
Tel: 0207 722 4730; email: Londrama@aol.com

Index